Sam Quek

There have been many people who've helped me achieve what I have in my life so far. I am thankful to all of them, especially former teachers, teammates and coaches. However, this book is dedicated to my family, who are the most important thing in the world to me. Thank you for all your love and support, and all the sacrifices you made so that I could fulfil my dreams.

I hope I made you proud.

Sam Quek
Hope and a Hockey Stick

Sam Quek

WHITE OWL

AN IMPRINT OF PEN & SWORD BOOKS LTD.
YORKSHIRE - PHILADELPHIA

First published in Great Britain in 2018 by
Pen and Sword White Owl
An imprint of Pen and Sword Books
Pen & Sword Books Ltd
Yorkshire - Philadelphia

ISBN 9781526733498

Typeset in India by Vman Infotech Private Limited

Printed and bound in the UK by TJ International Ltd.

Pen & Sword Books Ltd incorporates the Imprints of Pen & Sword Books
Archaeology, Atlas, Aviation, Battleground, Discovery, Family History, History,
Maritime, Military, Naval, Politics, Railways, Select, Transport, True Crime,
Fiction, Frontline Books, Leo Cooper, Praetorian Press, Seaforth Publishing,
Wharncliffe and White Owl.

For a complete list of Pen & Sword titles please contact

PEN & SWORD BOOKS LIMITED
47 Church Street, Barnsley, South Yorkshire, S70 2AS, England
E-mail: enquiries@pen-and-sword.co.uk
Website: www.pen-and-sword.co.uk

or

PEN AND SWORD BOOKS
1950 Lawrence Rd, Havertown, PA 19083, USA
E-mail: Uspen-and-sword@casematepublishers.com
Website: www.penandswordbooks.com

Contents

Prologue

I first sensed it during the national anthems – the realisation that this was it. We were one game away from being Olympic gold medallists. I'd experienced nerves before throughout my international career but this was more than just butterflies in the tummy. It was different.

Everything had been building to this moment. For the team, it was the culmination of all our efforts for the tournament, our flawless record that had carried us to this showdown with the Netherlands, winners of the last two Olympic titles.

For me, though, it was more. This was my big chance. After the heartache of missing out in Beijing in 2008 and the agony of London 2012, when it seemed the entire nation was having a party to which I wasn't invited, here was the opportunity to make amends. All the hard work, all the sacrifices, would be worth it if we could return from Rio with a gold medal.

Was it the occasion? The knowledge that back home the BBC *News at Ten* was being delayed as millions tuned in to see if Team GB's women could emulate the heroics of the men back in Seoul in 1988?

Was it that at the back of my mind I knew it could be my last international match? Going into Rio I had been thinking that I had been doing this for ten years. If we didn't medal I was definitely retiring. Even when I was selected, I thought if we won gold I was going to call it quits. My dream would have come true. There would be no more targets, nothing more I had to achieve. This gold medal match could be my last game, in my last tournament.

Was it the frustration that I was starting the match on the bench? In hockey it wasn't that big a deal because we operate a roll on roll off rotation system, so everyone usually plays the same number of minutes in a match. I'd be on after seven minutes, but this was the Olympic final. The starting line-ups would be on live TV back home and I wondered if most of the 10 million people watching would think I was just a substitute rather than a full part of the team. I always felt I played better when I was on from the start, fresh from the warm-up. Coming on I'd have to get up to speed very quickly with the tempo of the match.

Maybe it was a combination of all those factors. Whatever the reason, I was starting to feel overwhelmed.

Hockey was prime time. The nation was watching. It was our moment.

The formalities out of the way, the match started under a bright blue sky on a sunny, if breezy, evening in Deodoro, in west Rio de Janeiro. Although the stands weren't remotely full, due to the ticketing issues that had plagued the whole tournament, behind the dugouts the Dutch fans were making their customary racket, matched superbly by the British fans, friends and family and the many others that had been following our story. Among them were my devoted parents, Albert and Marilyn, and my boyfriend, Tom Mairs – hard to miss in his Union Jack Morphsuit and hat, beating his drum. In the opposite stand, a large contingent from Team GB – including the men's rowers and the rugby sevens women, who'd defied expectations by narrowly missing out on bronze – were also making their presence felt.

Out on the vivid blue pitch it was a cagey opening. The Dutch girls, imposing in their charcoal grey and orange, were heavily pressing our girls – kitted out in our favourite red – as we knew they would, forcing us to play the ball. No one wanted to make a mistake and I sat there watching the girls, itching to get on.

After three minutes there was activity on the bench. Karen Brown, our assistant coach, who until 2016 was our most capped player and winner of the bronze in Seoul, was starting to get the subs on. Constantly consulting her iPad programme that told her who was due for rotation, Karen worked methodically down the line – the forward sub first, then midfield, the screens, before, lastly, the defence.

I got the nod.

'Okay Sam, go on for Crista, but you're playing left half.'

Finally!

I left the dugout area, turned right and faced the pitch. Even though the dugout was right next to the pitch, standing on the sideline – at the halfway line where you entered the fray – the perspective was entirely different.

Now the nerves really began to kick in.

My hand was shaking. I couldn't keep my stick still.

What the hell was happening?

Each week at Bisham Abbey, our state-of-the-art training centre in Berkshire, on 'Thinking Thursdays' head coach Danny Kerry ran us through a whole host of scenarios: 'You are two down with ten minutes left, devise a strategy to get level', or 'You're a player down, how do you see the game out without conceding a goal?' It seemed we'd developed a coping strategy for every eventuality so we would never be caught unawares. As I stood on the sidelines I couldn't recall him ever saying 'You are coming on after a few minutes in the Gold Medal Olympic match and you're shaking with nerves … how do you calm yourself down?'

This was totally new.

'Oh my God,' I thought, 'I've never experienced anything like this. Why am I feeling this now?'

I couldn't ignore it. It was threatening to completely overwhelm me. There were no routines to fall back on, and that made me worry even more.

I remembered a breathing technique, which I'd read about and used to do very early on in my career. Take big, deep breaths in for six seconds, out for three seconds. I was making it up but I just thought, 'You need to take deep breaths and refocus.'

I was coming on for Crista Cullen, who was over on the far right side, in my usual position. When I came on, I would slot in at left back and Giselle Ansley and our captain Kate Richardson-Walsh moved over to cover until there was a suitable moment in the match for me to move over to the right. That aspect of the substitution didn't bother me too much because I could play right or left, but I had to remain focussed as whilst the positions may seem similar, they require very different techniques as all your passing and running angles change.

This particular sub was taking a lot longer than normal because the match was so cagey. There were turnovers. It was back and forth. I was getting more and more nervous.

'Crista, Crista,' I shouted across.

Finally I took to the pitch. My Olympic final was under way. If my 10-year-old self could see me now!

In any game, I always felt my first touch was huge. If it was a bad touch, I'd think, 'Right, now that's out your system, you can press on,' and if it was a good touch then I'd think 'That was decent, you're going to have a good day today.' On the hockey pitch was where I felt most confident and able to express myself. So why was this happening now?

Whenever you go on the pitch, for the first few minutes you are knackered. Your heart rate goes up, but then you get your first touch and you're up to speed with the tempo. I knew once I got that out of the way, I'd settle, I'd get my second wind and then I'd be well and truly into the game. For three or four minutes, though, the ball was being played around and I still hadn't touched it. I was running around feeling knackered and was starting to panic that the game was passing me by. People were shouting my name and giving tactical instructions. Ordinarily, I'd be able to process it but with so many nerves the information became jumbled.

The ball went off for a sideline deep in our half near to me. I looked up but I couldn't see a pass on. I found playing on the left tougher than playing right back, because you are playing across your opponent's forehand. There's less space because they have got their stick on the right-hand side of their body. Normally there is always a pass backwards and we can recycle the ball until an opportunity to pass forward opens up. Teams don't usually high press, but we were sat so deep that the Dutch were all over us. They had someone threatening the ball back to Kate, who is my safe and easy pass. Passing to her though would put her under real pressure. If their centre forward got a touch or intercepted it we could be in big trouble. With Kate blocked off, my go-to pass was Unsy – Laura Unsworth, at centre half. On the pitch we had played side by side for almost all my career and off the pitch we had lived together for many years. We had developed an understanding that didn't require words; usually a look or a gesture was enough for each of us to know what pass the other needed.

I passed it towards her without appreciating she was also under so much pressure. She was tackled instantly and the ball was turned over to the opposition. It was a really crap pass. Kitty van Male, their centre forward, then had the ball and started dribbling into the top of the 'D', the zone in which she could take a shot at goal.

Instantly I knew I'd made a mistake.

'Sam, you idiot,' I thought. 'You've given this away. Why did you pass it there? Go and win it back. You can win it back.'

My only thought was getting that ball back. I sprinted to catch her. I could still be the hero and catch her with a big sliding tackle.

I dived and went to ground but missed the ball and completely wiped out van Male from behind.

I looked up to see the umpire signalling a penalty stroke.

Oh shit!

The first time I give away a penalty in my entire international career – and I do it in an Olympic final.

None of my teammates challenged the call. That said it all. It was a very messy tackle but thankfully I didn't get carded. The umpire must have taken the view that Kate was covering and it therefore wasn't a given that van Male would score.

In any normal match I would have done what we call channel – getting alongside her but not making a tackle and just making sure she couldn't get across my way. I could have run her onto Kate's stick for her to make the tackle. Sam in any other game would have done that, but Sam in an Olympic final – a very nervous Sam – had just made a completely rash emotional decision.

You idiot!

It was like I was having an out-of-body experience. Mind and body were not in sync. Normally I'm in the zone, composed.

I saw Kate and Unsy looking at me. I knew exactly what they were thinking: 'You're better than that. That was so silly; you'd never normally do that.' It wasn't a look of disappointment, frustration or anger. It was just, 'Come on, Sam, that was sloppy.'

'Sorry guys,' I said.

Nobody said anything. They didn't have to.

'Oh my God, Sam, what have you done?', I thought.

I felt I'd let the team down. I'd let the country down. The looks from Kate and Unsy just amplified that.

The next morning's newspaper headlines flashed through my mind: 'Quek costs GB gold.'

In the run-up to the game we'd talked about the strength of the Dutch, and their ability to score at will. We had to keep the game tight and hope we could take our chances at the other end when they came to us.

For the opening few minutes we'd done precisely that. We still had a long way to go. But gifting them a penalty was the last thing in our game plan. In a game of this magnitude, handing them a soft lead would be horrendous. They had more experience of these types of occasions and an early goal would settle any of their nerves even further. It would be a dream start for them. For eight years I'd waited for the chance to show what I could do on the biggest stage of all. Was I now going to blow the most important moment of my career?

Maartje Paumen stepped forward to take the penalty. The sight of her sent shivers of dread through my body. She was the best drag flicker in the game. Absolutely lethal. She never missed. Whenever the Dutch got a flick or a penalty corner, they celebrated like they'd scored a goal because they had that much faith in her.

We had one of the best keepers in the world in Maddie Hinch, who I knew was capable of making exceptional saves, but this was asking a lot, even of her.

My only hope was that Paumen somehow missed the target or Maddie pulled off a wonder save.

I stared at the ball thinking, 'Miss, miss, miss, miss …'

Paumen prepared to flick. I could hardly bare to watch.

Were our gold medal dreams about to start slipping away?

Chapter 1

Humble Beginnings

In order for you to understand how I came to be on a hockey field in Brazil representing my country at the Olympic Games, I should first give you a sense of where I came from. My story began, not in the hospital where I was born, but in the salubrious surroundings of Baileys dance club in St John's Precinct, in the heart of Liverpool. For it was there, in 1974, that Albert Quek from Singapore met Marilyn Higgins from Everton.

The chances of them meeting were pretty slim. Albert was only visiting Liverpool on a navy ship, while Marilyn was juggling life as a businesswoman with her own children's boutique and being a single mother with a young daughter, Maxine. They were both around twenty-one when they happened to be in Baileys on the same night.

Albert asked Marilyn to dance. Marilyn found him quite attractive but it wasn't a case of her fancying him from the off. It was just a dance in her eyes. At the end of the night he asked her for a second date. And it's just as well for me, my twin brother Shaun and my older brother Mike that she said yes. For that young couple became our mum and dad.

That all-important second date, when they got to know each other a little better, was to the cinema to see the latest James Bond movie, which I figured out was *The Man with the Golden Gun*, as it was released that year. That led to some more dates until my dad had to leave on his ship once more. At the time my mum had her boutique – called Maxine's, after my sister – on Townsend Lane in Anfield, and it was doing really well.

They kept in touch over two years by letter because back then there was no such thing as picking up the phone to call long distance. Every so often, Dad would come back to Liverpool and they'd meet up. It wasn't until 1976 that he decided to stay in Liverpool to be with my mum. When I asked my dad if he would have stayed in the city, regardless of whether he had fallen in love with my mum, he said, 'No. It was just for your mum.'

Maxine was only four when they got together permanently and my mum says it's so important to emphasise how my dad embraced my sister and raised her as one of his own.

Mum had been living in a little flat at the top of a building. Dad got a job selling offal to supermarkets and restaurants. He was working for the gentleman who owned the business, earning five pounds a day for three days a week, so just fifteen pounds a week. Despite this meagre arrangement, Dad grew the business and found new contacts. However, soon his boss decided to sell the business and did so without consulting my dad or giving him a chance to take it over. Obviously they couldn't have afforded it but given the effort my dad had put into building the business up he was hurt at the way it was handled. He continued to work for the new owner but in the meantime Mum scouted out warehouses with walk-in freezers and cold storage with a view to setting up on their own.

They moved into a little terraced house in Coniston Street in Everton. They found it through a housing trust and, although modest, it was the first home they'd had with their own front door. Compared to where they'd lived before it was massive and they were very excited. It was within walking distance of Mum's boutique, but she gradually grew disillusioned with her business. Although the shop continued to do well, it had been broken into an astonishing twelve times.

Mum and Dad tried everything to deter the thieves. They put grills on the windows but on one occasion the crooks actually dug in from next door. It got to the point where Mum couldn't sleep properly for fear of getting another phone call to tell them it had been ransacked. When that did happen they would leg it round to try to catch the thieves red-handed. My mum used to get frustrated with the people on the main road because often the shop was targeted on a Sunday when it was closed. There was a pelican crossing right outside the shop and people watched it being broken into. All it would have taken was one call to alert her, so they could perhaps have stopped the majority of the stock being taken. The thieves would literally leave with anything they could get their hands on. One time, their house was also broken into. They pulled up while the burglary was in progress, which was enough to disturb the crooks and they ran off.

Sadly, it seemed it was that kind of area where if you were seen to be doing well you became a bit of a target.

Ironically, Mum and Dad were by no means well off. They were working as hard as they could to build something of their own. They existed on such a tight budget they practically lived on Spam and rice because it was so cheap.

When they found suitable premises, Mum sourced a second-hand van and after selling the boutique, she and my dad decided to strike out on their own. Dad quit his job and, with Mum's brother John Higgins and his wife Dawn, they set up their own food supply business, Quick Products. They got the idea for the name after a man mistakenly thought my dad was called Mr Quick. Mum thought it sent out a statement – quick products; get them fast and efficiently.

The four of them were doing everything by hand – processing all the produce and making deliveries. The warehouse was freezing and Mum remembers it as the toughest time, working in sub-zero temperatures to satisfy orders. I guess that's where I got my 'tough' mentality from.

Dad said to me that when he was a child growing up in Singapore he hardly ever saw his father, who worked away a lot. His mother was left to raise the children on her own– my dad had five younger sisters and a brother. He always vowed to work hard enough so that his wife would be able to dedicate her time to looking after their children. He has always lived by something his granddad said: 'If you have a good pair of hands you'll never go hungry.'

That gave him the motivation to work hard and apply himself to whatever he did, 100 per cent.

In 1982, Mum gave birth to her second child, Michael.

Six years on, she was pregnant again – this time with twins. Mum went into labour and on 18 October 1988 was admitted to Mill Road Hospital, not far from the city centre and about a mile away from Liverpool Football Club's famous Anfield stadium. Before I entered the world, however, I was centre stage in my own little drama. My placenta had stopped working and I wasn't getting enough oxygen, so the doctors had to get me out quickly. Three minutes later, my twin brother Shaun also arrived safely. By strange coincidence, my mum's sister-in-law, Sheila Higgins, was pregnant at the same time and gave birth to our cousin Phil about six hours after Shaun and I arrived on the same ward. From that day on, Shaun, Phil and I were referred as the triplets, particularly throughout our early years.

Sadly, Mill Road Hospital doesn't exist anymore, but before it closed in 1993 it was well known in Liverpool and the surrounding areas because during the blitz in 1941, which devastated the city, it took a direct hit one evening when a bomb exploded in the rear courtyard, next to the maternity unit. Many mothers and their newborn babies were killed. It was testament to the spirit of Liverpudlians and British grit that after such devastation, the maternity unit was rebuilt and remained for another fifty years. I like to think that perhaps even the history of the building in which I was born also helped shape the type of person I grew up to be.

As if having two newborn babies wasn't enough to contend with, when Shaun and I were just a month old, our parents moved from their Coniston Street terrace to a three-bedroom, detached house in West Derby, a suburb in the north-eastern side of the city. The house was in Newby Grove, and although it was still quite small, we had our own grass garden and our own drive. It was in a cul-de-sac off a main road, so the perfect setting for a family with young children. To my parents, being able to move there was a big deal and Mum recalls how proud she was that they had managed to afford a detached house at the time. Shaun and I shared the small room upstairs, while Mike had his own. Maxine, who was eighteen years older than me, was living in her own place and had a full-time job by the time Shaun and I came into the world.

West Derby was seen as quite posh, certainly compared to the area we'd moved from. It was once better known as the location for the '90s Channel 4 TV soap opera *Brookside* and more recently for the amazing Alder Hey Children's Hospital. Among the area's most notable former residents were Pete Best, the Beatles' original drummer, and the late, great Bill Shankly, legendary former manger of Liverpool FC.

My mum and dad tell me I was a laid-back baby – until it came to feeding time. The moment I was hungry I wanted to be fed and Shaun would always have to wait for his turn because I would be screaming. They used to put us in a twin pram and if I lost my dummy and Shaun was sleeping next to me I would nick the one out of his mouth.

I remember some very random things from my early childhood. By the time I was two I could whistle with unusual precision. One time I was out with my dad and got him into trouble when I let out a loud wolf whistle and a woman turned around. She thought it was my dad. My mum still finds this hilarious.

One of my earliest memories was watching my very first film in Newby Grove. It was Disney's *Pinocchio* on video. I remember getting emotional at the moment the wooden boy's creator Geppetto was looking for Pinocchio. I can vividly remember getting upset and trying to understand why I was crying. I felt embarrassed crying in front of Shaun and remember running out of the living room into the corridor where the staircase was on the side of the house and sitting on the bottom step, trying not to cry, but failing.

I also recall my brother and I both had prams. As we were on a cul-de-sac it was very safe for us to play on the drive. I had a toy duck, which I called Ducky, and Shaun had a bear called Teddy, because it was a good old-fashioned bear with arms that moved quite rigidly. Granted, they weren't the most imaginative names, but we were only four years old. My mum had originally bought me a pram but Shaun wanted one, too. It was probably the only time in my early life when I chose a girly girl thing to do, but it wasn't a case of mothering the duck. We used the prams as go-karts. We used to strap our teddies in and have races down the drive.

My nana had a dog and my mum says that when I was a toddler I was so scared they had to lock the dog away before I would go into her house in Anfield. My mum and dad would go in with the bags and my twin brother and Mike, and then they'd come out and pick me up. I used to shake with fear. This is so strange to hear now because it is the complete opposite of how I am today. I am totally obsessed with any dog. Growing up, I had the most amazing Border terrier called Jake, and now I have two dogs – Max and Ollie – who are like my children. I must spend hours each day just playing with them or hugging them. I have an affinity for them that feels much more than owner and pet. I also enjoy being a supporter of Merseyside Dogs Trust. Last year I even got the opportunity to name one of their rescue dogs. I called him Rio. I think my 4-year-old self would have called him Doggy, though.

My first pet was Charlie, the mynah bird. My mum loved birds and he used to mimic what she said. He would say 'Hellooooo?' in a long, lazy drawl and 'Okay, byeeeeee' because that's the way my mum ends a phone call. Like me, he could also wolf whistle. I think he too got my dad into trouble a few times because it was really loud. I say 'he' because we were all convinced Charlie was a boy, until ten years on he laid an egg and we had to change its name to Charlene.

When I was old enough, I went to a nursery called St Mary's, which was just around the corner from where we lived. My mum shared with me a story from then, of the time she came to pick Shaun and me up one day and I was acting strangely. I couldn't really speak properly at that age and was making an 'arh, arh' noise, then pointing to Shaun. Mum couldn't understand what I was trying to say but something about my actions concerned her. Weeks later, one of the nursery teachers, whom my mum was quite friendly with, randomly came up to her and asked, 'Has Shaun or anyone said anything about any experiences that they've had with the other nursery teacher, because there's been a few instances of people reporting that she's been quite physical with some of the kids?'

My mum replied: 'That's really funny you say that because Samantha's been randomly saying "Shaun, arh, arh" when I collect her.'

The next day at nursery, the teacher lifted me up to peer through the glass of each of the four classrooms, as teaching was taking place. At the first room she lifted me and asked, 'Shaun, arh, arh – that one?'

I went, 'No', and shook my head.

We then repeated this sequence as we moved to each window in turn. When we got to the last classroom and she said 'Shaun, arh, arh – that one?' I pointed directly to the teacher and went, 'Shaun, arh, arh.' They investigated this and apparently the teacher had been smacking the kids, but was managing not to leave any noticeable physical marks. It makes me sad and a bit sick to think about it, but even at such a young age I was so intuitive and protective of Shaun.

When Shaun and I were five, my sister Maxine decided to move with her husband over to the Wirral, the peninsula between the river Mersey and the river Dee. Mum was helping her look at houses and they were eyeing up a particular house in Beryl Road when my mum saw there was another one about five doors down. Maxine went to look at that too, but it was my mum who took a shine to it. My sister ended up going for a house about a mile away, in a completely different area, and my mum went for the house she'd seen with Maxine. She hadn't even been thinking about moving house.

This was a really significant time in my childhood, because while I had never felt poor, it is clear we were obviously at the lower end of the financial scale when compared to the rest of the country. My mum and dad had worked so hard to grow their business and give us a better life and the move to the Wirral, to a house that Mum and Dad still live in to this day, really felt like the accumulation of those efforts. My parents' work ethic was instilled in me.

When the day came to move, as Scousers call it, 'over the water', I was desperate to claim the front passenger seat of my parents' Mercedes E-Class. It was my mum's pride and joy – she loves cars – and she was going to be driving the children over, while my dad took the van packed with all our stuff. The front seat was usually for grown-ups, but we were allowed to sit in it if there was only one adult in the car. I remember arguing with my brothers over who should get the seat, with Mike claiming he was the oldest, me playing the girl card and Shaun claiming it was his turn as he never got a go. That's because Mike always claimed to be the oldest and I always played the girl card. When we got in the car, we found out the bloomin' mynah bird had got it above all of us! He was in his cage in the front, while the three of us were all strapped in the back. So we all immediately disliked the idea of a new house. The journey only took forty minutes but I remember it felt like an eternity.

As we pulled up on the driveway to the house on Beryl Road, a relatively busy road, I can remember a feeling as though we were visiting someone important and that this wasn't my home. It was a big, white-painted house, with stones on the driveway and nicely cut trees in the front. There was also a garage, which my dad explained was a house for a car. I remember when Dad opened the front door and thinking how tiny the hallway was, until I was told this was 'a porch', a room where you would put your coats and shoes before going into the house. It seemed very posh because I had never had a porch, nor had our car had its own house before.

The house itself, in comparison to Newby Grove, felt like a castle. The rooms were much bigger and Shaun and I were told we could each have a room of our own. No doubt my parents thought that would be an advantageous selling point to warm their children to the idea of a new house that was away from our friends. However, Shaun was my best friend, and the idea of not sharing a room with him immediately turned me off and I wanted to go back to my old house. That was until I saw the garden.

Beryl Road runs parallel to a very small river, which acts as a natural boundary to the houses that back onto ours. The river is awkwardly situated, as the distance between it and Beryl Road meant that the land was too small to sandwich in a new road for a row of houses, each with its own back garden. This meant that our new home had an oversized garden. It was roughly three quarters of an acre – or, as Mike, Shaun and I viewed it, almost half a full-sized football pitch.

We had no way of knowing then, of course, but it was in that garden that the first seeds of a sporting prowess that would lead me all the way to Rio were sown.

Chapter 2

No Girls Allowed

'Hey chink.'

It took me a moment to work out who the girl was referring to. She was really tall, with short blonde hair and had a very pale, stern face.

'You smell like a Chinese takeaway.'

It was then I realised she was talking to me.

At Hillside Primary School, Wirral, the playground was split in two – one side for the lower school and the other for the upper school and the older kids. Cross the tramlines on the tennis court and you were in their domain. Being in the lower school I watched where I went.

She was still there taunting me, pulling at the sides of her eyes to make them look Chinese.

Up until that point I hadn't been aware my ethnicity was any different to anyone else's. This was all new. Not only were we at a new school with new people, but this type of attitude was completely alien.

Even though I was only five years old, I remember not being massively fazed. I don't think I cried or made a big fuss.

It wasn't a big hoo-ha, but it came up in conversation with my mum.

'She shouldn't be saying that to you,' Mum said. 'If she says it again, go and tell the teacher. But just ignore it.'

That was how we were brought up. It wasn't a case of 'Don't fight back', it was more, 'Just ignore her, she's being silly. Be the bigger person.'

From what I can remember, I think it was sorted out quite quickly. I don't recall feeling that I was being bullied but I did feel a bit intimidated. It only happened once or twice. I think I ended up going and telling the teacher. I can imagine the girl probably got told off and warned never to do it again because that seemed to be the end of the matter.

It was my first year at primary school and we only spent one year there before our parents moved Shaun and me to the private Birkenhead School in Oxton.

Before we had moved over from Liverpool to the Wirral, my older brother Mike was already going to a school in Birkenhead called Prenton

Prep. Dad's business was doing well and my parents were keen to get him into a good school before he sat his eleven-plus exams.

When we moved schools, Shaun went to Birkenhead boys' and I attended the girls' school. For the first time, we'd be in different schools and we'd be apart until at least the sixth form.

It was just one of the many changes we'd had to get used to since moving from Liverpool. Although they are very close geographically, there's a friendly rivalry between Liverpool and Wirral. Liverpudlians believe themselves to be true, proud Scousers and consider people from the Wirral 'Woolybacks', or 'Wools' for short. Apparently the term dates back to when workers from out of town at Liverpool Docks were identifiable from the traces of wool on their clothing, from carrying woollen bales on their backs. Basically, though, it means you're a plastic Scouser. Even if you were born in Liverpool, like we were, it doesn't seem to matter.

Over the years, the boundary lines have been more clearly defined thanks to, believe it or not, wheelie bins. Upon their introduction nationally, Liverpool City Council elected to have purple wheelie bins, presumably to make them more visible and help the bin collectors, whereas Wirral Borough Council elected to have green wheelie bins, most probably to have what they deemed as unsightly bins blend in more to the surrounding areas of greenery.

Even now, if I'm away from home and happen to suggest I am a Scouser or from Liverpool within earshot of a fellow Liverpudlian, they will immediately challenge me, asking what colour my bin is. When I say green, they will say, 'So you are a Wool then?' or 'You're only a Plazzy-Scouser'.

Green bin or not, I will always maintain I am from Liverpool and I am equally as proud a Scouser as any purple bin owner. It was strange to think that living over the water could make such a difference.

Some things didn't change, particularly when it came to the important matter of football. Although my mum's family are all Everton fans, my dad supported Liverpool and he brought my brothers and me up to be Reds. So you can imagine derby day in our house, when the extended family come round, it can get pretty competitive. I got my first Liverpool strip when I was seven. I recently found a picture of me at that age looking really proud in my full kit.

At that age, I lived for playing football with my brothers. I'd come home from primary school, get changed and head into the garden. My brothers – and cousins when they came over – made no allowances for me because I was girl and I wouldn't have wanted them to. It was never an issue. I got stuck in and they treated me like one of the boys. When my cousins came over, I'd go in goal. Mainly, though, it would be me and Mike or Shaun having a kick around or playing a game called 'heads and volleys'. We would be out for hours, and would only come in when it got so dark you couldn't see the ball. I remember that I used to come in with the sweat dripping off me.

My favourite player growing up was Steve McManaman and I'd pretend to be him, and would give a running commentary during our kickabouts: 'And it's McManaman racing down the wing…' Shaun's favourite was Robbie Fowler. 'And McManaman crosses for Fowler, who shoots and scores!'

I didn't understand the difference between a state school and a private one. The main thing that was different was the uniform – little grey trousers and a shirt. Ties weren't compulsory but my parents always wanted us looking smart, so Shaun and I would always wear the tie, the jumper, the lot. You could only get my uniform from a shop called Watson Prickard in Liverpool, which now doesn't exist. For Shaun's uniform, there was a shop in the school grounds where you had to get all the attire, which included those little old school caps kids used to wear.

We had thirty kids in our class at Hillside and in my first class at Birkenhead I had just thirteen, which made a huge difference. We'd gone from fighting for attention to a much more academically focused environment. We were also very lucky because the sports facilities at Birkenhead were excellent. Back at Hillside, physical education was taken by the form teacher and was your traditional bean bag and hula hoop-based exercises. At Birkenhead we had a dedicated PE teacher called Allie Johnson and the facilities seemed out of this world. We had our own swimming pool, tennis courts and playing field and we experienced a variety of different sports. Even at that young age we were playing sports like lacrosse, albeit with plastic sticks.

Allie Johnson, whom I still speak to now, was one of those teachers who loved trying to get the best out of children and wasn't afraid to push them if she spotted potential. When I first tried tennis I liked it. I was pretty useful with a racket. I was only eight or nine but Allie pushed me to join a tennis club, so I became a member of Birkenhead Lawn Tennis Club. I played a few matches but I quickly found I didn't enjoy it. If I missed a shot or hit it into the net I'd hear sniggering behind me. I remember playing one girl and every point I lost, her mother and sister burst out laughing behind me. The experience made me realise that I preferred to be around people and, rather than be out there on my own, I wanted to be part of a team.

That was what I hoped football would give me. After all, I just wanted to play. I thought my dream was coming true when Shaun and I joined Wirral Panthers, the local football team in West Kirby. When we first started going to training we were still too young to play matches but it was great fun just to train and play inter-squad games. I hoped if I was good enough I'd get my chance one day.

I guess growing up I was something of a tomboy. Unfortunately, young girls then and even to this day seem reluctant to continue sport into their teenage years. They get teased for being sweaty or dirty, or called lesbians simply for enjoying sport, which is really quite sad. I don't think there's anything wrong with being a tomboy. I never wore dresses and although I had my own group of girl friends, I just wanted to go out and play football with Shaun and his mates. Just as my brothers and some of my cousins would do, some of the lads would put big tackles on me because they didn't like getting skinned or tackled by a girl. That helped toughen me up and I liked that Shaun and his friends just accepted me as one of their own.

When I reached nine or ten and the Panthers joined a local league, the fact that it was a boys' league didn't mean anything to me. I was one of the team. What difference did it make?

At first, not much.

I played a couple of games and was having the time of my life. I played left midfield, which suited my ability to take a pass and make things happen. Shaun was behind me at centre back. I loved it.

After the first couple of games, I started to hear comments from the sidelines. When I first showed up with Dad, no one paid any attention. I just looked like one of the other kids having a practice before the game started. When we got ready to play, however, and I got my kit on like the other players, that's when the comments started.

'Oh my God, there's a girl playing football … they've got a girl on their team … check this out.'

It was like I had three heads or something. Apparently it was unheard of in this league.

People walking past started to stop and stare. I was certainly attracting some attention.

It didn't faze me though; I just remember thinking, 'This is just the way it is.' Perhaps on some level I became relaxed with the concept of having an audience but it was a bit strange.

I was aware that they were only looking at me because I was a girl. I think even at that age it made me want to play better because I had the attitude, 'Well, I'll show you, I'm not just here to make the numbers up, I can actually play because I'm a girl.'

I was also aware that some of the opposition boys didn't know how to handle it. There were some lads who clearly didn't want to tackle me, or mark me because they were too scared to hurt me, or they just felt embarrassed and they didn't want to.

On the flipside there were lads who would go in so hard and make terrible tackles just to see if I could handle it. I was quite mindful of it, though, and being on the receiving end of that kind of attention helped to speed up my reactions so I wouldn't get caught in possession. I made sure I got the ball out of my feet quicker. I was never the kind of player to try to take on a million people. My style was 'get it and give it'.

I enjoyed the competitive nature of the games and thought I held my own. Unbeknownst to me, some people had other ideas. After about four games it emerged that a few complaints had been made to the local Wallasey Football Association that the Panthers had a girl playing for them. The local FA's response was to tell the club I couldn't play.

I was nine years old and effectively banned from playing in a children's league. It sounds incredible in today's era where boys and girls play regularly together up until a certain age, but clearly enough people were unhappy with it and the FA's response was to uphold their complaints rather than challenge their prejudices.

I was gutted. I remember thinking, 'Why can't I play?' It seemed unfair to think it was just because I was a girl.

My mum and one of the other player's dads, John Denham, who ran the team, tried to take it up with the local governing body, saying that the rule book said girls can play with boys up until the age of eleven, when they hit physical maturity.

Their response was that it was a boys' league and a boys' cup. Girls couldn't play. John and my mum went down to the FA in London and they confirmed that I was allowed to play until I was eleven. When they came back up north they had a meeting with the local FA again and a representative from London came up. The result was that the local FA had to allow it. Unfortunately, the ruling came too late.

While all the arguing had been going on, I had continued to turn up at training and could only watch the matches on a Sunday. The manager made me the water girl because he wanted to keep me included, but it wasn't the same. I just wanted to play.

Although I was clearly frustrated, I didn't make a big drama out of it. I think I was a tough little cookie even at that age.

When the ruling came through there were only two games remaining in the season. One was a league game but the final match was a cup final in Noctorum, up the road from where we lived.

I was allowed to play and the manager made me captain for the day. All the mums went to such an effort, getting balloons for the moment when we ran out of the changing room. We all got special new T-shirts and it was on a big full-sized pitch with proper goals.

We were playing a team called Greenleas. Before the game started, I went to the centre circle and shook hands with their captain as we had our photos taken. The funny thing about that photo is that the lad only came up to my chest in height. Physically I could actually give a lot of the boys a run for their money because girls hit puberty a lot quicker than boys. I even remember towering over Shaun for a brief period.

The final was a close match and we were trailing, I think 2–1, when the manager took me off a few minutes before the end. I was gutted but I imagine they wanted to give me a round of applause as a send-off because it would be the last game I'd play for them.

When I turned eleven, I joined a girls' team. There were two local options. One was Greenleas, whose boys' team had beaten us in the cup final, and whose girls' team were playing at a high standard in a more established league.

There was also Tranmere Rovers, who at the time I didn't know much about but obviously had a rich history, and also had name recognition nationally as their men's team were playing in the second tier of English football, pushing to get in the Premier League.

My brother Mike was all for me joining them. 'Sam, 100 per cent go to Tranmere,' he said, 'because when you're telling people who you play football for, no one will have a clue if you say "Greenleas on the Wirral". But if you say "Tranmere Rovers", everyone will be like, "That's decent". Straight away it gives you credibility.'

I'm glad he said that to me because it was so true. I was there until I was sixteen/seventeen, and that was exactly the reaction I got. I'm not saying that's the sole reason you should have for choosing a team but it gave me a boost, particularly after the experience I'd had.

Tranmere had a good setup. I remember going down for my first training session with them feeling so shy. I probably felt more nervous going to this session than I did turning up to the lads' team. At least then I'd had the comfort blanket of my twin brother being there and I'd known loads of his mates anyway.

I had to go to a small artificial pitch at the back of Tranmere's stadium, Prenton Park. It was probably a quarter of the size of a full pitch but I'd never seen so many girls playing football. There were two female coaches, too.

It was my first experience of proper competition because there were girls who had been at Tranmere for a while. This was their stomping ground. Instantly I could tell there were players who were a lot more skilful than I was. We had to dribble around and do keep-ups until the coach clapped her hands. I was terrible at keep-ups. Pass me the ball and I'd know where my pass was going before I even got the ball. I knew where the space was and things like that. My game was completely different to these tricks and flicks and in that first training session, I felt so terrible that I couldn't do all the things we were asked to.

In a sporting context, it was the first time I felt intimidated. I knew I was going to have to prove myself and show that I was good enough to be there. Some of the girls asked me what school I went to. When I said Birkenhead, they gave me grief: 'Oh, you're a posh girl. You go to a private school.'

They were all from state schools and because I wasn't, this made me different. I remember thinking, 'How can I be a posh girl?' I didn't feel like a posh girl. I also didn't speak any different to them and I lived pretty much in the same area. None of that mattered though. To them, if you went to a private school, even if you were only there thanks to an extraordinary effort from your parents, you were a posh girl. It was a gang mentality and I was a little different in some way. To argue would have been pointless.

Being singled out only added to my feeling of nervousness. I was thinking to myself, 'Am I enjoying this? Do I really want to be here?'

I was never one to give up just because something got hard. I continued to go down every Tuesday and train there, and over time, as I got to know the girls better, it got a little easier as I began to find my place within the group.

Tranmere's matches were on a Saturday so I could still go and watch Shaun's team play on a Sunday with my parents. It was like a family day out. Mum would catch up with her mates as the team was made up of Shaun's school friends, so she already knew a lot of the other mums from the school gate. They would bring their flasks of coffee and some nibbles and have a good catch-up on the sidelines. Meanwhile, my dad and the other fellas would help with the warm-ups and put the nets up.

When it came to my football matches we'd meet outside Tranmere stadium, where a double-decker bus would be waiting. The parents would be on the bottom and the players on the top. You had to pay £12 each for a seat on the bus and the club provided us with the kit, but we had to hand it back after the games. Although they had a good setup, compared to some of the clubs we were playing, Tranmere seemed a pretty poorly funded team.

We used to play the likes of Liverpool, Everton and Aston Villa. Being a red, it was thrilling for us to come up against a Liverpool side. I hadn't even realised they had a girls' team when I first started playing. When we played Everton, I always wanted to beat them even more than any other team!

Towards the end of my first season, Tranmere Rovers' men's senior team reached the final of the League Cup. This was particularly exciting for me as the nation was talking about Tranmere Rovers, the team I played for. It backed up Mike's advice to me that Tranmere's name recognition would be much more than Greenleas'. The game was the one of the last matches to be played at the old Wembley Stadium before it was knocked down ahead of its refurbishment. Our team let us keep our kits so when Dad and one of his mates took Shaun, me and one of Shaun's friends to the game, I wore my kit. Tranmere were unlucky to lose 2–1 to Leicester that day. I was thrilled to go to a proper football match.

But the experience of that game paled in comparison to the next match I went to – at Anfield, the home of my beloved Liverpool FC.

It was May 2000 and the occasion was the testimonial for Ronnie Moran, a club legend who had served as a player, captain, coach, assistant manager and, briefly when called upon, caretaker manager.

I was just so excited to finally be going to the home of my heroes. In the run-up to the day I planned my outfit meticulously, because it seemed to me, from watching the telly, that the fans wore their strips over their hoodies.

Just walking through the cobbled streets on the way to Anfield was a thrill. Many of the old terraced houses don't exist anymore because of the regeneration project around the ground but back then it seemed like we were stepping through hallowed streets.

I can still remember the feeling of walking to the ground, holding my dad's hand with a little bit of apprehension that I didn't want to lose him. Everybody around me was really tall. Before we even reached the ground, I was loving the atmosphere, and the fact that you could buy scarves and badges on the walk-up to the stadium. We bought chips and gravy outside and, even to this day, I still get chips and gravy in the very same shop before I go into a game.

We were sitting in the Kop and I loved it. I didn't feel scared or worried by the noise even though all around me men were cheering and shouting. I chanted along with the songs without really knowing the words.

I fell in love with it. After that I wanted to go to every game.

As luck would have it, I did get the chance to savour the unique atmosphere of Anfield many more times – and often in the company of greatness.

When I was part of the boys' football team, the son of Liverpool's all-time leading goal scorer Ian Rush was part of our team. Shaun became very good friends with Jonathan – or JJ, as he was known – and Mum grew close to Tracy, Ian's wife at the time. They became really good family friends to the point where, from around 1999 to 2005, we would go on holiday together, staying at his villa in Portugal.

At that age I didn't realise what a legend Ian was. It was only from the fans' comments and reaction that I started to think, 'Wow, he must have been good.'

That's when you sit back and think it's a bit surreal. It was only at Anfield that I realised how famous he was. I'd go to the games mainly with my dad, Shaun, JJ and Ian. It was an amazing time because we got to go to the players' lounge after the game and meet all my heroes. I used to get my programme signed every week, even though I'd got many of the same signatures just the week before.

This was 2001, when Gérard Houllier was making Liverpool a force to be reckoned with. In February that year, we won the Worthington League Cup by beating Birmingham on penalties. With Wembley out of action the match was held at what was then the Millennium Stadium in Cardiff.

Liverpool were back in Cardiff in May that year in an FA Cup final against Arsenal – and we'd be there to see it. We didn't go with Ian this time; instead my dad got three tickets to take Shaun and me.

I was so excited. I remembered from the Tranmere final at Wembley seeing all the cars decorated in the club colours for the drive down so I used the week before to prepare. I wanted to make sure the colours clearly made it clear it was Liverpool and not Arsenal, so I got red and yellow ribbons and tied them to the aerial. I got two new scarves and put them out the back passenger windows and got another one that said 'Liverpool FC' to lie across the back window. I also put a flag on the parcel shelf.

We woke at 5.00 am to leave at 6.00 am. I was so proud going down as a Liverpool fan. I sat up so my shoulders would face outwards so everyone could see I was wearing a Liverpool shirt. I had Dad put on U2's *Beautiful Day* – the song Sky Sports used to play in the build-up to live games – as we approached the ground.

Our seats were in the corner at the end Liverpool would be shooting towards in the second half. After all the excitement of the build-up, Liverpool were on the back foot for a lot of the match and when Arsenal scored in the seventy-second minute, we started to fear the worst. However, Michael Owen popped up with two brilliant goals. When his worldy second went in, we were right in the corner he ran to for his flip celebration. I was on the end of the row next to a big, sweaty gentleman and he picked me up in all the commotion. Incredible scenes.

Four days later, Liverpool were in the UEFA Cup Final in Dortmund against Spanish side Alavés. In a nine-goal thriller, the Reds emerged victorious 5–4 after extra time to complete a unique cup treble.

Two years on from that historic season, Liverpool were back in a Worthington League Cup final against Manchester United, once again at the Millennium Stadium. This time we did go down with Ian Rush and JJ. I remember that Ian had his two tickets nicked on the walk up to the stadium. Our seats were next to his so we waited until the last minute and the police took us up because whoever was sitting there would have bought them illegally. Sure enough, there were two men sitting in their seats, who were then ejected.

Liverpool went on to win it 2–0, Michael Owen hitting another four minutes from the end. It was the perfect end to an amazing season of watching Liverpool. That year I'd been to as many games as I could, when my own matches allowed.

Playing for Tranmere had been a steep learning curve. There were some players who embraced me and didn't view me as a threat because they were confident in their own ability and then there others who did see me as a threat and therefore didn't even look at me, let alone speak to me.

Some of them wouldn't even pass to me. Even at that young age, I was thinking, 'Why isn't she passing to me?' And then when she did pass to me, if I gave it away, I'd feel terrible. It was a lot to learn and grapple with.

Even the coach at times took the Mick that I was a posh girl. 'Oh get up Sam, you're a posh girl, you'll have to get used to how we play here.'

It was just banter, but I could easily have taken it the other way.

Sometimes the Mick-taking was justified. They used to rib me for taking a briefcase to school. I probably deserved that. Who takes a briefcase to school?

It's all part of being in a team and it was good for me to experience that and learn how to handle it. It would stand me in good stead later in life.

Unfortunately, I began to enjoy the whole experience less and less. I'd developed into a defender at Tranmere but wasn't an automatic first pick. We'd travel to places like Birmingham to play Aston Villa and I'd sometimes be left on the bench because the coach rarely wanted to change the defence, unless there was an injury. And if I did get on it would only be for the last ten minutes or so.

Besides, another sport that had always been secondary to football in my eyes was coming to the fore. I was starting to show some prowess in a game that would take over my life in ways I never dreamt possible.

Chapter 3

Thank You Mr Cartmel

The first my mum knew was when she came to pick me up from football and another parent came up to her.

'Your Sam played well in the match the other day,' the woman said.

Mum smiled. She perhaps assumed she was talking about football.

'She's a brilliant hockey player,' the woman added.

Mum was stunned as she didn't even know I played hockey. I was ten at the time and had been playing matches at school. Being at Birkenhead was the first chance I'd had to hold a stick and I had taken to it quite easily, but I was so consumed with love for football at the time that it didn't really register. That's why I never thought to mention it to my parents.

I'd got into hockey because during school lunchtimes there were clubs for all sorts of sports, from netball to lacrosse. I went to hockey and straight away I slotted into centre midfield. I loved that pivotal role, being able to get up and down the pitch, helping with defence and setting up attacks.

Our matches were held on a Wednesday afternoon. For the next game, Mum came along to see for herself if I was any good. She says that even at that young age I stood out. 'I'm not being biased,' she said, 'but you could just see your vision on the pitch, the way you passed to people and your tackling.'

What I hadn't realised was that, whilst Mum was never massively sporty as a child, she was always picked for the school hockey team and became captain. She used to love playing hockey.

I'm intrigued about where my sporting ability came from. I always assumed, if anything, it came from my dad's side as he was always into sport. He was a very competent swimmer and represented his school and Singapore state in the pool. He was a keen cyclist as well. In addition, one of his sisters, my Auntie Sally, used to play football for Singapore when she was twenty.

But Mum had a greater influence than perhaps I gave her credit for when I was growing up. Her attitude when it came to sport was important. She never said to me, 'Don't worry, it's the taking part that counts.'

Don't get me wrong; she never took it to the extreme of saying 'You must win', it was more a case of, 'Come on Sam, you can do it'. She used to encourage me but never told me it was okay to lose. I think that helped instil in me a desire to win. If I lost, Mum wouldn't come down hard on me. She'd say if she felt I was unlucky but she encouraged me to do my best and gave me the confidence that I could do it. If I have any children in the future I think that's how I would like to be with them.

In my younger days we played to win. It didn't always work out that way but win or lose, we learned important lessons. I hear some schools these days don't announce winners and instead issue everyone with medals. It's all about the taking part that counts, which doesn't seem right to me. You have to learn how to lose as a child and how to conduct yourself while dealing with a loss. The same goes if you're a winner. You need to know how to behave, how to commiserate with your opponents and not rub the loss in their faces. If children are taught that everybody wins, then how is that going to set them up for the rest of their lives? When it comes to them going for a job interview, there will only be one winner. A company isn't going to give a job to everyone that applies.

Thankfully, Birkenhead wasn't like that. We took our sport seriously but made sure it was fun, too.

I owe my first PE teacher, Allie Johnson, a debt of gratitude for pushing me on. After watching me play in the school matches and being impressed by my natural ability, she put me forward for the Wirral county trials for the under-12 team.

'I think this would be a brilliant experience for Sam,' Mrs Johnson said to my mum. 'Send her to the Wirral trials. I think she's got a good chance. She's a very good player. Even if she doesn't get in, I think for the future it will put her in good stead because I can see her going for more and more trials.'

The trials were held at the Oval Leisure Centre in Bebington, which I later found out was where *Chariots of Fire* was filmed. I turned up with my mum not knowing anyone. There were lots of girls, all older, from a host of different schools. There were some faces I recognised from Birkenhead but they were in the year above so I didn't know them. I started to feel nervous.

The trials lasted the full day. Once we'd registered, an official handed me a coloured bib with a number on the back and we were then put through different drills and all the time someone was standing there with a clipboard assessing our ability.

I don't think I got the concept of what a trial really meant or what team I was even going to represent if I did make it through. I think I just found it a bit strange. Being unsure of what was happening meant I kept quite quiet. But when we were arranged into teams for games I came alive. I've been like that throughout my career. Put me on a hockey pitch and I'll always shout for the ball, pass and run like my life depended on it.

It was so long ago, I can't recall if we were told there and then or they sent us a letter afterwards, but amazingly, given my age, they selected me. The team was Wirral County, which would be competing in the forthcoming Merseyside Youth Games.

I didn't know then but my selection was thanks to a coach who would have a major impact on my life – Peter Cartmel.

Peter seemed quite old, certainly to a young girl, and he was tall – about 6 feet 5 inches – was skinny and spoke in a very soft voice. He'd be hunched over and wore Dunlop trainers with an old school shell suit and had a club bag that he carried around like a handbag. Due to his quirky mannerisms and the fact that he wasn't married, a few people over the years would question his sexuality, but he was just very eccentric. And he loved his hockey and teaching. He lived on his own in Aintree and taught at Kingsmead School, in Hoylake.

It was Peter Cartmel who had selected me. Later on it came to light that some of the other selectors, among those another PE teacher whose pupils were also trying out, didn't want to select me because I was too young, and it was Mr Cartmel who put his foot down and said, 'No. She's young but she's good enough. She's good enough to represent.'

Knowing that someone had that much faith in my ability meant the world to me.

The first time I was called up to represent the Wirral I was very nervous. The Merseyside Youth Games, held at Wavertree in Liverpool, were a huge deal and I remember feeling tiny compared to everyone else – not like the days of turning out for the boys' football team. It was a beautiful, sunny day and I wore a little cap to keep the bright light out of my eyes. My skirt was pulled up over my waist and the hockey stick was way too big for me.

Thankfully, the Birkenhead girls took me under their wing and looked after me. I was going to need their support because there were girls from other schools, including Kingsmead, and one girl in particular obviously decided she didn't like me. She was from West Kirby. She was basically a little cow. Never mind not passing the ball, during our match she hardly even looked at me. When she did, she shot me daggers. If I said something, she cut me down. It was far worse than anything I'd experienced with the girls' football.

Maybe, again, it was a case of jealousy, or she felt threatened, but whatever the reason she went out of her way to intimidate me. Once more, I had to do what I felt was right and try not to let her affect me. I had to concentrate on my own game and do my best to justify my selection because Mr Cartmel had stuck his neck out for me. I wanted to repay that faith.

I don't think much was expected of me as I think they wanted me there more for the experience than anything else. The set up was a round robin group stage of about four matches and the winners from two groups would go through to a knockout stage. We were playing teams like Knowsley, St Helens and Liverpool South. I started off not getting a lot of pitch time but when I came on I made such an impact that as we progressed through the games I was featuring more and more.

Mum said some of the parents weren't happy. She could hear comments on the sidelines about why a 10-year-old was seeing so much action. She also said she heard one pushy parent say to their child, 'If she can do it why can't you?'

Mum said I stood out because I made up for my lack of inches on the others by being fast. I could get from one end of the pitch to the other before anyone caught me. She also said I was team player, never selfish. Even if there was a weaker player, I would try to set them up and make them look good.

We actually ended up winning that tournament and it was my first taste of success. I had won my first proper winner's medal.

The following year was big in more ways than one. Not only did I move into the secondary school at Birkenhead but I also continued my progression with hockey. I had the same county trials that I'd had the year before but this time I was in year seven and was a lot more confident, and I knew a lot more of the girls because I'd moved into the senior school. The county team had changed somewhat. There were still a few of the girls from the other schools but I came out of my shell a little and felt relaxed enough to have a conversation and joke around while we were warming up.

The Merseyside Youth Games that year were held at the Oval in Bebington, so it was a pitch I knew and was also a lot closer to home. I played a key role in the tournament and we won gold again. I remember the *Liverpool Echo* dedicated a pullout section to the games and carried photos of all the teams across four pages. It was my first proper press cutting. Mum and Dad kept it and I remember hoping it would be the first of many write-ups.

Following that success I joined Mr Cartmel's club side, Mini Panthers. I think it was just coincidence they were also called Panthers, like the boys' football team I had played for. They met after school on Mondays for training and Mr Cartmel used to run it himself, largely out of his own pocket, although parents paid a small sub. Nick Clark, an ex-England player, helped out with the coaching and kids from all over the Wirral would come to learn hockey. Come rain or shine, we'd turn up, pay our two pounds and he would lay on the sessions. Mr Cartmel was a very good coach and everyone loved him because he was such a nice guy. That said, we all knew when he was angry about something because he had this big, massive, booming voice. He hardly ever had cause to use it but when he did … wowzers!

He used to take us to play games against other clubs and every so often we'd go to tournaments and would normally win. He had us so well drilled, it wasn't just a free for all; we learned proper tactical elements of the game.

My weekly schedule was starting to mount up. From the age of twelve I was going to Mini Panthers after school on a Monday, on Tuesday I had football, Wednesday it was lacrosse, more football on Thursday, Friday was a day off and then I'd have football on a Saturday. My parents must have been knackered driving me around everywhere. And it was to get even busier.

Another key influence on my hockey was my secondary school PE teacher, Moira Concannon. She encouraged me to join a more senior club. I was spoiled for choice locally. My main options were Oxton or Neston, but Mrs Concannon believed I should join Chester. It was further away but they had a women's team in the national league and she thought I'd benefit from the higher standard of competition that their setup would bring. Chester met on a Wednesday night from 6.00 to 7.30 pm. If I made it into their team, they played matches on a Saturday afternoon. So, potentially, I'd have football in the morning and then hockey in the afternoon.

It's just as well I never had any other hobbies besides my sport. I always regret not taking up a musical instrument when I was younger as I'd love to play one now, but I'm not sure how I would have fitted one in. While I was still in primary school I tried to join the school orchestra but really it was a bit of a ruse. It was during the winter months and it was so cold in the playground that a friend and I figured if we joined the orchestra we'd be able to sit inside in the warmth. We turned up and the music teacher put us on percussion. I didn't have a clue what I was doing, so I only lasted about three sessions.

I was also fortunate that my sporting activities didn't seem to impact negatively on my studies. Academically I was doing fine. I was never the cleverest person in the class – I was more of a 'B' grade student than an 'A' grade – but my results were steady throughout my school life.

It was also probably a blessing that I didn't have much of a social life outside my sporting activities. Don't get me wrong; I had friends but I had been too focused on sport to have much consideration for other teenage girl obsessions.

I had still been a bit of a tomboy, although when I hit thirteen I did make a bit of a concession and started to change. I guess the first sign that boys and girls were heading down a different path came in year seven, around the time girls hit puberty and some of them started to wear bras. There was a period when the biggest dilemma was, 'Do you wear one, do you not?' It sounds pathetic but it was such a drama. In the summer it was obvious who was because when they took their school jumper off you could see whether there were straps showing or not. All of a sudden it became cool, so everyone was wearing one whether they needed one or not. I'd started wearing a bra in year seven so I was starting to become a little more conscious of how I looked.

The next big moment came when Shaun and I turned thirteen. My twin brother and I always used to have joint birthdays – I don't know how our parents coped! Anyway, for our joint thirteenth, Shaun invited boys from his school and I invited the girls. It was a pretty epic party, if I do say so. There were about sixty kids in total and it was the first time I ever ventured into a dress. Even then it was a sporty, cotton number, not what I'd consider fancy or girly girl, just a simple grey dress with a white cardigan, and I insisted I wore it with trainers. I wasn't going full-on proper girl just yet!

We were at that stage in life where my mates were into getting dressed up way more than I was. I thought I'd better do something to stop them taking the Mick. I can actually recall feeling really nervous about what people would think, because I was always in jeans or trackie bottoms.

Despite the clothes I wore, I always looked feminine. My hair was always long and I used to spend time getting it just right. This was the era before straighteners were everywhere and my mum used to iron my hair. It sounds daft to describe it now but you used to have to lay your hair out on the ironing board, your mum put the iron on your hair and you pulled your hair out. There was no other way to straighten your hair back in the day. If you tried to do that now, people would be like, 'What on earth are you doing?'

And of course it was important to look good when we went along to the local discos. They were called the Frenzies, which happened in the civic hall every month. Tickets for a Frenzy were in high demand and people made sure they got theirs as soon as they went on sale in the local library. It was the big night when we were in our early teens. People would coordinate them with their birthday parties and you'd see them arriving in Limousines, which we did when we were a bit older. Everybody got dressed up and this was the time I really started wearing dresses and became quite conscious of the way I looked. I started experimenting with make-up and we felt like proper grown-ups when we went out.

Having said all that, I was a late bloomer. I wasn't that interested in boys. All of my friends had snogged someone long before I had. I was very picky back then. I still am in fact.

I don't mind admitting I was a bit of a prude. There was a way to do things and the way you initiated a snog was to get your friend to go up to someone you liked and get them to tap him on the shoulder and say, 'Will you get into my mate?' The lad would pretend to shrug his shoulders like he was doing them a massive favour and say, 'Okay then.' That was the cue to start snogging. It was very sophisticated!

So many of my friends had their first kiss that way, but not me. I did have a few lads approach me and ask but I would always say no. And I never asked anyone to snog. I was way too prudish. Plus my brother would be there with his mates. I preferred to be the instigator, or the negotiator.

So there was a lot going on in the busy life of a 13-year-old when I decided to follow Mrs Concannon's advice and try out with Chester Hockey Club.

The club was very welcoming. I didn't have to face a trial situation; they were happy for anyone to come along. I was training with the fourth team anyway, which comprised girls of different ages, so there wasn't a great deal of expectation.

That said, I was naturally keen to impress and never gave anything less than 100 per cent, so I went along wanting to get stuck in and show the coaches what I was capable of.

It was a dark Wednesday evening and we were training under the floodlights. We started warming up, everything was fine and I was feeling good, getting into my stride. We did a bit of stick work and I was looking at the other girls, trying to get a sense of how I would measure up against the rest of the fourth team.

When we started playing a match situation everything changed. I went to take a pass and completely missed the ball. 'That's odd,' I thought. Then it happened again. One moment I'd see the pass but then I'd lose the ball. I literally couldn't see it.

What was happening?

I rubbed my eyes, trying to work out what was going on. No one around me seemed to bother. It was the first time they had seen me play and I think they probably thought that was my standard.

I knew I'd had issues with my eyesight for a few years but during games it had always been fine. And there had been no problems when I played football.

I started to feel a bit concerned. Was there something seriously wrong with my eyes? Was it going to affect my ability to play hockey?

Chapter 4

Teenage Trials

'Are you okay, Sam?' My mum and dad had been watching training.
'Why didn't you pass it there?'

'Because I couldn't see anything,' I said.

I felt as though I was going blind because I couldn't see the ball at all.
For the remainder of the session I'd been squinting so hard but still couldn't
make it out.

Mum made an appointment for me to go back to the opticians and in the
meantime I wore glasses to play hockey, which obviously wasn't ideal. You
wouldn't be allowed to do that now. I was okay in the daylight – I could see
a bit better, if a little fuzzy – but at night, under the floodlights, I was lost.

Mum asked the optician about contact lenses. As I was still quite young
we couldn't assume I'd automatically get them. Thankfully I could – and
wow, what a difference it made. I could see!

Almost overnight I went from being a good player to an excellent player
because I could see the ball so much more sharply. I could trap balls that
were coming at me fast, I could see passes clearly – and the difference at
training was amazing because my confidence soared.

When I was still thirteen I made the ladies' fourth team. I was the
youngest there by some considerable distance. My shirt number was '46'.
There were other teenagers but I found that the older women took me
under their wing. Mrs Concannon was right; joining a proper women's team
helped my game and made me a lot more mature. We still had a laugh but I
learned more about how to hold myself, how to behave. If I got frustrated or
angry I quickly had to check myself because they'd either tell me off or be
like, 'Come on Sam.' They had no time for teenage tantrums.

When you've got an older woman telling you 'Right, forget that' or 'That
was really good', it helps shape you into a more rounded player.

When I broke into the team, I was still playing football for Tranmere
Rovers, so Saturdays became my own private race against the clock.

Tranmere's matches would be over in Allerton, Liverpool. On a Saturday
morning I'd get up, have some breakfast and Dad would drive me over. I
would have to be there for about 10.00 am for the match starting at half past.

The games weren't full ninety minutes but we were moving into eleven-a-side matches, where previously they had been seven-a-side, so it was pretty full on. We would finish at about 11.30 am and, while everyone else headed for the changing room, I'd race to the car to get changed. Dad would park as close to the pitch as possible to save us a few minutes. I'd kick my muddy boots off and he would be banging them together while I started to get ready for hockey. I'd still be switching into my hockey gear while he was driving off.

We'd pick up some food on the way to hockey. In an age of sports nutrition and carefully balanced diets this probably sounds terrible but we would always pass Harry Ramsden's, so we'd pull in there, have a quick fish and chips and then head over to Chester for the match. Let's just say you can get away with it at that age!

I'd get to Chester in time to start the match at 3.00 pm and that would be my Saturday.

On Sunday it was Shaun who would go and play football and we'd go round to watch him. My mum would come to my matches as well when she could and she would be there as well on a Sunday. Both our parents gave up the majority of their weekends for us. It was a big sacrifice on their part.

I can remember playing football against one team from a pretty rough area and it all kicked off. Their players were committing some terrible fouls during the match. Our forward went up for a fifty-fifty ball with their keeper, who started rolling around on the floor and then had a go at our striker. More of their girls waded in, then the parents from the other team ran in to fight and half the parents from Tranmere raced on to try to break it all up.

My mum was there and as I was at the back she stood to the side of me and said, 'You stay there Samantha. Don't you even think about it.'

'I'm not thinking about it,' I said.

I was never the type of player who would get the red mist. If someone came in and hit me hard I didn't get up and kick off. I would stand up for myself and say something like 'That's an absolute disgrace', but I would never physically lash out or get in anyone's face.

After the melee died down two parents from each team got carded and had to go and walk away.

Even at games where the kids were as young as six and seven, there were parents losing the plot. That Tranmere match was the only one of mine where parents were sent off. However, Shaun's team played matches where rope was pegged around the pitch to stop parents encroaching onto the playing side.

You don't really get the same at hockey. I think that's because discipline is a big part of the sport. If you give a referee abuse they'll card you, send you off for a minute. I've been carded because the referee thought I was swearing at her, but I was cursing myself. In situations like that there's no point in standing arguing with the referee, like you see in football with players surrounding the officials. In hockey now there's the self-pass rule so if you stop to complain, your opponent's already got the ball and started running away with it. So you don't actually have the time to remonstrate. It's one of my favourite rules and I would love to see professional football bring it in.

The only scrapes I got into were on the injury front. Playing hockey can sometimes feel like you're taking your life in your hands when you're facing eleven fired-up women armed with sticks.

I never liked to make a fuss about injuries. I'd had the odd whack to the face when I was younger, an occasional stick in the ribs, but I always felt a bit embarrassed if I went down. I think that comes from the days of playing football in our back garden with my brothers and cousins. They expected the girl to cry if she got hurt and I didn't want to ever prove them right.

I once took that attitude to the extreme when I suffered my worst injury – which came not from playing hockey, funnily enough, but in a game of rounders. It was during a North West school tournament in Blackburn and I was the bowler. I didn't realise I'd been hurt and so I didn't mention anything to my mum when I got home.

A short while later my friend Eleanor rang up. 'I'm just wondering how Sam is?' she said.

'She's having a nap. How do you mean?' my mum replied.

'Well, Sam got the ball smashed in the side of her head after she bowled it.'

I couldn't remember anything about it, but I ended up having concussion for a week.

Upon joining Chester I finished with Mr Cartmel's Mini Panthers. In truth, I'd outgrown the club too. But that wasn't the end of my relationship with him by any means. He would remain an ever-present and important figure in my hockey development. So much so that I was honoured many years later, when I was around twenty-five years old, to be asked to speak at his funeral.

Now I was playing regularly, and thanks to the contact lenses, my progression was rapid. Within a year of playing with Chester I moved through the teams and was soon playing for the first team in the National League.

But although I benefitted hugely from playing with the club's best players, there was a downside to starring with women ten and twenty years older than me. After the matches the rest of the team dived into the showers. I was mortified. I didn't want to expose my 14-year-old body to these fully-grown women. They used to take the Mick out of me and called me 'Sweaty Sam' because I'd refuse to change from my kit, but I didn't care.

I think it took me until I was sixteen before I ventured in, and even then I kept my sports bra and knickers on. As I got older I realised I was being silly. No one even looks at anyone else's body but it was all part of growing up and at the time it seemed a big deal. I think all teenagers are more self-conscious than they really should be.

The upturn in my form led to a trial with Cheshire. The schools would enter the trials and the selectors picked a Cheshire team to play against sides like Lancashire and Greater Manchester in a summer competition.

Before my trial I spoke to Mr Cartmel and he gave me pointers about things I should do, which was very helpful. He would go on to do this throughout my career. He'd write a little note: 'Don't forget to do this, and if you believe that you're in the right then follow your heart.' His writing was so ornate and perfect, with distinctive little flicks, so that when a letter came in the post I'd instantly know it was from him and always felt excited to open it. He really was one in a million.

Ahead of the Cheshire county trials, I remember going to Taskers sportswear and seeing equipment from a brand called Dita. I was used to playing with a standard Slazenger stick from JJB Sports. I thought, 'Whoa, this is a proper professional stick.'

My dad was with me and we didn't really understand the different features of professional hockey sticks, such and the bow or bend in a stick and how the lengths varied.

'Go on, we'll treat you,' Dad said. 'You're doing so well, you can have it for your Cheshire trials next week.'

At the trials I couldn't wait to try it out. It looked so cool. We hadn't long started when I went to cross the ball and chipped it right into a girl's face. Luckily she had a gum shield in because it caught her right in the teeth. I felt so guilty.

I tried again but the bow in the lower part of the stick just made the ball rocket into the air. I played with it for an hour and reverted back to the old stick my parents had advised me to take just in case.

It didn't do me any harm, however, as I got selected, and those Cheshire trials led to the North of England trials, although this time I wasn't so lucky and was passed over for selection. I was fuming as I thought I'd played well but there was always the following year to try again.

Around this time my hockey and football were vying for my complete attention.

Tranmere had a school of excellence for the best under-15 and under-17 players on Merseyside. I can remember playing with the likes of Jodie Taylor, who was the top scorer in the women's European Championships in 2017 and is now ever-present within the England setup. I could see my football career taking off and I was offered the chance to play at a higher level, which I took. However, my game time soon became limited, as a punishment of sorts, because I kept missing training to play in various hockey matches that were scheduled on the same nights. The coaches didn't like that football wasn't my only priority.

Trying to succeed at sport when you're going through your teens is a difficult task. It wasn't just football that briefly threatened to curtail my hockey prospects. It was hard to stay focused when you're at the mercy of external influences.

After my slow start on the boy front, I finally found out what the fuss was about at a Frenzy disco by snogging my first fella. I fancied one particular guy and spoke to him at every disco. I remember we finally snogged and my mates all going, 'Oh my God, you've had your first kiss.'

My parents picked me up at 10.00 pm, when it was over, but I didn't dare talk about anything that happened at the Frenzy. God forbid. A few months later the same boy became my first proper boyfriend. It seemed like we had something special for all of a few weeks but we split after a month.

It was when I was fourteen that I also had my first drink. Like most teenagers you started with little tipples and trying to nick an alcopop out of the fridge when you were having a sleepover. My friends and I only drank when there was a house party but unfortunately for me, these mostly fell on a Friday night, when I had hockey the next day. Twice in the early days of drinking I woke up after a party feeling a bit sick and not wanting to go to hockey. My mum and dad were adamant. 'You made a commitment to your team, you've got yourself into this state,' they said. 'You have to go.'

So I did, and I somehow got away with it.

One time I was at a house party and two of my mates got drunk and went walkabout on the local streets. I'd had a bit to drink but realised I'd better go and look for them. I found them paralytic on the ground by a park bench. At first I didn't know what to do because everyone had gone from the house party. The only thing I could do was call my mum. She rang the mums of the girls and they all came and we made sure the girls were all right.

Although the incident had sobered me up, I was still a bit drunk, but Mum said, 'I'm so proud that wasn't you today.'

I remember feeling really quite guilty, but this was only one of a handful of times I ever really ventured from being generally a very well-behaved girl.

It was actually far too easy to get your hands on booze at that age. I was fifteen when I got served in a shop because they thought I was eighteen. I was so nervous and grabbed a chewing gum from the side of the till in an effort to look more casual.

The shopkeeper asked me my age but when I replied 'Eighteen', he just asked, 'When?'

'Last month,' I said. That was all the confirmation he needed.

Even though I'd felt drunk a few times when I was fourteen, the first proper hangover I had when I was on holiday in Gran Canaria with my brother Mike, my sister Maxine and her two kids. I was fifteen, and when Michael, who was twenty-one, was buying some beer, I pestered him to buy me an alcopop. That night he taught me how to strawpedo – the art of using a straw in a bottle so you can neck it quicker. I tried to do it but couldn't. It was coming out of my nose but I thought I was so cool to be drinking with my older brother. The hotel had a nightclub in the basement and I had a few more drinks there. I was so hung-over the next day from being sick. Thankfully, it was a learning experience and I learned not to overindulge.

Having a busier social life meant I needed more money to fund it, so I took on a part-time job working at my sister's café at a Total Fitness gym. I liked having my own money and some independence, and I don't remember ever asking my parents for money from the age of fifteen onwards. I was getting a monthly pay cheque for £360 and I thought I was rich! I remember being in the café and one lad saying to me, 'God Sam, you're never still.' Maybe it was my dad's work ethic but I always felt I wanted to be doing something. I couldn't just stand there staring or chatting like some of the others did. I used to get so bored if I did that, so if there was a table that needed cleaning, I'd clean it straight away, and I'd always be just brushing the floor, or tidying the counters or restocking the fridges. I wanted to be the best I could be – no matter what I set my mind to. Everything was a competition.

The usual teenage trials and temptations might have briefly threatened my commitment to hockey but my fortunes were about to take a turn in a direction that showed me the potential rewards to all the hard work and training.

At the next North of England trials I made the cut, and was selected to be part of the squad. I found myself playing in a tournament that pitched my region against the finest players that the country had to offer and my performances were being noticed at a higher level.

Not long after starring for the North, a letter dropped through our letterbox in Beryl Road. Some national scouts had spotted my potential and it was an invitation to join some of the country's hottest young under-16 prospects at Bisham Abbey, the national centre for hockey.

It was the chance I'd always dreamed of – the chance to play for England.

Chapter 5

Making the Grade

I couldn't feel my hands. It was so cold my bones were shaking and my teeth were chattering. The sleet had turned to hail, which was bouncing off the ground.

Welcome to England!

When I'd imagined what it would be like to get my first taste of what life might be like in the international setup, this wasn't it. I'd never known training like it and I ached in muscles I never knew I had.

Bisham Abbey was the home of England Hockey and the centre for a number of other elite sporting institutions. The facilities were second to none. Everything was organised to military precision and one of the coaches in particular must have modelled her persona on an army drill instructor.

'Why are you all taking so long?' she yelled, her Dutch/English voice ringing through my ears. 'Right! The last three to put their shin pads on will be doing a lap race around the pitch. The first one round will get to stop, the second two will then run off and if you are last you will have to do an extra one on your own.'

Oh. My. God.

I was always slow putting my shin pads on because I wanted them to be just right. 'Sod it,' I thought. I tried to speed it up but it was no good. I was in the last three.

We were marched to the side of the pitch.

'One lap. No cutting corners. Round the back of the goals,' the coach yelled.

The physio was joining us … apparently for the fun of it.

'Go!'

We were off. I might have been a slowcoach getting ready but I wasn't going to be doing two laps of the pitch. I flew round and absolutely smashed it. I came first by quite a margin.

Being made an example of weirdly worked in my favour. The coaches got to see how fast I could run and how seriously I competed, regardless of what the competition was.

In those two days at Bisham Abbey I learned more about training and myself than in several weeks in a team setup.

Forty girls had been invited to the trial. That number would be whittled down over several meetings until they arrived at a suitable squad. The under-16s took in players in two age groups – girls that were fifteen and girls that were sixteen – and a vast majority of the 16-year-old girls had already been to Bisham Abbey and had represented England the year before.

For the whole time, the rain, sleet and hail didn't let up. I was soaked through and I felt constantly scrutinised, like every mannerism was being analysed to gauge if I was England material.

I must have been though – because I made it into the squad that would represent my country in Berlin that summer against Europe's finest nations.

My 15-year-old ambitions had just been given rocket boosters. I was the definition of proud, and my parents were ecstatic. Mum was so excited she rang up our local paper, the *Wirral Globe*, and they ran an article on my selection.

The tournament was a mini four-nation contest in Berlin, featuring hosts Germany, Netherlands, Spain and England. Germany and the Dutch had formidable squads and boasted a good record against us. I was so thrilled to be going on my first hockey overseas trip and to be able to represent my country.

When it was time to leave I was very excited. We were flying from Heathrow and when the time came for my dad to drive me down I was buzzing to put my England kit on. I was kitted out in the full tracksuit. We stopped at a service station and I made sure everyone could see I was off to represent England. Even the kitbag was England branded. It was the real McCoy, not replicas like you could buy in the shop. I was so, so proud.

By the time we met up I was a little more relaxed because by then I knew some of the girls a bit better and was more comfortable in their company. I was going to be away for a week. The tournament was held over three or four days. After we landed we had two days of training and then into the competition. My mum and dad were coming out to watch and I couldn't have been happier.

It was the first time I had a daily planner to adhere to, so we had to wake up at a certain time, have breakfast at this time, a morning walk at that time. Even the idea of a daily planner was all very exciting back then. It felt really professional. We were staying in university halls so we all had single rooms. I was petrified I'd miss the wake-up call so I hardly got any sleep at all.

In an effort to bring us closer together the coaches organised some team-building exercises. The older age groups, the under-18s and under-21s, were also there so we were grouped with a 'big sister' from each for a quiz. Two girls from my age group came up to me during our allocated social time – Kirsty Mackay and Lindsay French. Lindsay had a very strong Yorkshire accent and Kirsty had a very strong Blackpool accent, yet they walked up to me and they said, 'Go on, speak. You're a Scouser.'

I thought, 'What are they talking about?'

I couldn't believe they were giving me a hard time about my accent – although it was the ideal icebreaker! Long gone were the days at Tranmere Rovers when I was considered the posh girl. Kirsty, Lindsay and me hit it off and became good friends after that.

When we were going through training and held a practice match the coaches put me in defence, at full back. I didn't think much of it; I was just happy to be there, but I would have rather played in midfield. During the competitive matches that followed I was also put in defence, and I grew to enjoy it. My strengths – tackling and being able to pick out a pass – were well suited to the position.

Our opening match was against the Germans. They were very powerful and it was a different level of hockey altogether from what I was used to. I knew immediately that if I was going to be able to compete at this level I had to raise my game.

Oddly, given everything else that was going on, I remember there was a stand selling bratwurst sausages near the pitch, and throughout the whole match – and for all of our games – all I could smell were those sausages. It made me feel sick. Even today, if I smell food near to where we're playing, it makes me feel queasy.

If my memory serves me right, we came third overall. I'll always remember the Spain match as I was straight strike at the top of the 'D', and I scored my first ever goal for England at that tournament – a sweet moment that will live with me forever.

Now that I'd had a taste of international hockey I wanted to make sure it wasn't going to be a one-off. I was pretty happy with the opportunities being part of Chester Hockey Club had given me, but fate was soon to intervene.

I hadn't long turned sixteen and was in the Total Fitness gym in the Wirral with my sister, running on the treadmill, when an older woman came over. She was probably only twenty-five but to me, then, she seemed older.

'You're that hockey player from the Wirral, aren't you?' she said.

I suspected she'd seen the piece my mum gave to the local paper but before I could answer, she added: 'I can tell you're that hockey player because I can see the shin pad marks.'

What she meant was that because we wear shin pads and socks we have the biggest tan lines. All hockey players have them – really brown knees and white shins.

She introduced herself as Kate Hendrick. She was playing for Bowdon Hightown, a team near Manchester, and had England caps at under-21 level. Bowdon were in the Premier Division of the Women's Hockey League.

'Why don't you come down and train with us?' she said. 'Even if you can't play with us on a Saturday, come down and get used to the group and a new environment.'

Okay, I thought, this is interesting. I chatted it over with my parents. My mum thought it would be a really good idea because it would be amazing to play at that level. At the time they had Nikki O'Donnell, who was playing in the senior team, Sally Walton, who was a highly rated prospect, and their player-coach was Tina Cullen. Tina was hockey royalty. She had gone to two Olympic Games and had scored over 400 top-flight goals.

If I joined Bowdon Hightown I would be moving up about five or six leagues to play in the Premier Division. It was a massive opportunity.

Their training was also on a Wednesday evening but when I explained the situation to Chester, they were brilliant. They understood I was stepping up a level and were happy for me to head over to Hightown after training. They were based at Altrincham, about twenty-five minutes' drive away from Chester. The plan was that I would train with them for a season and join them if I improved sufficiently to meet their standard. Initially I did double sessions and then split my time between the two clubs.

Turning up for my first session at Hightown was reminiscent of my recent England experience. Once again, I was slow to put my shin pads on and the last person, besides me, to get ready was Tina Cullen.

'Oh my God,' I thought, 'that's Tina Cullen!' As we were last out I would be warming up with her. I was like a rabbit in the headlights. I normally viewed warm-ups as an important thing to get right. Right from the off I wanted to make sure I was getting the pace of the ball and passing well. But with Tina I thought I had to be so on it. Every pass I thought should go on her stick.

Watching Tina in training was a real eye-opener. She was the best player I had ever seen live. The things she could do in training were mesmeric to me. The angles she could score from, her balance, her skill. It was a stark reminder of how much I still had to learn. I felt confident with my game, but putting me up against Tina made me look a real amateur. Bowdon was the place to be if I was going to get to that next level.

I reverted to my shy self when I first started there. One of the first people to speak to me before I trained was a girl with curly blonde hair tied back into a ponytail. I noticed she was wearing football trainers and to my horror she was wearing full Everton kit. When she spoke she had a proper, thick Liverpool accent – not like my slight twang. Her name was Ria, and she was lovely. We are very good friends to this day, so much so she will be a bridesmaid at my wedding, and we still laugh about that first encounter.

Once I saw the standard at Bowdon I was glad that I wasn't going to be joining them straight as a 16-year-old. I can imagine I would have spent a lot of the season sitting on the bench. In the meantime, I continued at Chester and remained in centre midfield, despite England playing me in defence.

The boost the additional training gave to my career was huge. I was selected for the England under-16 side that competed in an eight-team tournament in Poland later that summer. That helped cement my place in the setup. We flew from Warsaw to Krakow, and then to a small place in the middle of nowhere. It was so remote in fact that I think the locals had rarely seen someone who was oriental or black. My fellow squad member and friend Abi Harper, who was mixed race, and I were treated like celebrities. People were taking pictures of us. Either that or maybe they just thought we were so incredibly stunning, of course!

My hockey life was in a time of exciting change. And the same could be said for school.

In my GCSE results I got an A* in PE, the highest grade, and the rest were Bs, except a C in French. I was a little bit embarrassed because I didn't get more A's, whilst Shaun got several A*s and two A's. I was happy, though, because my results were enough to get me into Calday Grammar School, in West Kirby, for my sixth form. I'd made the decision to leave Birkenhead because I wanted to study PE and I could only take it there in the lower sixth form. I also wanted to take psychology, but it was only available via Skype tutorials. Instead, I ended up taking sports studies, human biology, geography and psychology at Calday. At that stage I had my heart set on becoming a nurse.

For my GCSEs I didn't really have an exam technique or know how to properly plan a revision schedule. I'd basically been winging it. I used to revise a week before my exams started and thought I'd be fine. I used to do a timetable but basically it consisted of two hours of this, two hours on that etc. That wasn't enough – as I was soon to discover.

Although my weekly schedule was lighter because I had abandoned football, instead of increasing my study time, I used the time I had free for the part-time job. In addition, I was still playing a lot of hockey and had been selected once more for the North of England side. As well as the England under-18s, I was picked for the national under-21 side. I was the youngest player in the squad. Best of all though, was when I was selected to be part of a Great Britain side that would travel to Australia to take part in the 2007 Youth Olympic Festival in January. The games, held annually in Sydney since 2001, were for athletes aged up to nineteen, and that year featured twenty countries competing in fourteen sports over twenty disciplines.

Everything about the games was designed to replicate as close as possible the real Olympic experience. So we were treated to a kitting out day, where the athletes gather to collect their gear for the tournament. After the excitement of receiving the England kit, this was almost even more special, donning the red, white and blue colours of Team GB for the first time. It was the furthest away from home I'd ever played before and certainly the highest standard of hockey I had been exposed to up to then.

We arrived at a grand school building, which was doubling as our holding camp, before we moved to the games' village. In the GB team were many of the young hopefuls tipped for future stardom, like the diver Tom Daley and gymnast Louis Smith. The hockey and gymnastics teams were among the first to arrive. After a few days we moved to the university halls, which became the athletes' village. We all attended the official opening ceremony that featured school children from New South Wales. I thought it was amazing. It gave me goosebumps imagining what it must be like at a real Olympic opening ceremony. Maybe I would get to sample it next year at the proper Olympics in Beijing?

When the competition began, we were facing three other teams in the hockey tournament – Australia, China and New Zealand. We played well and made it through to a gold medal match against the host nation. It was a tight match but we battled to a 4–2 win – and the gold medal!

Our success was one of thirteen golds for Team GB. Louis Smith picked up one of the others, while Tom Daley, only twelve at the time, won silver in the synchronised diving with his 16-year-old partner Callum Johnstone.

At our medal ceremony I clutched the gold and dared to dream that one day I might know what it was like to hold the real thing. It was a hugely exciting and satisfying moment.

But not long after arriving back home, I came crashing back down to earth. In the last few weeks and months, hockey had completely taken over my life. Something had to give – and it was my schoolwork. I'd completely neglected it. My AS exams – those we sat in the first year of sixth form – were looming and I didn't have much time to study. I tried to devise a revision schedule but it was too little, too late.

I couldn't believe what I was seeing when the results came out. I'd ended up with three E's and a D. To my horror, I then realised that those results counted towards my final A levels. I'd honestly thought they didn't really matter.

After my last results my parents were disappointed and had stern words with me, making sure I realised that my chances of going to university were under threat if I didn't make a big change. I imagine they were very cross. They had sacrificed a lot to give me a private school education for many years and what did I have to show for it? It was all very well enjoying the success with hockey but in 2007 there was no money to be made from playing the sport professionally.

I'd thought I could handle the twin pressures of hockey and school but it looked like I was mistaken. If I didn't pass my A levels there would be no university degree. Then what would I do?

Suddenly, my future was in jeopardy. Was my hockey to blame?

Chapter 6

Uni Mates and a Hockey Great

I was really up against it. It had come as a complete shock that my A levels were a points-based system so the AS results contributed significantly to my final grades.

Going into my last year at Calday, I now needed predicted grades to secure conditional acceptances at universities. In preparation for my final year, I dropped geography because I just wasn't enjoying it, so that left me with psychology, human biology and sports studies. I went to my psychology teacher and asked if she would predict me a B.

'I can't do that, Sam,' she said. 'How can you go from an E to a B?'

I swore that I would work hard and eventually she said if I performed well in the next two modular tests, she'd give me a predicted B for my UCAS higher education application forms. That helped me get conditional acceptances for nursing at Manchester, Liverpool and Leeds Metropolitan universities.

That at least gave me a chance. All I had to do now was work my socks off over the next school year to get the results I needed to turn this situation around. I had to prove that devoting so much time and energy to hockey wasn't going to be detrimental to my career prospects. Juggling these twin priorities was going to be tricky – but at least I didn't have to worry too much about that over the summer.

It was then I was taking part in my first significant tournament with England – the under-21 European Championships in Catania, Sicily. On a personal level, it was an amazing experience. I started the tournament on the bench but the further we progressed the more I was involved. Given I was still only seventeen and had been bumped up to the under-21 squad I was thrilled with my performances. We finished runners-up, narrowly losing the final to Germany. I had the added bonus of parents being there in Italy to watch us win the silver medal. I was very fortunate throughout my career to have my parents watching me whenever their time and budgets would allow. I always played a lot better when I had someone watching me live because I wanted to impress. One of the sacrifices they made for me was always taking their annual holiday in whatever country I was playing in. I only realised this when I was older, because when I was younger I naively thought that watching was part of their holiday, as opposed to coming to watch me and having to make that their holiday.

At the end of the tournament everybody let their hair down. Drinking was forbidden on tour but someone must have smuggled a bottle of vodka in for the end of tournament party. Although I was still only seventeen, my friends Kirsty, Lindsay and Ashleigh Ball, whom I was going to be playing with at Bowdon Hightown in the forthcoming season, vouched for me. Someone mixed the vodka with some lemonade and handed it to me to drink. I gingerly took a sip.

Ugh. It was about 90 per cent vodka, 10 per cent lemonade. 'I can't drink this,' I protested.

'Go on. Drink it!'

Being urged to take a drink was about the closest it came to an initiation with the national team. It was disgusting. There was certainly no drinking culture within the squad – although it was fun to be letting off steam after a tough tournament. It was my first experience of going out after a tournament to celebrate with my England hockey teammates.

Unbeknownst to me, after the tournament, Karen Brown – the assistant coach for the women's team who had a little say in the under-21s – said to my mum, 'Don't tell Sam this, but I think she's a fantastic talent and I wouldn't be surprised if she made it into the senior squad soon. I think she's had a fantastic tournament.'

True to her word, Mum never told me this until years later. She didn't want me to get too big for my boots. It was probably just as well she didn't tell me. I was certainly desperately hoping to be involved in future squads and dreamed of winning a full England or Great Britain cap one day, but in my immediate future I had to concentrate on my studying.

In that final school year all I did was work. Every lunchtime, I was in the library. On Mondays and Tuesdays I'd stay after school for two hours to study. I was determined to get the grades required to go to university. Even today the thought of those E's embarrasses me.

I didn't have a social life to speak of, which was doubly frustrating because I'd passed my driving test not long after I turned seventeen but wasn't able to fully utilise it. All my time was devoted to studying and hockey. I had already sacrificed a lot and put in a huge amount of effort to get where I was. Whenever in my life I forgot why I was dedicating so much time to hockey, I would always think of everything I had already endured, how far I had already come and what I had already given up; that would always return me to centre and refocus me.

When the new season began I was playing for Hightown and had left Chester Hockey Club completely. I was a little sad to leave as they had been brilliant to me and gave me a platform that had led me to international recognition. However, it was time to spread my wings and see if I could cut it in the Premier League.

Bowdon were unusual in that they played a 4–4–2 system. Most teams favoured a 4–3–3. I played centre midfield, so I was one of two in the middle and I was given licence to roam further forward to help set up attacks and track back to cover the defence. I loved it. The standard was a step up, as you would expect from a team several divisions higher, but I relished the challenge and when I met up with the England teams I didn't find the jump in quality the same as I had done previously.

Sadly, the pressure I'd put on myself to turn around my academic fortunes and the demands from hockey meant that for the first time, I experienced the sort of sacrifices sportsmen and women have to make to succeed.

When I moved schools to Calday, I left a few of my old friends behind. Geographically, the two schools are only fifteen minutes apart, but with so much academic work going on and my hockey, those friendships suffered and sadly fell by the wayside.

The problem I had with making new friends at Calday was that they didn't know or appreciate my history. They hadn't seen me rise through the ranks and the hard work I had put in and therefore they didn't understand why I would miss social gatherings or birthday parties. They didn't realise that if I was up late on a Friday night, I played significantly worse on the Saturday morning. I just couldn't afford that risk. I couldn't treat the faith so many people had put in me and the sacrifices they had made for me with such contempt. I was in it for the long term. I had to be mature, I had to have a steady head and I couldn't give in to peer pressure.

Don't get me wrong, I wasn't lonely or anything, as I still had the air of popularity that comes with being a fledgling international athlete. I think people liked to associate with that. It gave me almost a local fame, having my picture in the paper and my name upon the school honours board. It wasn't a false friendship, but it did feel that way sometimes. I didn't establish any deep, meaningful, lifelong friendships from school and I longed for a group of friends who understood me as a person, who knew where I had come from. I wanted friends who appreciated that I was hurting by missing the party of the year and rather than being angry at me, friends who understood that and were proud of me.

As we approached exam time all of those considerations I put to one side. This time there would be no second chances. Mess these up and I was in a heap of trouble. Finally I had found an exam technique that worked for me. I used to write out all my information in paragraphs, then condense that paragraph into a sentence and then into a bullet point. I just remember writing … constant writing of notes.

I felt reasonably confident sitting the exams but I'd been there before and ended up disappointed when the results came through. I couldn't take anything for granted.

Finally the day came for the exam results to be issued. I could go into school to get them but before I left the house I just kept pressing refresh on my UCAS form. If I'd got the results I needed my university acceptances should change from 'conditional' to 'unconditional'.

Refresh, refresh, refresh. Come on, come on.

It froze for a second and then loaded. There it was: 'Unconditional'.

That's when I knew I'd made it. I was in. I'd managed to get a B, C and a D, which was enough – just – to get me to university.

Phew!

Panic averted, I could get on with my life … actually, to be more accurate, I could get on with hockey.

First up was the European Championships in Italy with the England under-21s. Shine there and do well in the youth games and I could put myself in the frame for the Beijing Olympics in 2008.

Bring it on!

Chapter 7

Moving On Up

I was so nervous I couldn't touch my breakfast. Even on the way down the M40, when we stopped at Warwick services I tried to eat something but I physically couldn't manage it. I did however manage several trips to the toilet!

This was the effect that being summoned to meet with the senior England team for the first time at Bisham Abbey had on me. It was basically just a training session, a chance to be introduced to the England team. But that was what scared me – some of the names I'd be mixing with, like the captain, Kate Walsh, and Helen Richardson, Lucilla Wright and Rachel Walker. They were huge figures in the sport. Obviously I'd seen some of them in action when playing for Bowdon Hightown, but this was different.

My dad drove me down and we got there ridiculously early, but I couldn't just walk in. I said to Dad, 'Can you park in the pub opposite the entrance and I'll wait and see if any of the people that I know are there first?'

I didn't want to be too early. I wanted to arrive ten minutes before we had to be there, so I could casually rock up – not pitch up an hour before. Good God, I didn't want to look *that* keen.

I was one of three newcomers into the setup. When we started training, I was scared stiff of people like Lucilla Wright and Rachel Walker. They were the type of characters whose attitude was that the newbies had to earn their respect before they'd give us an inch or talk to us.

I passed the ball to Rachel but it was about a yard out of her reach. She just stood still and left it. The look she shot me said, 'I want it on the end of my stick.'

Part of me thought, 'Oh my God, what a diva,' but the overriding message was, 'Bloody hell, this is a different level of expectation.'

That attitude didn't let up for the rest of the session.

I daren't talk to the other established players because I felt intimidated by them, both by their status in the game and also by the mixed reception I got as a new player. They certainly weren't throwing the new girls a welcome party for joining the squad; it was much more like they were staving off an invasion. I imagine they thought I could be a threat to their position. I was going to have to earn my stripes, so I kept my head down at first. The last thing I wanted them thinking was 'Look at this youngster chirping up straight away', and then them becoming even less welcoming the next time I joined up with them.

The big announcement would be the one in September. That was when a squad representing Great Britain on a tour of Argentina that November was decided. Only players who made that tour would have a chance of being in the training squad for the Beijing Olympics the following year.

By then I'd have started university. The question facing me over the summer had been where?

Passing my exams meant I had the options of Liverpool, Manchester or Leeds. A further dilemma I had was whether to continue with my plan to do nursing. Would I really be able to juggle the demands of a nursing course, with the many hours of placements it would entail, with potential tournaments, tours and hockey practice?

I chose Leeds Metropolitan University because I wanted to move away from home and have a full student experience, but not have to travel too far, which was why I hadn't opted for somewhere like Edinburgh or down south in Kent.

After deliberating for weeks about whether I could commit to nursing, at the last minute I rang up Leeds Met and said, 'I have been offered a place on your nursing course. These are my grades; any chance I can do a sport and exercise science degree instead?'

To my amazement, even though the course was full, they not only offered me a place but they threw in a full sports scholarship as well. It was all down to my hockey CV. I was delighted.

Having a scholarship meant I could use the university's excellent sports facilities for free, they provided a mentor if I had any psychological issues and a conditioning coach to help with fitness, and they gave me a grant of about £1,000 to help with kit, travelling and other expenses.

Unfortunately, however, now that I was training with the senior England squad, I couldn't use the university's facilities. I had to use an English Institute of Sport (EIS) facility, the nearest of which was in Sheffield. This was because England Hockey wanted to ensure I was using the best possible equipment and had access to properly qualified staff, and that my progress could be monitored and uploaded to their central data hub.

The start of any student's life at university is the freshers' fortnight where they ease themselves into their new surroundings, meet the people with whom they'll share the next few years and, naturally, get smashed as often as possible!

Sadly, for me, the fresher festivities would be curtailed because the sports studies course demanded that newcomers go away for a three-day outdoor residential weekend in Anglesey, North Wales. It was a compulsory course and I tried everything to get out of it. I didn't fancy going rock climbing in the freezing cold, so for the first time in my life, I tried to play the international hockey card, claiming there was a real risk of injury. I wondered whether the word 'international' would impress them sufficiently to spare me the sniffly nose and chapped fingers that would no doubt follow. Their response? 'No, you have to come.' Fair enough; they probably realised I was trying it on.

The course was on Friday, Saturday and Sunday. Friday was also the day the squad for Argentina would be announced – at midday. I prayed there would be Internet access where we were staying so I could see if I'd been chosen.

I sat on the coach down to Wales not knowing anyone and cursing my bad luck, wondering why I didn't get a coach's letter to exempt me. Surely if they wanted me to train at an EIS facility gym, I could have convinced them that it was a bad idea to go on an adventure pursuits weekend with the university. Damn. I stopped daydreaming of what I could have done differently to avoid the course as soon as we arrived.

We were split into groups alphabetically and allocated chalets to stay in that each had eight bunk beds. Of course, I needn't have felt sorry for myself. I roomed with a girl called Mel, who turned out to be lovely. On that trip I also became friends with a girl called Katie and another called Jess. Little did I know that these were the three girls I had longed to meet during my time in Calday – the type that got me and understood what I did and what I was hoping to one day achieve. We all became lifelong friends and I was maid of honour for Mel on her wedding day.

Mel was very unassuming, with a dry, blunt sense of humour. People would often mistake her for moody at first, but she cracked me up and we became very close.

Katie had the thickest accent that I had heard in my life – it was thick, thick Yorkshire. 'Y'rite, Sam?' she would always ask. She was the funniest of the four of us and there was never a time she wasn't up for a laugh. She was a really positive person.

Jess was from down south and was really caring. You could always go to her and she would listen to you and sympathise, but domestically she was a nightmare. The girl couldn't boil an egg. Luckily for her, Mel assumed the role of mum, so Jess made it through university unscathed and well nourished despite her slender frame.

In my second and third years of university the four of us lived together. It was one of the happiest times of my life. They understood me and my schedule. The best way to explain this was that without them I would have missed out on a big part of university life. I remember that the student nights on Tuesdays at Tiger Tiger in Leeds were always very popular; but on Tuesdays I had training in Loughborough from 7.30–9.30 pm. They didn't let that be a problem. While I went to training they would get ready and go out for pre-drinks. As I made the hour-and-a-half trip back to university, I would text them when I was twenty minutes away from our house. They would then all come home and wait for me to put my key in the door. What then occurred was like something out of a Hollywood movie. My sweaty kit would be stripped off as I was hauled up the stairs and pushed into a pre-run shower. I would then be dragged out and a pre-determined outfit would be thrown on me and as one of the girls dried my hair, the other painted my nails. Mel would then throw a toasted sandwich of some sort down my neck so I didn't go out on an empty stomach.

In fifteen minutes flat I was ready to go and we would head out, all the while knowing that I would usually have a two-drink maximum as I was likely playing university hockey on the Wednesday afternoon. They were great times.

Back to that very first activity weekend, we had a jam-packed schedule that included challenging team-building exercises. As soon as we were done on Friday afternoon, I sprinted back to the chalet, desperate to check my emails. Had I made the cut?

I had a basic Nokia phone at the time and although I could check emails on it, the Internet signal was awful. I kept trying to refresh my emails but it kept cutting out.

Come on, come on, COME ON!

Eventually they opened. The email was there. I was almost too scared to look. I scanned down.

There it was: Samantha Quek.

I'd made it. I was going to Argentina!

I was absolutely buzzing. 'Holy crap, I'm going to get my first international cap.'

I remember Mel was so thrilled for me. 'Oh my God. You're going to be playing for GB.'

I immediately texted my mum and dad, sister and brothers. They were all ecstatic.

We finished the course and came back to Leeds and while most students were gradually feeling their way into their new courses, my timetable was full on. I missed out on quite a lot of uni in those early weeks due to hockey training camps. On top of that, when I was back at uni, I had to start utilising the Sheffield EIS. I trained with a girl called Jo Ellis, who was also from Leeds. I knew Jo from Bowdon Hightown and she had also been in the England squad on my first introductory session. We got on well. In the mornings we'd get up at 5.30 am to be in the gym for 6.30 am.

It was a hectic few weeks before the squad met up again. Even my Bowdon Hightown matches would take up an entire day as I'd have to leave a couple of hours' travel time both before and after the match to allow for the traffic between Leeds and Manchester.

Hockey was now properly taking over my life.

I was one of six uncapped players in the twenty-four-strong Great Britain women's Olympic training squad that were going to Argentina. Of those six, Charlotte Craddock of Cannock, and Susie Gilbert of Birmingham University, were like me and had yet to win a full cap for either England or GB. Jo Ellis and Jo Hayley Brown of Canterbury had played for England before, while Laura Bartlett, who was a year above me, had seventeen caps for Scotland. It was expected that we would all get our chance at some point over the five-test series against the hosts.

Arriving in Salta, a province in the north of the country, was unlike anything I had experienced before. The police provided an escort to a pitch in the middle of nowhere. There wasn't a stand or any kind of structure. We had a week's acclimatisation, training and preparation before the first match and as we trained, the authorities began erecting scaffolding around us. It was supposed to be able to hold thousands of people but it looked pretty flimsy.

They announced the team for the first test match. Every uncapped player in the squad was picked – except me.

What the hell?

Why had everyone else got a cap?

The buzz I'd felt since joining up with the squad quickly disappeared as I was gutted. I knew though that I just had to accept it and wait for my chance, but the sense of disappointment only amplified when we arrived for the match to find the new stand packed with nearly 7,000 fans. It was unbelievable: easily the biggest crowd I'd seen for a hockey match. Argentineans love their hockey and the stand was swaying with all the jumping around they were doing, and the crowd were banging drums and setting off flares. It was nuts. Clearly health and safety wasn't as big a concern over there as it is here.

Once the action started the girls equipped themselves superbly against a team ranked second in the world, running out 3–0 winners. I was delighted for Jo, who scored our second, following up the opener from Leicester defender Crista Cullen, from a penalty corner. Charlotte Craddock had a dream first cap by scoring the third. I have been a team player all my life: team first and me second. That is how you are successful. That said, I remember feeling a tinge of jealousy that some of the other debutants had played so well. Maybe it would be harder for me to stand out when I got my chance. It was a selfish mentality, but one that came from the fact I wasn't established in the team yet; I was still auditioning and very nervous.

The second test was in two days' time. My despair at missing out on the first match turned to elation when the team was announced and I was playing. At nineteen I would be earning my first cap, and not just any cap – a Great Britain cap.

The tradition for all debutants is that in front of the whole squad they have to get up and collect a certificate to mark the occasion. Everyone then shouts 'Speech!'

The night before I wrote down some words on a piece of paper but I binned it. I didn't want to be standing there reading from a note. I just wanted to say something nice and not waffle on.

'I just want to say thank you for this opportunity,' I said, nervously. 'It's so great to be doing it with such an experienced group of people. I never thought I'd be getting this cap, especially when I was nineteen.'

I was obviously ecstatic to be playing but when I looked at the rest of the team I realised it was going to be tough. We were fielding a young side. Senior campaigners like Kate Walsh and Helen Richardson were rested. We'd be up against it.

So it proved as Argentina battered us basically for the whole match. I can't remember a more intense experience. It was trial by fire. We stood firm and managed to keep them out, battling to a very credible 0–0 draw. I was pleased with my own performance. One report even said I hadn't put a foot wrong. Head coach Danny Kerry also seemed to be delighted by the resilience we'd shown as a team.

Unfortunately that was as good as it got on that tour. Two successive 1–0 defeats and a 2–1 loss in the fifth and final decider turned the series in Argentina's favour.

When I look back on that trip, I can now see how it helped shape me as a player. I learned a lot, primarily from rooming with Kate Walsh. Young golfers look up to Tiger Woods, young tennis players to Roger Federer; young hockey players looked up to Kate Walsh. She was an icon in my eyes – a real legend of the game – and I held her in a celebrity-like status. I wasn't intimidated by sharing a room with her, but felt honoured. I remember looking at her and thinking, 'I want to be just like you – the model professional.' I looked at how she packed her kitbag and I started packing mine the same. I listened to how she spoke to other players with respect and calmness and I tried to copy that. If she went to bed at 10.00 pm, I wanted to go to bed at 10.00 pm. If she brushed her teeth before getting a shower in the morning, then that was the order I was going to do it in, too. She was my sporting hero. To this day, even though I count her as a very good friend after years of tournaments playing alongside her in the back line and joining her at countless social events, if I am ever asked who my sporting idol is, it's Katie Walsh.

During that trip I remember struggling with how I wanted to represent myself as a woman. I hadn't completely stopped being a tomboy and was becoming more interested in fashion and beauty. It was a time of personal evolution, which was strange considering that for the first time I was surrounded by a group of girls who were also tomboys like me.

I remember during that trip sitting on the hotel landing painting my nails and being confronted by one of the coaching staff saying, 'What are you doing? Stop being unprofessional.' It was a time of mixed signals. Not that long ago I was that girl who didn't want to be seen dead in a dress despite being encouraged to wear one and now, at university, I wanted to feel more girly. Yet here I was being told that wasn't the way.

Doing any sort of make-up or spending time on your hair was a no-no back then. The attitude was that if you were doing that you were not focusing on the game. That's all changed now – it's very much part of the pre-match ritual – but back in the day the image of a hockey player was completely different. I've had it a few times throughout my career, people saying, 'You don't look like a hockey player.'

I'd always reply, 'Well, what does a hockey player look like?'

More often than not they'd say, 'Short, butch, with short hair.'

I'm not sure what happened in the intervening period to change things. Perhaps it was the increased coverage of the sport, the rise of social media. It didn't make much of a difference to me. I never thought wanting to be the best and wanting to look my best had to be mutually exclusive.

On that first trip to Argentina there were a few things I had to get my head around.

I remember going for my first active recovery, or low impact session, and I put on a bikini, not thinking anything of it. Kate put on a one-piece swimming costume, though. She looked at me and said, 'Ooh. Have you got a swimming costume with you?'

'No,' I said. 'Why?'

'Because everybody wears a swimming costume and they might take the Mick.'

'I'll tell you what,' she said, 'why don't you wear that sports bra.'

I quickly changed into a Nike sports bra, which was baby blue so matched my bikini bottoms and made it look like I was wearing a sport bikini. I went down and everybody was in swimming costumes apart from me and one other girl. Kate was right and while she herself wouldn't join in the banter, she had recognised that I wouldn't have wanted to be on the end of it on this occasion, and I was thankful for the heads-up. Just one example of her being a very perceptive, excellent captain.

Sarah Thomas, known as Tommo, was that other girl in a two-piece. She was an established player and the only Welsh girl in the squad, so she was used to people bantering with her. She also had a wicked sense of humour and would give as good as she got. She didn't worry about wearing her little stringy bikini, despite some people jesting, 'Hey Tommo, off to the beach are we? Not a lot of support in that top.'

Fast-forward ten years and you'd be hard-pushed to find anyone not in a string bikini, but back then you were made to feel like a figure of fun.

Overall, my first senior international trip had been amazing. I probably returned thinking that while it had been brilliant to be involved it was really just an opportunity for me to gain some international experience. I'm not sure I fully believed a permanent place in the team was within my reach.

We'd only been back a few weeks when the email came through naming those who would be in the squad in the run-up to Beijing. Again, my mindset was very much like, 'Oh, you're lucky to be here and have the opportunity.' I was possibly guilty of looking further ahead and thinking London 2012 was what to aim for.

I was thrilled to be in the squad and to be involved in the training in the lead-up to the final squad announcement for Beijing. It made me believe I actually had a real shot at going to the upcoming Olympic Games: a staggering thought.

In May, three months before the Olympics got under way, we played Argentina again, this time over a two-game series in Reading, and I was in the squad. When they named the teams for the two matches I was down for the second game. I felt disappointment because it was clear the main players were featuring in both games, but it was still hugely exciting. My mum and dad and brothers were coming down to watch. I was very proud, representing my country on home soil.

We knew all about the strength of Argentina but this time I would be facing Soledad García, their star striker and possibly the best player in the world at that time. She was a two-time World Cup winner and had won two Olympic medals. She had been the difference in the first match, scoring a classy winner in a 3–2 victory.

Argentina were favourites to complete the whitewash. However, once the match got under way I felt no stress. I played one of the best games of my life, making every tackle. I had García in my back pocket. It was the first time I ever thought 'You can do this Sam. You can compete at the top level.' We won 4–2 to level the series. I just had to hope I'd done enough to impress the coaches.

Two weeks later, another email dropped.

'Congratulations to the sixteen players who will be representing Great Britain at the XXIX Olympiad.'

I looked down the list. My name wasn't there. Two reserves were allowed, who would be staying outside the village: a goalkeeper and an outfield player. I wasn't one of those either.

It went on: 'These players are also required to train with the squad until the squad leaves for Beijing.'

I was one of six players asked to train with the squad for three or four weeks because should anyone get injured, they needed people to play against.

Perhaps it was too much to have expected that I could make the squad in Beijing, being only nineteen and having only featured recently, but it was still disappointing, especially given my good performances. My gradual improvement and game against García had made me dream.

Looking back, I regret not pushing more, actually. I think my application that year was too blasé. I took it for granted that I was filling the numbers because of my age. I would have benefitted from having Mr Cartmel around to remind me of the words he'd said to me as a skinny 11-year-old playing with the bigger girls: 'If you are good enough, you are old enough.' Weirdly, it's a bigger regret now than it was then, because I quite quickly consoled myself with the idea I was just too young. But looking back, I probably was good enough to have competed in Beijing.

Still, I told myself, there was always London 2012. I'd be four years older and at my peak. What could be better? A home Olympics, with the world watching … that would be my time, and surely, I wouldn't have to worry about selection because by then I would no doubt be a well-established member of the squad. Surely?

Chapter 8

Jealousies and Rivalries

Brisbane, Australia, February 2008

This is the life, I thought, as I jumped on the king-sized bed.

We'd just arrived for the second leg of our test series against Australia. Our accommodation was a lovely hotel. The rooms were like little apartments, with a kitchen, living room and two separate bedrooms and a bathroom.

The main bedroom boasted the king-sized bed and an en suite, whilst the other room had two singles.

I was sharing with Kate Walsh and Helen Richardson. As soon as I walked into the hotel room and eyed up the bed situation I figured I'd chance it and try to bag the bigger one. Everyone was laughing. 'Check out Quek, the newbie; the youngster's got the en suite king-sized bed.'

Queensland had been our second port of call after Perth. We'd had great fun there, staying in apartments, and hosting our own series of *Come Dine With Me* nights in the different flats. We split into groups and using the food budget we had been supplied with, we went shopping and had to create a meal for the other flats. In my team were Sarah Thomas, Katy Roberts and Jennie Bimson. Our meal was a disaster! We became so obsessed with our watermelon centrepiece for the table that was meant to create the 'wow' factor that we didn't start cooking until very late. We told Katy to get cracking on the sausage and pea risotto. One of the components of risotto is white wine, and whilst the recipe only called for a little to be used, by the end of the cooking process the whole bottle had been used up ... and not in the risotto. It transpired that every time Katy had added a little to the risotto, she took a sip from the bottle herself. The results were hilarious – a wallpaper paste risotto and a drunk Katy. Despite some club hockey players having a reputation for being big drinkers, as international athletes we rarely drank and therefore had a very low tolerance. I think Katy only had two or three glasses, but she was singing all night. We really did have a laugh as a team during our down time.

I loved being with the Team GB squad, even though I didn't see that much game time during the series with Australia and I still wasn't entirely relaxed in the setup. It was the usual thing I'd experienced when breaking into all new teams, football as well as hockey – there were players who embraced me and there were ones who saw me as a threat.

I had to learn fast and accept that was the way it was. I wasn't going to get a free pass to their exclusive club. I had to earn it. But it was tough – and it could affect your play.

In those early test matches I was definitely playing within my shell. I felt I couldn't turn around to an established senior player, particularly when playing for Great Britain, and go, 'Why aren't you passing me the ball?' or 'Pass the ball, I'm on.'

Some of the more senior players were still giving me a hard time on the pitch, too. Even if they hit me a terrible pass they might have a go at me for not rescuing it for them. 'Come on Sam!'

It would take years before I'd have the confidence, in that type of situation, to respond with, 'Stop blaming other people for your mistakes, get on with the game.'

One particular player would always have a go at me despite their sloppy passing: same old story; anyone's fault but their own. While I took it from her in those early days, we were reunited at club level many years later and she hadn't changed. She barked at me, 'Sam, will you move! You could have got to that ball!' But by this time the mouse had learned to roar, so I gave her it back with both barrels: 'Are you still the person that can't stop blaming everyone else for your shit passes?' She stood dumbfounded and shut up. I often encountered that type of player throughout my career. Confidence in your own ability is essential, but when it turns to arrogance it's a dangerous thing. There were those who were seen as the best on merit and then those who were the seen as best in their own head. This girl was a talented player, but ultimately her arrogance was her downfall and after years in the international setup, she would soon be told she wasn't in the coach's plans, despite being in the age range to compete for the Rio Olympic cycle.

It was difficult for me going into that group of girls. However, I was determined to prove to everyone I belonged there. Although I was one of the girls taken to Australia to give the team extra players to train with, should anyone get injured there might be a slim chance of a late promotion to the team. It would be wrong to say I was hoping someone got injured, but equally it would be wrong to say I was hoping no one would get injured. That sounds terrible to say but I'm sure it's a feeling most sportsmen and women could relate to. Obviously, I didn't want to wish ill on anyone, but that slimmest of chances was the motivation that kept the six of us extras going.

From Australia we flew to Macau, the location in southern China of Team GB's holding base ahead of the Olympics. There we were treated to five star luxury for five days. Our hotel was simply gorgeous. I was rooming with Laura Bartlett and there was no race to bag the best sleeping arrangements as there were two king-sized beds. There was no requirement to train while we were there. Our job was to sample all the facilities to see where the athletes would be living and the venues where they'd be training. The hotel had its own hockey pitch, an athletics field and a golf range. We could do anything we wanted.

Macau was known for its casinos so we paid a visit to the Venetian. We couldn't believe how mobbed it was. They take their gambling seriously. I tried my hand at roulette and black jack – only stakes of £20 or so – but lost it all straight away.

It sounds as though we were having the time of our lives but it was while we were in Macau that we held an important meeting that would change the face of hockey. We all met in a basement conference room where Danny Kerry spoke for the first time about full-time training and a centralised programme. It meant those chosen would be training full-time with the squad and for the first time players would be paid a salary, with pay grades according to seniority and experience.

The proposal was for training to take place at Bisham Abbey, where England and GB hockey were already based. Danny opened up the floor to hear ideas from the girls and some people were making an argument to train at Loughborough, in Leicestershire, because it was more central geographically.

This was the start of a conversation that would revolutionise our sport. We were entering unchartered territory.

The plan was to roll out the first cycle of funding in 2009.

I was torn. On the one hand it sounded an exciting and progressive development but on the other, the idea of moving full-time to Bisham was daunting. I loved the idea of playing of hockey full-time but the thought of moving away from my university life and even further away from my family was something I hadn't considered before.

At the time I was travelling down to Bisham for weekend training and Laura and I rented two rooms in the home of Mr and Mrs Bennett, whose daughter Anna had played for Great Britain. It was kind of them to accommodate us in their farmhouse at Twyford, but staying in what was a family home wouldn't really work as a long-term solution.

I actually backed the idea of basing ourselves at Loughborough, where the university was a centre for sporting excellence, and the benefits of having it in the middle of the country meant that club players could still play for their teams in the north and south. I worried that if we went to Bisham, everyone would have to move down from northern clubs, like Bowdon, to play closer to home and that would benefit the southern clubs.

Still, it was exciting to even be involved in these discussions.

As the Olympics got under way and the senior team carried on with their preparations, I was one of two hockey players selected for a London 2012 ambition programme. Suzie Gilbert was the other. The idea was to replicate the Olympic Games' experience for a group of young British athletes and coaches tipped to make an impact in four years' time. Prior to Beijing, only 30 per cent of Team GB's gold medallists came from first-time Olympians. The hope was that by introducing athletes to the spectacle earlier it might improve performances when it mattered.

Whilst I had been very disappointed at not being chosen to compete in Beijing, those feelings evaporated when I was selected for the ambition programme. It really felt like the coaches were telling me that although I had missed out this time, I was more or less nailed on for 2012. It was everything I needed; instead of looking back at the disappointment of missing out, I was now looking forward to a home Olympics in 2012.

As much effort had been made as possible to give the ambition athletes the same experience. There was a mini kitting out event, which I couldn't make, but they sent all the kit out to me. We had more kit for this trip than we ever had at Bisham. In truth, this gear was a lot better than the GB kit I'd been used to up until then. Back in the day, it was a pretty mismatched kit, consisting of three T-shirts with GB on them – red, white and blue. We had no major sponsor – it was the days before Investec's involvement – so we had two pairs of shorts each, courtesy of Kate, who worked for sports brand Canterbury and had managed to get us some for free. We teamed this with just plain socks. Mismatched kit or not, to be honest, at that point I would have played in a bin liner and a set of clogs so long as it had the English lion or the GB crest on the front.

We certainly looked the part as we boarded the plane to head to China.

It was a bittersweet moment – pulling on Team GB Olympic branded kit for the first time. Obviously I was proud to even be in this position, but it was the words beneath the logo that got to me: London 2012 Ambition Programme.

I felt nervous wearing the gear; for some reason I felt I didn't merit it. I worried that someone would see the branding and assume I was part of the squad. I dreaded the question, 'Are you going to the Olympics?'

I'd have to say, 'No, not this time.'

We visited the athletes' village, saw the dining hall and inside some of the rooms. I secretly prayed we wouldn't see the hockey girls who had properly earned their place there, while I felt a bit of a tourist. However, I did bump into some of them when they were getting physio treatment.

They were like, 'Hi Sam, how are you?'

They were being perfectly nice. Perhaps it was that the team's hierarchy had now been established and I was no longer a threat to their positions in the squad. Or, more likely, it was that they knew how it felt to be in my position. I should have remembered they were young once too, but I just felt so self-conscious.

'Hi,' I said, hoping they wouldn't be able to detect the awkwardness in my voice. When we visited the dining hall and were grabbing food with our day passes, all the hockey girls were having food. Again, I felt so awkward because I wasn't close to anyone there. My closest mate, Laura, was a reserve, based outside of the village.

A host of ambition programme parties had been out before it was our turn so by the time we got there the Olympics were under way. I caught a couple of the hockey matches and did some touristy things like visit Tiananmen Square.

In terms of whetting the appetite to compete on that world stage, it definitely made me hungry and even more excited to be competing in 2012. I even let my mind wander and started to think about the other fifteen girls I would pick to play along with me. I thought about who would be retiring, as you usually lose about seven people each cycle, and who I would replace them with if I were the coach.

The girls experienced mixed fortunes at the Games, suffering a heavy defeat by Germany but winning two and drawing two of their remaining group games, eventually finishing sixth after losing 2–0 to Australia.

When everyone returned from China, Kate, our captain, wasn't there. It emerged that while they were in Beijing, Kate and Helen announced they were a couple. I think some people worried that it might have an impact on the team dynamic, especially given that Kate was our captain and Helen our vice captain. Would they challenge and question each other's decisions as a good captain and vice captain should? Would they separate themselves from the group a little? Were they almost too powerful as a couple now? Would their say be bigger than the team's? These might all be valid concerns perhaps for any other team, but this was Kate Walsh and Helen Richardson. I'd known them for years. They were far too professional to ever let their relationship affect the team dynamic and, as for becoming too powerful, Kate was already the boss amongst us all, and rightly so. She was our leader, we all respected her and followed her lead, usually unquestioningly, as she had earned that right, having led by example for many years. If you ever had a problem you could go to Kate and she would sort it, with no bias or agenda. She worked harder than all of us and put more in after hours than the rest of us combined. I never questioned for a minute anything negative would come from their relationship and ultimately I was happy for them as my friends. I imagine it must have been a very tough time for them, both personally and professionally.

Nothing ever changed in terms of what happened on the hockey pitch, and not really off it either. They still sat on separate tables for dinner, and went in different groups for training.

As I got older and played with them more I started taking the Mick out of them like I would any other teammate. For example, if they hit each other on the pitch and Kate put her arm around Helen to check she was all right, I'd say, 'Aw, look at you guys!'

They were always overly considerate to the feelings of the other girls. In the first few tours after they got together they didn't even share rooms because they were so worried about what the other girls would think. They handled everything so well. They are brilliant, to be honest – just class people, both of them.

That all played out in the weeks and months following Beijing. In the immediate aftermath, the Olympic side were rested. When we met up again to play as England for a flying two-match series against Germany in November 2008, it was a chance for fringe players to make their mark. That meant an opportunity for me to earn my first England cap.

I was quite an unusual case because most players get their first international cap for their home nation before turning out for Team GB. I already had a Great Britain cap and I was mega proud of that because not many achieve it that way round.

Although many of our senior players were rested, Germany had their full Olympic team at their disposal, including the legendary Natascha Keller, a gold medallist in Athens.

The tradition for England is the same as GB – players earning their first cap have to make a speech, but as we had about seven in one night, everyone kept it brief.

In the match our inexperience showed and Germany battered us, but it was a great feeling to get my senior England career off the mark.

Something I hadn't considered came to the fore that week. Several senior players who ordinarily might have been considering retirement from the international scene didn't do so, because they wanted to compete in a home Olympic Games four years later. Instead of the squad turnover being anything up to 50 per cent, only a handful left after being told by Danny they didn't feature in his future plans. However, I felt all I needed was one spot to free up and I would get my chance.

In order to make sure I was part of those plans, I threw myself into training. Largely I was back with the under-21s but my attitude was that if I kept working hard I could force my way into contention with the seniors.

Juggling training with my studies wasn't easy; in fact it was bloody hard work. I was always busy, and time seemed to pass so quickly. I'd be at Bisham Abbey on a Sunday, Monday and Tuesday, and drive up to university on a Tuesday night to the student house I shared with Katie, Mel and Jess. On Wednesday, I'd play university hockey and train at Manchester in the evening with Bowdon. I had seminars on Thursday and Friday back at university, following which I'd drive to the Wirral to spend Saturday with my parents.

I was starting to feel that I was letting a lot of people down again. I had missed parties and the like when I was in school and sixth form, but now I had such limited time outside of hockey and university that I was starting to feel I was neglecting my family. On the one day off I had a week, I had to drive home and find time to see Mum, Dad, Mike, Shaun, Maxine and her two children, Sam and Yasmin, who were much closer to me than your standard niece and nephew, as well as my nan, who was ninety-three, and also all the other extended family. In addition, I wanted to see my university friends who were being so great with me, and perhaps even have a relationship of some sort. Alone time? No chance!

It was a tough time. My family were always understanding but it was perhaps the first time that cracks started to appear. When I did arrive home they would say, 'Oh hello, nice to see you' or 'Hello stranger!' This used to both annoy and upset me. I knew they meant it lightheartedly but I was becoming more and more aware I was letting down people who meant the world to me. I was often super-sensitive to anything they would say. Deep down, I knew they would always be there for me and had my back.

I'd started seeing a rugby player called Gareth, whom I met on a night out with the girls in Seal Street, Liverpool. We'd hit it off so on Fridays I stayed with him. Gareth was from the Wirral and, like me, was into his sport. He knew all about training and fitness. He used to come and do my workout and running sessions with me. It was the first serious relationship I'd had. If I had a home match with Bowdon I would stay over at his on Saturday night. On Sunday morning I'd go back to my parents' house, and then it was back down the road to Bisham Abbey.

That was my life for the remainder of 2008 and into the next year. It was hectic but I was in the international setup and now a fully established, key player in the Bowdon first team, and we were doing really well.

In the 2008/09 season, Bowdon Hightown dominated the women's game, winning the Slazenger Premier Division by fifteen points from our nearest challengers, losing only once in the process. Indoors, we ended a 14-year wait for the National Indoor Hockey Championships title when we defeated Slough in the final at the National Indoor Arena, Birmingham, and went on to represent England in Europe. And in May we completed an historic treble by clinching the women's cup, beating a strong Reading team featuring a number of GB internationalists 2–1.

However, although at club level I was enjoying some incredible successes, in the international setup I felt in limbo.

That winter there had been the European indoor tournament. I was delighted to be selected but I was conscious that hockey was interfering with my degree. I'd missed a lot of university time in my first year and was worried about the same happening in my second, when my grades would really matter as they now counted towards my overall degree result.

The indoor event coincided with a work placement module I had to do, so I decided to go and have a word with Danny Kerry.

'Is it going to impact on my future selection if I don't go to this tournament?' I said.

'No,' he replied, 'it shouldn't. It'll be fine.'

It wasn't a choice I made lightly, but it was a choice fuelled by the panic of three years earlier, when I had got those terrible AS results at Calday and feared for my future after hockey.

I completed the module but then found I wasn't selected for the next England test matches or trips away. I became paranoid and wondered if it was because I missed the indoor. Even though Danny had said it wasn't an issue, I started to worry that the coaches might have thought I wasn't fully committed to the programme.

I started to view any little development as a sign I was being overlooked. Ten people from my age group, who all went to the indoor but had no other experience, got selected for the Champions Trophy in Sydney in July 2009, and I was the only one who didn't. It didn't make sense to me at all.

The logical reason was that the coach wanted to give some other youngsters some much-needed experience. However, I took it personally. I just kept thinking, 'What have I done wrong?' It was the first time I had felt like I was being dropped, but instead of responding positively and resolving to work even harder to force my way back into their plans, I felt like I was being punished and that Danny had just paid me lip service.

In my mind it was even worse than missing out on Beijing because although that was disappointing, I hadn't really expected to be there. But since the Olympic selection I'd had the experience of the pre-Beijing cycle and I'd been part of the ambition programme for 2012.

I spoke to my mum, my coaches at Bowdon Hightown and sounded out Peter Cartmel, my old mentor. They were all of the same opinion: Just go back to Danny, be honest with him and ask, 'Is it because I didn't commit to the programme for the indoor?'

That's what I did. I spoke to Danny. He reassured me that he just wanted to give some other girls the experience I'd had. That made me feel a bit better. But as hockey underwent its revolution later that year, I was soon to discover that my part in the Olympics was by no means guaranteed.

Another seemingly inconsequential development that year would have serious ramifications for me in the future. In the wake of doping scandals across several sports, the authorities had introduced the concept of Therapeutic Use Exemption (TUE), the process by which an athlete can obtain approval to use a prescribed prohibited substance or method for the treatment of a legitimate medical condition.

Hockey was no exception to the anti-doping rules. A few of the players carried inhalers but it was important to show they did need them for medical reasons, so we were all sent to Loughborough University for testing. You were hooked up to a ventilator machine and your peak expiratory flow – how you breathe normally – was calculated. You then did sixty seconds of very fast breathing to replicate exercise and your peak flow was calculated again. The difference between those two readings indicated whether you needed an inhaler or not.

In my case, the difference was quite significant and the result showed I needed an inhaler. Yet, in all my time playing hockey, and football, I'd never felt I needed one. I'd never felt tight in the chest or short of breath.

I was prescribed an inhaler and the advice was that I should always carry it around in my hockey bag along with the TUE form just in case we were drug tested. I didn't have cause to use it and for years hardly gave it a thought. I never for one second thought that one day someone would try to use its existence to damage my reputation.

Chapter 9

Mental Torment

Whenever I pulled on my country's shirt I felt immense pride. But to do so as captain was massive.

Missing out on selection for the senior team that travelled to Sydney for the Champions Trophy was gutting. However, being made captain for the under-21 side that would challenge for the Junior World Cup in Boston in August 2009 was something that will live with me forever. It was a massive tournament. For every player, regardless of your experience, it's one step from the senior squad.

We were taking a relatively young team across the Atlantic and straight away the coach made me captain because I was a lot more experienced than the majority of the team.

I'd been a little bit apprehensive about going back into the under-21 squad. The experiences I'd had with the seniors meant I was tactically so much further ahead of the rest of the team. In that situation you don't want to go in all guns blazing, telling people to do this, do that. You have to tread a fine line between knowing when to command your teammates because you want to win and holding back because they're still young. I wanted to try to emulate Kate's style with the seniors. I had soaked up everything I could from her and I was determined to lead by example.

On a personal level, I wanted to make as big an impact as I could, but those plans lay in tatters when, during our first game against France, I went over in a tackle and a French girl fell on top of me. The most excruciating pain shot into my left shoulder. On the floor I tried to sit up but couldn't because of the pain and I started to panic. Had I done some serious damage?

I came off straight away and the physio assessed the problem. I'd snapped a ligament in the acromioclavicular or AC joint at the top of my arm.

Although I was in agony, the team were performing well. In that first match we'd thumped France 5–0 and had battled to a 2–2 draw against South Korea in our second. A final 2–0 win over Chile saw us progress to the medal round.

After sitting out the two matches, I was desperate to return to the team. I was in so much pain but tried to get through the fitness test. To prove my fitness I had to do roly-poly forward rolls and a wheelbarrow race to make sure that if I fell over I could land properly. They heavily strapped the shoulder and I was confident I could put weight through it. Finally, I was deemed fit to play.

Once I took to the field against India, I realised I was still in pain. It was impossible to play my best hockey. Going into tackles I couldn't reach out with my left arm. There are a few pictures of me trying to make tackles with only my right hand on my stick, which is a complete no-no.

Despite this, we won the game. We then went on to beat the United States and reached the semi-finals, where we faced Argentina. I gave it my all, and in a very tight game we pushed them all the way, but narrowly lost 1–0 after extra time. I felt a little guilty, wondering if I had done what was best for the team by playing with an injury.

We tried to raise our game for the bronze medal match but after another close contest with South Korea, we were defeated 2–1. Fourth place in the Junior World Cup was a great achievement, but it could have been so much better.

The same couldn't be said for the seniors, sadly, in the Champions Trophy, finishing last of six countries with no wins from five matches. We were only spared relegation because we were hosting the tournament in 2010. The senior team performed better in the Euro-Hockey Nations Championship in Amsterdam, finishing with the bronze medal.

The seniors clearly weren't ticking on all cylinders and Danny wasn't going to be shy about making changes. Despite me not being included, I felt, given the inconsistent results, it was only a matter of time before I would be asked back to help out.

The centralised funding that had been proposed a year earlier came into force at the tail end of 2009. I was excited and a little relieved to be part of the first programme. Players received certain allocations for different levels of seniority and experience. That meant around twelve players were on 'A' category funding, the highest level for the most senior players, and ten people were on 'B', the secondary level. I was in the 'B' category so for me it meant around £1,000 a month, which was great, but it didn't exactly mean you could start rocking up in a Range Rover. Also, we were living in Marlow, with very high rents and very high retail prices. I'd have got a lot more for my money if I were still in Leeds or Liverpool!

While we were still down at Bisham part-time, Laura and I had moved from the Bennetts' house into a maisonette above a garage in Henley-on-Thames. After we went full-time the owner of the maisonette offered to us, for a favourable rent, a flat he rented in Marlow, which was much closer to our hockey HQ. After six months we moved to a better flat, which was a lot more expensive but nicer, and closer to Marlow High Street. It was great having our own space but with rent and bills totalling £700 a month it was a big difference from the £20 a night we had been paying to stay with the Bennetts. I was still reliant on a student loan and on top of that my parents helped out with petrol money.

Being part of the centralised programme was certainly a step in the right direction but I believed moving to a new club might give me the best chance of being involved at London 2012.

Reading was the closest club to Bisham Abbey, only twenty minutes' drive away. More importantly, a strong core of the England and GB teams played its hockey there. Kate Walsh, Helen Richardson, Laura Bartlett, Emily Maguire from Scotland, Alex Danson and Beth Storry, the England goalkeeper, were all there, so I saw it very much as an opportunity to get to know better the GB players and get used to playing with them. By playing consistent club hockey with them, I was able to learn more about how Helen wanted to receive the ball and also build strong connections with Kate and Emily, whom I would be playing alongside in the GB backline.

A move there made complete hockey sense but I also hoped sent out a statement, especially if Danny, despite saying otherwise, really did have questions over my commitment to the programme.

I went to Danny Kerry and asked him if it would benefit me moving to Reading and he agreed, but said it was a decision only I could make. I also spoke to Kate, and she was up for me moving there. The Reading coach was Simon Letchford, whose wife Lisa was part of the GB team in Beijing. They were also very encouraging. It felt like the right move.

To make the switch, I notified England Hockey that I was leaving Bowdon, and Reading did the same. England Hockey then organised the transfer. I felt really bad leaving Bowdon Hightown. They had brought me through when I was younger, had moulded me into a good player, and I felt so at home there. I felt I owed them so much more than to just leave and, although it wasn't my first hockey club, I had more of an affinity with Bowdon than any other I had played for. It was a decision that made me so sad, but one I had to make. It was another one of those inevitable sacrifices. I vowed that one day I would be back though.

Reading's arch rivals were Leicester, who boasted effectively the other half of the England team, with the likes of Crista Cullen, Anne Panter and Jennie Bimson.

For the first time in my club career I played in defence. The back line was Kate, Emily and me at right half, the right inside midfielder was Laura, and centre half was Helen. Up front, I was passing to Alex Danson. I got to know them better on the pitch and off. As a result I felt more confident when I went to Bisham and became more of the character I am at heart, someone who was quite relaxed and joked around.

Quickly I seemed to be back in the international frame and was delighted to be selected to join the England senior team for the indoor series against Scotland in Paisley. In our opening game I scored the winner with literally the last flick of the game from a penalty corner. The series was drawn 2–2 but it was great to be back involved.

It couldn't have come at a better time because 2010 was going to be a massive year. Not only was there the World Cup in Argentina in September – the tournament that only the Olympics ranked higher than – but also the Commonwealth Games were being held in Delhi a month later. I was desperate to be involved in both, but particularly the Commonwealth Games, as it was the only other multi-sport tournament around. In terms of experiencing the village and organisational side it would be an invaluable experience. It was also generally considered amongst the senior players that being selected for Delhi would pretty much indicate who was going to the 2012 Olympics. That only increased my desire to be there.

This was the start of a long-running Olympic obsession for me. Even though I should have been excited about potentially competing in my first international multi-sport tournament, in a fascinating country like India, I only viewed it as a stepping stone to a bigger prize. All I saw it as was a stepping stone to the Olympics.

Moving down south wasn't all plain sailing. It meant I was doing the final year of my degree away from Leeds and I'd be further away from my family and friends. Ultimately, it also spelled the end of my relationship with Gareth. We continued to get on great but we'd reached a stage when we were moving in different directions and growing apart. He was six years older, was ready to settle and was saving for a house, whereas I was 100 per cent hockey focused and wanted to travel. We might have been able to have made it work, but he would have had to have given up his life for me, because it wasn't going to happen the other way around. I wasn't going to forget all the hard work and sacrifices I had put in up to now. We split on good terms, each of us understanding we had different ideas of where our lives were at the time.

On the club front, I thought I was adjusting to the move well. I felt I was developing an understanding with the players around me. Reading had a good season and we were up there challenging for the league title, before losing in the play-offs. We also reached the cup final, narrowly missing out to Leicester, who edged the final 2–1, which particularly annoyed me because of our rivalry with them.

I was pleased with my form and hoped the club setup would boost my chances of being involved when the England team was announced for the Champions Trophy in Nottingham in July. This time there was no elation when I opened the announcement email – only dejection. My name was not on the list ... again.

Although I wasn't able to influence proceedings, the girls gave a far better account of themselves than they'd done a year before in Australia. They finished with an extremely credible bronze medal, beating the eventual champions Argentina in the round robin. By now my confidence in being selected for 2012 was starting to seriously wane, despite previously thinking it was a certainty.

I continued to hope things might be different when the World Cup squad was announced – after all, what else can you do? However, more disappointment was in store. I also wouldn't be on the plane to Argentina.

Again, the girls that did go performed well, coming away with another bronze medal, losing to Holland in the semi-finals, but beating Germany 2–0 to take third place.

I felt a pattern was emerging. I knew this feeling all too well – after suffering the disappointments of Beijing and Sydney. Short of a miracle, my hopes of going to Delhi for the Commonwealth Games were going to be dashed as well. And so it transpired.

Missing out on three big tournaments at that stage of my career was crushing. I felt I'd been doing okay, but obviously it wasn't good enough. London 2012 was two years away, so I still had time to turn it around. I maintained I was talented enough but not making it into the squad for Delhi shattered my already fragile confidence.

I was so confused. Signs were clearly pointing that I wasn't in the coach's plans for 2012, but why would they have put me on the 2012 ambition programme? Why would they have put me on the paid centralised programme? Also, that centralised programme was graded on a traffic light system, where if you were on green, you were safe, on amber, it was a warning that you could soon be dropped from the programme, and red meant you would soon be dropped. It was done like this to give you sufficient warning that you would need to make other plans. I was never anything but green. I had been captain of the under–21s and felt a level above that standard, and was also giving a good account of myself in training. My personal life was fully geared to hockey. There was quite literally nothing left to sacrifice. I had been fully committed, so what was going on?

I sought Danny's advice again on what aspects of my game I could work on to improve.

'Focus on your ball retention,' he said. 'When you get it, try not to lose it.'

The feedback was constructive but I took it the wrong way. Whenever I played next and the ball came to me, all that was going on in my head was, 'Don't lose the ball, don't lose the ball.'

And what would happen? I'd inexplicably give it away. It became this big issue in my head.

It didn't help that we still trained as a full group, so the girls selected for the big tournaments were training with those that weren't. For the most part, those in the squad tried to be respectful but they couldn't help letting their excitement show, and it was impossible to avoid the excited chat about what they were taking or the typical girl stuff like checking who was taking a hair dryer and things like that.

I'm sure there was an element of sympathy for the people left at home but at the same time, the players that were going needed to focus on their own game and how they'd perform. And for those of us who were missing out, although we were gutted, we couldn't show we were upset at not being selected.

At Bisham Abbey, a video analysis room with six computer screens was the place you went to study your performance and the tactics of your opponents. If I wanted to improve I needed to examine every aspect of my play and work out how to cut out the mistakes. In the files was footage from every single one of my international games and all my training sessions. I was prepared to pour over every clip.

If I was ever going to compete against the best at the highest level, then I had to go back to basics. It wasn't going to be pretty.

Chapter 10

A Pain Like No Other

It was like starring in your own nightmare version of *You've Been Framed*. I was watching seemingly endless video clips of my performances, but focusing solely on mistakes. I'd reached out to England's team sports psychologist Tom Cross to look at my game, identify weaknesses and try to rectify them.

We spent ages in the video analysis room at Bisham. When I'd asked Danny Kerry what I could work on to improve my game to get myself back into his thinking, he said: 'Get clips of yourself, whether it's in training games or just five-a-sides, when you play in actual matches, and every time you give the ball away, write down why you think you gave the ball away. And note down what scenario was it: Should you have passed? Should you have dribbled?'

So that's what I was doing. I wanted to show I was doing everything I could to improve. So, with Tom we created a massive spreadsheet after pouring over dozens of clips. We looked at whether I was playing on the left or right, whether I gave possession away in a pass or dribbled and lost it, or whether I misplaced a pass off to the sideline. Watching endless replays of your bad moments is quite sobering. It makes you wonder how on earth you got to that level. These were ten seconds of clips from sixty minutes of match, but it was hard to think of it like that.

The next column would be what I would do next. Did I win it back, get into the right position or defend the situation properly? If there were clips I was unsure of and didn't realise what was actually the right decision, I'd go to see Danny. I must have looked at over fifty clips but I'd go to Danny with five and say, 'Here I passed it but it was turned over. Was that the right decision?'

I had hoped that by analysing my performances it would make me a better player and make split decisions easier to judge, but it ended up having the opposite effect. We'd talk through each clip but I was overthinking, overanalysing everything, and the smallest things became big issues. With every hit of the play button, my confidence lowered more. When I played, I tried to work out what the right decision should be every time I got the ball.

It was like I was replaying every clip in my head, trying to remember what the right thing to do was.

I had to face it – I was in a downward spiral.

It didn't help that I was paranoid that Tom, our psychologist, might be relaying my insecurities back to Danny.

While I was pouring over videos and getting myself worked up, the England squad in Delhi battled to the bronze medal, just missing out on the gold medal final by losing 1–0 to Australia.

When the new season started I once again tried to focus on rediscovering my form and trying to force myself into Danny's plans. It helped that Reading enjoyed a great season, winning the league play-off final against Leicester 3–2. This was particularly sweet, being revenge for the year before.

I stopped trying to overthink every pass and my overall play improved. I wasn't really thinking about whether I'd be selected for England in the summer.

Then, out of the blue, I was selected for the Champions Trophy in Amstelveen. I was absolutely buzzing. It would be my first international tournament. In the run-up to it I played some of my best hockey. My conversations with Danny had become more open and that helped restore my confidence. I was back.

We arrived in the Netherlands and played a practice match against Australia. I played really well. I was making my tackles and was doing well on my passing. We were working on a new system. Usually we operated a numbered passing system where we'd never miss a player out. Imagine a back four, numbered one to four from left to right. If I was the right back, I was number four, so I could only pass it short to the person on my left, the centre back, who would be number three. I would never miss them out and play a longer pass to the number two centre back or the number one left back. It was a system designed to keep a rigid back four, make no mistakes, and let the more creative players create. It went against my natural instincts as a midfielder to try to find a pass to open up the attack.

With the new system we tried a more free-flowing system, where you didn't always have to pass to a specific player. It changed our playing angles, which resulted in a fast passing game that required more accuracy. We didn't win the game but I came off pleased with how I had played and thinking I had given a good account of myself in a practice game going into the tournament.

As soon as we came off the pitch, Danny got us into the dressing room and bollocked us all. He then turned to me.

'How many times do I have to tell people, like you Sam, about not missing a person out on the transfer?'

I couldn't believe it. In my head I thought, 'What are you talking about? We specifically discussed working on getting the ball out the pocket and transferring it quickly.'

I never said anything, though. It was obvious he was seriously pissed off. Danny's not an aggressive style of coach but he's not shy about letting you know when he's unhappy.

From thinking I'd played well, all of a sudden I wondered, 'Did I play well? Maybe I shouldn't have done this or that.' The last thing I needed was to be questioning myself again. My natural game was already a fraction slower than it would usually be as I was second-guessing myself with every move – not a great way to be heading into an important tournament.

For that tournament we had a total of eighteen players. Eleven started but only five were allowed on the bench for each match, so two would have to sit in the stand. For the first game against Argentina Danny put me in at sixteen.

My mind was working overtime again. 'Why aren't I starting? Is it because I'm still new to the team and I've not played in a tournament?'

So many questions. I couldn't quiz Danny because I didn't want to be seen to be high maintenance. I felt like I was starting to lose my mind.

The match started and finally I got on for my first competitive international action. I couldn't have asked for a tougher baptism, given Argentina were the reigning champions. I'm not sure whether the occasion got to me, or the conditions – it was lashing with rain. Perhaps it was that my mind was awash with self-doubt, but I was making rookie errors. Coming up against Soledad García, I felt undaunted as previously I'd done well against her, but she caught me out with some cute play, putting the ball onto my foot in the 'D'. I could have avoided it and a penalty was called. I should have been wise to the move.

Argentina didn't score but my confidence was now completely shattered.

In truth, too many of us were off colour that day. Argentina took the lead thanks to a moment of individual brilliance from Luciana Ayma, the seven-time World Player of the Year. Although that was the extent of the scoring, we never really looked like getting on level terms. Argentina had the bulk of the play.

'Some people brought their B games today,' Danny Kerry said after the match. 'We need to be much better tomorrow.'

I was one of the players who hadn't played well, but it was a small relief that I may have an immediate chance to atone for my performance.

Our next opponents the following day were South Korea, a much weaker team than Argentina, but I wouldn't play a part. Danny had selected me as one of the two to sit in the stand.

My head had now completely gone. It was just an endless series of peaks and troughs. I couldn't take it. I was very low, but when something gave me a reason to get excited again, I would get a boost, only to fall even further as the next disappointment came along.

More questions swirled in my mind. The team would probably do better than the day before because they were now against a much weaker opponent. Would the coaches account for that or would they think dropping me made the team better?

Rather than concentrating on how I could cut out the mistakes, I started to feel sorry for myself and aggrieved that there was some sort of personal slight on Danny's part. I thought it was unfair I wasn't getting a proper chance.

The girls fought out a 2–2 draw against the Koreans. Our last pool match was against China. We needed a win to be sure of qualifying to the medal matches but we could only manage a 0–0 draw. Once more, I started on the bench but came off to earn my second competitive cap. You would think I would have taken confidence from the clean sheet – I didn't.

We had to hope that Argentina did us a favour against Korea but that match was drawn so we were out of contention for a medal.

I again sat out our non-medal match against Germany, which we won 1–0, but finally started the next game against Australia, which we won 3–2. We played Australia for the second time in three days to decide who was the best of the rest outside the medal matches, and we triumphed again 2–0. The team had improved as the tournament went on and our fifth place finish achieved our pre-tournament target of qualifying Great Britain for the 2012 Champions Trophy. That was crucial as the tournament was seen as the perfect preparation for the London Olympics.

As I reflected on my first major tournament I should have been thrilled to feature in some games, but instead I felt dejected. I dwelled on the fact that my appearances had been sparse. My mum and dad came over to watch me and I felt embarrassed that I'd hardly played. Is this what they had spent their money on, to come and watch their daughter sit on a bench? They were used to seeing me be the star of most teams I played in. Now I felt I was barely even a part of the team. They used to be so proud of me. 'Look at me now,' I thought, 'I've let you down at the final hurdle.'

I knew I had to sort my head out and get positive. Easier said than done. The next tournament was the European Championships in a month's time in Mönchengladbach, Germany. Again I motivated myself by thinking that would be my chance – an opportunity to show what I could do if given a consistent run of games.

During training one day, Karen Brown, our assistant coach, called me in to watch over some video. She started playing the García clip from the opening match of the Champions Trophy.

The footage still haunts me now.

There's García, running down the left-hand side. I'm at right back, channelling, channelling, channelling. We're in the 'D' and she just puts it on my foot.

'If you're going to be playing international hockey,' Karen said, 'you need to be a bit more astute to this.'

It was constructive advice but again I didn't take it as that. I was so paranoid about any little criticism that I took it personally. In my head this only meant one thing: You're not going to the Europeans, Sam.

The email announcement should have put me out of my misery. However, missing out on selection for the Europeans told only part of the story. 'This is just like it was with the Delhi Commonwealth Games,' I thought. 'If I'm not going this time then they won't select me for London.' It didn't matter how much I tried to convince myself differently; it was obvious. How could they pick me for 2012 when I'd only been to one tournament and only played two or three games of senior international hockey in four years?

Even though you tell yourself, the stark reality is, it doesn't sink in. It just swirls around in your head. It's a constant internal monologue: Well, you're not going to London because realistically, how are you going to get selected? What was the point in giving everything up? Cut your losses now, Sam, don't waste another year of your life. You're already embarrassing yourself. Time to realise it's never going to happen. You're not as good as you think you are.

This was my thought process, almost every night before I went to bed, and every morning once I had woken up.

The more I tried to process it the lower my mood sank, but I refused to let anyone know just how depressed I was.

England came away from the EuroHockey Nations Championship in August with a bronze. The team wasn't changing much. London 2012 was growing ever more distant for me.

I went back to Bisham in September 2010 and tried to keep working and training hard.

In the Olympic year, the Champions Trophy was held in February. Great Britain entered, courtesy of England's performance a few months earlier. I wasn't selected for that squad. They went on to win the silver medal, our highest ever placing.

Again the internal torment went on: 'See, Sam, the coaches are right, a silver medal in the Champions Trophy is amazing, they must have a really good team now you are not in it.'

The team was performing well. Anyone could argue the coach's selections were indeed justified. The only way I would make it to London was if someone in my position suffered an injury or a loss of form.

I always want England or Great Britain to win, but it's human nature to want to be involved. And if you're not involved, you want there to be a reason why you should be involved next time, whatever that may be.

As far as hockey was concerned, I had lost all concept of what was real and what was fake.

Unlike most other jobs, there are always players competing with for your position.

I always felt Emily Maguire might get the nod over me for British teams because she was Scottish and it helped show the other nations were represented. Again, this was a case of paranoia. Emily was a very talented player and when selected she was always there on merit. I liked her a lot but there were only so many defence positions to fill, so someone was always going to miss out, and I would rather it was her than me. No doubt she felt the same, too.

Around that time, Anne Panter, a solid right back, was returning from a car crash where she had needed two knee operations. Her fightback to fitness was amazing, and her story attracted a lot of attention. 'Another person that would be selected ahead of me,' I thought. Again, though, Anne was always selected on merit, not sympathy. My brain was just in overdrive.

Each squad announcement reinforced my fear that my Olympic dream was dying – perhaps forever. Added to that frustration was the torture of watching the Olympic Park take shape.

The opening ceremony might still be months away but as soon as the pitch was laid at the Riverbank Arena in Stratford – the venue for the hockey tournament – we went down to test out the facilities. We'd travel by coach down from Bisham every Thursday and go through the massive security process into what then was literally a building site. Once we cleared security, we'd get changed and be escorted on the bus over to the hockey pitch. All that was there was a portable toilet, temporary office and the pitch. We'd do a two-hour session in the morning, and then have a lunch break and another two-hour session in the afternoon.

When we first started using the pitch there were no side barriers so the ball just ran over into gravel. When first laid, a hockey pitch will be bouncy, so the organisers let club teams play on it to get the surface to bed in so the pitch would run faster and have less of a bounce.

With each passing week the arena was taking shape and we could see the stadium and smaller venues getting bigger and bigger. The cycling velodrome was one of the first to be completed and I remember seeing the images of my dream become reality.

The stands that over time surrounded the hockey pitch were huge. It would be the biggest venue I had seen, but I doubted I would ever play a competitive match there.

During the time we were training there we were constantly reminded, 'This is the Olympics, it's coming to London, and this is what you are training for.' Every news cycle had an update on the progress of the facilities, and every newspaper was starting to have 'ones to watch' sections about athletes set to compete in the games. The pressure was ramping up.

Every Thursday we'd get on a coach from Bisham and travel down. Those of us not selected for a warm-up test series had to go and watch from the stands. It wasn't a pleasant experience. It was bloody awful, in fact. I shed tears into my pillow most nights. I was clinging onto the slimmest hope that anything could happen. I still believed I deserved to be on the team.

Living with Laura Bartlett at the time made it doubly difficult because she was getting selected for every GB squad. I was happy for her and was pleased for her. It was tough though, particularly the times when she was away at a tournament and I was stuck back in the flat.

Sometimes when the selection email came out for the test matches it was obvious she was going, because she was a good player. We were friends before we were teammates and were comfortable enough in each other's company. She wouldn't pander to me and helped me not to feel sorry for myself. I probably should have been more positive and happy for her, but I just didn't feel positive or happy. I wouldn't be like, 'Oh congratulations!' I'd just be like, 'Alright, good luck' when she left to join the squad.

Any other feelings were just pushed to the side. That was when playing hockey felt most like a job. I became a bit closer to the other girls who weren't selected. Often it would be a group of six of us who missed out and we would still be training at Bisham when the rest of the squad were away. When I looked at them I never felt they took missing out as hard as I did.

Perhaps they didn't feel they should have been selected? Perhaps they didn't care as much as I did? Or perhaps they were now experts at hiding the tracks of their tears, as I was.

Once the final test matches were out of the way, the squad for the Olympics was due to be announced. It was only May, so the opening ceremony was still several weeks away. I clung to hope, but in my heart I had prepared myself that I wasn't going to get selected.

Hope was the only thing that had kept me going for so long. The faint idea that maybe, just maybe, was what got me up and out in the morning, every day for the last few years. I was running on fumes at this point.

The momentum was building. The Duchess of Cambridge arrived for a photo opportunity and played hockey on the new pitch. She was wearing a Team GB top and peach jeans, and we all stood there watching as she hit a few balls for the cameras. She was lovely and was clearly excited for the forthcoming games. Suddenly there was press interest on us training and we were being asked what we thought of the new stadiums and facilities.

On Tuesday, 8 May at 8.00 am, the announcement came. We all agreed on a time when it was going to be. I decided I wanted to be at home. I didn't want to be around anyone because I knew in my heart of hearts what was going to happen. I lay in bed and set my alarm for eight o'clock. I didn't need to; I got no sleep that night. In fact, I hadn't slept properly for ages. At ten to eight I was looking at my phone … refresh, refresh, refresh.

Finally, it came through. I wasn't in the sixteen, nor was I in the reserves.

To be honest, I didn't feel anything at first.

It was a crazy moment that I can't quite explain. I was experiencing relief that I finally knew the outcome, but at the same time the fumes of hope I had been running on for so long were finally extinguished.

All the questions that had been swirling in my mind instantly disappeared. They didn't matter anymore; nothing mattered anymore. I was numb – and I mean numb. I felt like a 10-ton lorry could have run me over and I wouldn't have felt a thing.

Time stood still and all my senses stopped working for a moment. I don't remember a sound, nor what was said to me, or what I was looking at … not a smell, or anything I was saying. I was just … blank.

After a few seconds I realised that I was gutted, and I mean gutted. I literally felt hollow. I remember crying, but it was an unemotional cry, because I knew 'It's the reality', and I had known it for so long, but hope had made me think otherwise.

There was no hope now.

Although I'd been expecting it, to see it in black and white just brought it home. And then there were waves of other emotions.

If I had given everything for six years, I could have, over time, made peace with missing out. But deep down I knew I hadn't. I had been limited by my own mindset, my paranoia, my lack of self-belief. I can't pinpoint when exactly it happened, but at some point the self-assured, optimistic, relatively happy 19-year-old woman who had been on the London 2012 legacy programme, with a burning desire and determination to be at the next Olympics, had become a paranoid, negative, scared, self-doubting, almost self-loathing Olympic obsessive.

I felt I had nothing.

I felt I had mortgaged my future for hockey, letting my grades slip and my relationships fade away. I had no savings, no job, and no home of my own. I was more distant from my family and friends than ever. What was my future to be when I had nothing to show for my past or present? What did I have to show to all the people who had put their faith in me, the hours my parents had spent helping my development? What could I show as the results for all the sacrifices I had made – all the missed births, funerals and marriages? What was I going to show to my family and friends when it was a case of 'Here you go … this was what all that was for … a handful of international caps'?

I felt so embarrassed. It was all everyone was talking about: 'My mate's going to 2012', 'My daughter's training for 2012'.

The number of people you have to tell when you don't get selected is horrible and although they are truly upset for you, they never really understand the depths of your sadness.

It was only going to get worse.

The greatest party was about to hit these shores. And I wasn't invited.

Chapter 11

Here's What You Could Have Won

It didn't matter where I looked; there was no escape from it. Union Jacks were everywhere. The nation was still buzzing from the Queen's diamond jubilee that had taken place earlier in the year, so the shops had remained well stocked. Patriotic fervour was approaching fever pitch.

We were one week away from the opening ceremony. At the Olympic Park, for the last training session before the tournament began, you could see everything had come together. The flagpoles were up, banners were hung and it was all anyone was talking about.

The sixteen girls in the squad were bouncing off the walls with excitement. Who could blame them? It was a unique moment in their lives and they were all there on merit. For the rest of us, though, there was no let-up. What people don't realise is, when you aren't selected for the Olympics, things don't just stop. There was a period of twelve weeks between selection and Olympics starting where you were expected to still train with the squad and help them prepare. It was the last thing on earth I wanted to do. Everything in me wanted to just stay in bed and stick two fingers up at GB Hockey. However, I had a duty to my teammates to help them. Where hope was no longer a motivation, doing the right thing was. But it was so, so hard.

I particularly found it tough being around my rivals for the defence positions who had been selected – Emily Maguire, Anne Panter and Sally Walton. They had all performed well when called upon and merited their selections, but I couldn't help thinking, 'What does she have that I don't?'

It didn't matter how much it was spelled out that I hadn't made the final cut for selection, that old devil called hope crept into my mind once more. If someone got injured, maybe I would be the replacement? It wasn't a case of hoping someone got injured, not at all, but it was being around the team, sensing their excitement, that made me dream again. If I did somehow get selected, all the things I had worried about when I opened the selection email would be fixed in an instant. I clearly still hadn't accepted the reality.

Up until that last session we'd trained as normal. But that final Thursday at the Olympic Park was different. I still felt numb. As bad as it sounds, even before the countdown had begun for the whole event, I just kept thinking, 'I can't wait for this to be over.'

For everyone it was a home Olympics. It was huge. For me, it just felt like torture.

Traditionally, the last session before a major tournament was the toughest. Everyone had to do it, not just the sixteen in the squad. Before we'd left for the Champions Trophy in Argentina I remembered a few of the girls had to stop early because the session was so tough. I always vowed I would never do that. My attitude was always, 'I'm going to prove that I'm fitter than anyone and show them I could just as well be on that plane – or in the Olympic village.'

That day we started with a punishing one-on-one routine on a half pitch where two players would compete head to head. Then it was straight into an eleven-a-side practice match for ten minutes, and after that, straight off to the sides, shin pads off and a running session. Normally we were told, 'Right, we're going to do three sets of ten reps.'

On this occasion they didn't tell us how long we'd be running for. We just had to keep running until we heard the second whistle, then we could stop. No sooner had we stopped than we were told to get to the baseline as quickly as possible, otherwise we'd miss the next whistle.

We were knackered and just wanted to drop to the floor, but we couldn't because we had to get to that baseline.

Ordinarily, I thrived on being pushed harder, but not today. Not after the crushing disappointment.

'This is a joke,' I thought. 'Nothing's going to change now. Why are they doing this to us?'

Fitness-wise, we were one week out of the Olympics. They could have just said, 'Right, those of you who are not selected, thanks very much, on your way.' They could have then kept working with everyone who was going.

If the workout alone wasn't bad enough, we were also doing it on the Olympic pitch. Every time I caught sight of those five bloody rings or London 2012, it screamed: 'This is what you could have had.'

I realise the coaches' thinking was to show how tight we were as a unit, that we were all in this together.

On any other day I'd get that. But that day I just thought, 'Fuck you'.

It just went on and on. And then it happened. The emotion I'd failed to show properly since the announcement now bubbled to the surface. The session stopped near the halfway line. The final whistle sounded and

I walked over to the other side of the pitch. My legs were weak, my whole body was heaving. I dropped to my hands and knees.

Then the tears came. Great gulping sobs, because I was knackered and felt like I was going to hyperventilate.

I remember Dave Hamilton, our strength and conditioning coach, coming over and patting me on the back to say, 'I'm so sorry but well done.'

He was only being nice and it was good of him to notice something was up but in my present mood I just thought, rather unkindly, 'Go away, can everyone just go away, can the world just please go away!'

I walked to the baseline where Katie Long, one of the other players who hadn't been selected, was. She was upset as well. I put my arm on her back and squeezed her shoulder. We were both on our hands and knees. We didn't even look at each other but I think we both knew what the other was thinking.

The tears were still streaming. I didn't feel upset. It was more anger and frustration – mostly with myself. I kept thinking, what more could I have done?

There was no time to wallow in self-pity. It was time for a group picture at the end. I didn't want to show I was crying. I already had people coming up asking, 'Are you okay?' The last thing I wanted was pity. I got my shit together and tried to pretend it was just sweat. It was a hot day after all, but I'm not sure if anyone bought it.

By the time the photo was taken everyone else was laughing and joking. I put my happy face on. I had become good at doing that.

That was the last time I saw the girls who would feature in the team until they were on the pitch playing in front of an ecstatic home crowd in an Olympic Games.

When the day of the opening ceremony arrived – on 27 July – one of my friends, Nicky O'Donnell, was having a leaving party as she was moving to New Zealand. I was quite grateful to have something to go to because I didn't want to sit at home feeling sorry for myself. I was still suffering from a mixture of emotions. It had been sixty days since selection, but because I hadn't had a break from hockey nor the Olympic fanfare yet, I hadn't had time to deal with how I truly felt. It sounds so pathetic to say, but I was grieving … grieving for the loss of my dream.

I walked into the pub where everyone was meeting and every screen around the bar began to show the ceremony. There was obviously no escape from it. As the ceremony went on, people were getting more and more excited. It was a strange feeling, like I was detached from it all, amid all the excitement.

There were some hockey girls among our group and as the teams came out they were going, 'Can you see the GB team? Here they come. Can you see the hockey girls?'

The plan had been that everyone was going to go on to Mojo, a bar where my twin brother Shaun was manager. Before the ceremony ended I went over there on my own while they all agreed to catch me up.

There were no TVs in Mojo and I just sat there with my brother chatting. I probably drank more than I would normally. I had texted my sister Maxine and older brother Mike. Later they told me that Maxine had said, 'Get over with Sam now,' not so I didn't do anything stupid; just to make sure I was okay. So Mike ended up coming out and meeting me and we just chatted, not about the Olympics but anything and everything else. My family did everything they could during this time. We are so close, and while I knew they were worried about me, I was determined to keep them at arm's length. I actively avoided them, partially through embarrassment and partially because their faces served as a reminder of the people I had let down. Looking back, I was so lucky to have had them there for me.

The women's hockey started two days into the tournament. The players who missed out were told they could watch the matches, so I felt it was expected of me to do so. I also didn't want anyone to see just how upset I was. By going to the matches, perhaps they would think I had dealt with not being selected much better than I had.

For Team GB's opening match against Japan, I went along with Katie Long and Susie Townsend, who'd also missed out on selection. It was the evening match and the Riverbank Arena was packed. The Games were only two days old but already you could tell the nation was being swept up in the excitement.

Earlier in the day the Netherlands had got off to the sort of start you'd expect, beating Belgium 3–0, and China had beaten South Korea 4–0. It was vital the girls got off to a good start.

Whilst we had been told we could come to watch the Games, we weren't supplied with tickets, which at the time I didn't care about as I had enough on my plate, but looking back, I think it was a disgrace. Throughout my career, the powers that be only ever gave you a family allocation of two tickets to each game. Even if you asked for more, they wouldn't be provided, even to purchase. Given how many people had helped us as athletes to get to where we were and what they had given up, all I wanted to do was invite them to a game as a thank you, but I was only ever supplied with tickets for my parents. If anyone else was to come they had to buy them separately if they were available, and then sit in a completely different section. It caused a lot of off-field issues at times and was an unnecessary distraction that we could have had more help with.

Although tickets to the 2012 matches were like gold dust I was able to get some in the friends and family section. I was quite literally paying to see my nightmares played out in front of me.

Despite my heartache, we decided to make a day of it so we headed for a bar called The Cow. It was such a gorgeous day and the atmosphere was buzzing. There were people from all over the world.

It helped lift my spirits. It was fun because at the end of the day I was there with my mates and we were drinking in the sunshine. From there we went into the park and there was a Pimms bar just outside the stadium. That was where we started bumping into people from the hockey world. That was interesting. About half the people I met found it so awkward to even make eye contact with me, let alone acknowledge me. Then there were those who would blatantly blank me. That, for me, was terrible.

I wanted to collar them: 'I haven't been selected, I haven't got a disease, I haven't done anything wrong.'

Even some of the parents whom we'd known and had gone on tour with before obviously found it excruciating. You'd think they would have a sense of how it felt.

I met up with Tina Cullen, who had by now become a good friend and was still coaching at Hightown. Even though she was one of GB's best ever scorers she knew what it was like to not be selected. She had a few comforting words.

By the time I got into the stadium, I was pretty tipsy! We were sat behind the goal. The arena was packed and the crowd was rowdy. Every mention of Team GB got a huge cheer. It was like everyone was infected with a collective euphoria.

Weirdly, my mind wandered back to the time when I wasn't allowed to play for the boys' football team as a child, and instead had to watch from the sidelines. It felt exactly the same. I was watching my friends play, but I wasn't allowed to join in. Ironically, I think I accepted it in a more mature way when I was just a kid.

The girls got off to the perfect start, racing into a 4–0 lead before half an hour had even been played. I was thrilled for my flatmate Laura Bartlett. She hadn't made the starting eleven but was on after a few minutes. Not everything went GB's way, however. Kate Walsh was hit in the face with a stick and went off injured. There was no more scoring but the team was off the mark, which was the important thing.

Their next match was in a couple of days' time but for the remainder of the games I went on my own. I couldn't bare the idea of having friends or family come to watch that weren't teammates, in a sort of 'This is what you could have won' sense. Although the whole atmosphere around the games was amazing, that made it even harder to accept. To think you might have been involved in that. I wasn't just physically alone, I felt mentally alone, as though I had no one independent that I could open up to and not feel embarrassed or laughed at for feeling so down.

South Korea were next up. Kate had undergone surgery on a fractured jaw but had astounded everyone by returning to the village and hadn't ruled out appearing again later in the tournament. Again, the girls got off to a flyer, going 3–1 up, but the Koreans came storming back to level it. Two quick goals swung it back in Team GB's favour. A further victory over Belgium gave them a great chance of making the semi-finals. Kate was back in action for the penultimate pool match against China. Unfortunately, she couldn't inspire the team to victory, and the narrow loss to China, and in the final group game at the hands of the Dutch, meant they finished second in their pool so faced the tougher of the two semis against Argentina.

Many of my memories from London 2012 are blurry because there was such an amazing buzz around the Olympic Park, and although I often turned up on my own, I'd meet up with people I knew and sank a few drinks.

For one of the games I did have a companion with me – and he caused a bit of a stir! He was a mate and manager of LeBron James, one of the most famous and successful American basketball players of all time. He was over because LeBron was in the US men's basketball team. Rather randomly, I'd become friends with him after meeting on a night out in Liverpool the year before. LeBron had become a minority shareholder in Liverpool FC and visited Anfield for the first time in 2011. My friend and I got chatting to his mate and he seemed interested that I was a hockey player. We exchanged various messages and I even went to visit him in Barcelona, where he took us to where LeBron and the rest of their NBA party were. We had a bit of dinner with them all. It was nuts. After that we'd kept in touch and when he came to London he texted me, like, 'Yo, take me to a hockey game.'

I took him to a match and as we were walking up the stairs some people were like, 'Have you seen the 6-foot-something black American guy Sam is with?' He used to be a basketball player, too, in college, so was dead tall. It was funny seeing people's reactions, because I had never brought a guy to hockey before, let alone one who stood out so much and was completely different to my exes like Gareth, whom I had described to them previously.

My mum proud as punch with her 3-month-old baby twins. I'm the one on the left!

Mum and Dad enjoying a night out in 1989. Mum's always loved her fashion!

Giving Shaun a birthday kiss on our third birthday.

I've always struggled to control my hair - even for one of our first school pictures.

My Birkenhead High School's uniform. Note the house captain badge; I guess I've always been a natural leader.

Steven Gerrard was always one of my favourite Liverpool players. I would have never have thought fifteen years later I'd be shaking his hand and having a casual conversation with him!

Just a typical family BBQ five-a-side. I like to think I scored the winning goal here!

At my very first Merseyside Youth Games in 1999, aged ten. Could have done with a smaller t-shirt! (I'm on the left.)

Another year's experience, a bigger smile and another gold medal! (Back row, 4th from left.)

Buzzing with my first-ever gold medal. (Merseyside Youth Games 1999.)

Warming up on the sideline ready to represent my school hockey team.

Year 6 Leavers' Disco. First time I ever wore a dress; you can't see but I've trainers on! (Back row, 6th from left.)

Another oversized playing shirt. This time in the colours of Tranmere Girls U15 team. I've clearly had a growth spurt! (Back row, third from left.)

My mentor, coach and good friend Peter Cartmel. He came to support me when I was playing for England under 16s in the summer of 2004.

Playing for Bowdon Hightown in the 2007/08 season vs Leicester. PA Images

Playing for GB on home turf against Argentina, a few weeks before Beijing Olympic selection. PA Images

Playing in Reading colours in 2010 vs Canterbury. Still loving the bun and headband combo.
PA Images

An Australian sandwich during the final of the 2014 Glasgow Commonwealth Games!
PA Images

Playing with confidence for GB during the Champions Trophy as I knew I was already selected for the 2016 Rio Olympics.
PA Images

Celebrating with family after winning European Gold.
Nick Robinson

Shouting words of joy up to my parents and Tom in the stands. PA Images

The fastest I've ever run in my life! We did it; Hollie had put the ball in the back of the net!
Getty

My dream becoming a reality: the best moment of the Games – singing the anthem with a gold medal around my neck! Getty

Unsy and I grabbing our one and only 'celeb' selfie with Novak Djokovic just before walking into breakfast.

The Legend, the boss, the world's best coach: Danny Kerry.

Jet-lagged and bloodshot eyes after finally getting to see that my nana was recovering well in hospital after her stroke.

At the surprise party when I landed back home from Rio after the best flight of my life.
Victoria Tetley - *Liverpool Echo*

Jess, Mel, Katie and me, ready to hit the town after I got back from *I'm a Celeb*. We never miss our annual reunion where we reminisce about our student days.

Being surprised by Tom, Max and Ollie wearing matching Christmas jumpers as they arrived at Heathrow to welcome me home after a trip away.

The strong females of my family. Back: *(left to right)* me, mum, Yasmin. Front: *(left to right)* Nana, Auntie Ann, Maxine.

My brothers taking me for a good feed after returning from the jungle! Mike, left, Shaun, right, and my nephew Milo, who was born on the same day as I won my Olympic gold medal.

I could have never have dreamt I would be part of such a fun group winning a National Television Award for *I'm a Celeb.*
Rex/Shutterstock

Cheering with relief that I'm out of the jungle!

Beaming with pride as I was awarded my MBE by Prince Charles at Buckingham Palace.
PA Images

صلة الرياضية
SELA SPORT

SPORT
INDUSTRY
AWARDS
2018

DOW JONES
SPORTS
INTELLIGENCE

SPORT
INDUSTRY
AWARDS
2018

SPORT
INDUSTRY
AWARDS
2018

EY
Building a better
working world

BT

SPORT
INDUSTRY
AWARDS
2018

Coutts

SPORT
INDUSTRY
AWARDS
2018

صلة الرياضية
SELA SPORT

Attending the BT Sport
Industry Awards, now as a
full-time sports presenter.
PA Images

The semi-final was another evening match. There was such a feeling of anticipation. Elsewhere in the Games, the Olympic fever and goodwill had propelled other athletes to exceed expectations so the hope was that the women could do the same. GB's men's team had also reached the semi-final, so both sides had a great chance of a medal.

I was a mess of mixed emotions for that game. A gold or silver medal could do wonders for our game. They were also my mates so obviously I wanted them to do well.

On the other hand – and this sounds awful to admit – a part of me didn't want them to get a medal because I wasn't part of it. Not being part of the team was one thing but not being part of the most successful women's team would be another. That seems so terrible and not a lot of people would admit to that, but I was clearly still very bitter.

The crowd was willing the team to do well but playing Argentina was always going to be tough, even with a passionate home support behind you. The girls fell behind quite early on but Argentina's second – and the goal that would prove to be decisive – came in controversial circumstances. The girls were appealing for a foul when Carla Rebecchi played on and scored – and the officials waved away all British attempts to refer the decision. It was a sore one to concede and I knew then it was unlikely they'd make it through to the gold medal match. Full credit to them, they battled to get back into the game and an Alex Danson goal gave them hope, but it wasn't to be.

I remember feeling a little bit of relief that they weren't going to be getting a gold medal but the final whistle went and all the girls fell to the floor on the pitch – and that's when it hit me.

I started to cry because I knew exactly how it felt when you fall short. I knew how much they had put into trying to win gold, and even though I was watching from the stand I felt how much they were hurting.

How had I let the bitterness of not being selected make me so selfish that part of me didn't want to see my friends succeed?

What had I become?

I was genuinely breaking my heart for them. It was terrible to see them that way.

The men also lost their semi-final to the Netherlands so bronze would be the best either team could hope for. Achieving that would still be incredible.

The girls had a couple of days to pick themselves up from the disappointment of losing the semi-final, but Kate's fighting spirit seemed to epitomise their determination not to leave the Games empty-handed. She was inspirational, first setting up Alex Danson to score from a penalty corner and then heroically blocking a shot from penalty corner when it looked like New Zealand were certain to equalise. Two further goals from Crista Cullen and Sarah Thomas meant New Zealand's goal back was only a consolation strike.

Bronze might not have been the colour the girls were hoping for when the tournament started but it was the least they deserved for the way they'd played. It equalled Team GB women's best performance at an Olympics, following the bronze won in 1992 in Barcelona.

I was genuinely so happy for them. It was the weirdest feeling, however, watching them celebrate. The Duchess of Cambridge, who had become one of their most vocal fans, was there to congratulate them.

It was the girls' moment – and deservedly so.

Those of us who hadn't been selected were just ordinary fans like the other members of the public. No one knew, nor cared, whether I was part of the wider team.

They took their lap of honour in front of packed stands cheering their appreciation and I doubt they could even see me in the crowd. I wanted to go down and hug them because they were my mates but I couldn't because I didn't have a pass. I couldn't just go down to the side of the pitch. I was just a spectator.

As I watched the celebrations, one thought was in my head: Did I have the fight left in me to compete for my place in Rio?

Chapter 12

Rediscovering Me

So put it in all of the papers,
I'm not afraid
They can read all about it ... read all about it ...

That song by Emile Sandé was the song of the 2012 games ... For a nation it seemed to encapsulate the Olympic experience. Everyone loves it. Me? I can't stand it. To this day, I can't listen to it.

As London 2012 drew to a close, I had four weeks off. Anyone not selected for the Olympics was off the programme. I'd have to return to Bisham in September and prove myself all over again. Until then, I had four weeks off.

During one of our final training sessions with Suzie Townsend, Maddie Hinch and another girl, Dilly Newton, were telling me that they were booked to go to Thailand – just to get away from the post-Olympic hype.

'That sounds like such a good idea,' I said.

'Do you want to come?'

I had no plans.

'Yeah. Sod it.'

So that night I booked a return flight. We'd be flying out the day after the closing ceremony. The night before I left it was on the television. I was half watching it with my dad but I was on my phone at the same time and that song came on. And they played a montage of the highlights and there was slow motion of the girls.

That was enough.

The next morning I went down to Heathrow, met the girls there and flew off.

I had such a belter of a time. I'd forgotten what it was like to feel really happy, have fun and be carefree. Being stressed led to me playing badly, which in turn got me down. I used to wake up not wanting to go to hockey training and then I had the period of not getting selected. It was just a never-ending downward spiral.

Lying in the sunshine, without needing to be up for training in the morning, I thought, 'I never want to be in that position again. I will never let myself get so unhappy.'

I was going to stop letting other people's actions affect me so much. In the long term had to rediscover my faith in myself and my abilities, and in the short term I just had to stop being so miserable.

When I landed back in the UK I wanted a permanent reminder of that mindset. So I thought, 'I'm going to get a tattoo.' I went to a tattooist in Marlow. I wanted something in Thai script because Thailand is where I had done my reflecting. While I was on holiday I'd met a Thai girl at a bar one night and it turned out she was only back in Thailand visiting her family because she was actually married to a Scouser and now lived in Liverpool. It was a strange coincidence. She added me on Facebook so when I got home I contacted her to ask if she'd check over the script I had in mind. I wanted it to say 'Live your life, be yourself'. I was concerned that if I just trusted the Internet it might have said 'hamburger' or something. Thankfully she said it did say what I wanted. I got it on my side underneath my arm so it can't be seen if I have a bra or bikini on. I've never been one to flaunt it. It's something private, just for me. It's to remind me never to let myself get to that place again.

When it was time to return to Bisham I had decided I was going to take on another cycle. At the time, I am not really sure what my reasoning was. Perhaps, aside from the excruciating heartache and the daily reminder of my years of failure, it was the easiest option. I didn't have to worry about a full-time job, or about entering 'the real world'. I was only twenty-four, I had another Olympic cycle in me and I was probably yet to reach my peak. I also had a huge chip on my shoulder and if I channelled that determination correctly, remembered not to get carried away or let factors outside of my control affect me, I could still one day be an Olympian. I was thinking more clearly and I felt I had my spark back.

I suspected some of the senior players would be retiring after London, or told they wouldn't be part of the future plans, so there would be more opportunities. Kate certainly wasn't retiring but Anne Panter, after that remarkable recovery from her car crash, was stepping down. There was still a solid core of back players. Unlike after the Beijing Olympics, I realised that I wasn't going to be handed a place on a plate. I was going to have to work even harder than ever before, but I was prepared to.

Everyone who wasn't selected for 2012 had to go into the initial selection phase. I had to go and prove that I was better than the new people who were putting their name into the selection hat, including club players, people who had never represented Great Britain before, the girls from the under-21 squad coming up. I had to show I was better than all of them because they were the new breed and they would be as hungry as I was four years earlier; but they couldn't be as hungry as I was now.

I had to go through three rounds of trials before I came up against people who were eventually going to be on the programme. I wasn't in the greatest shape of my life; those days wallowing in bed and at the London 2012 concession stands had taken their toll.

In November 2012, there wasn't the centralised programme so we were attending Bisham for weekend camps.

Having completed my degree, to earn some money I got a job in a gym in North Wales, as a sales manager. I was in charge of marketing, memberships, promotions and seasonal deals. It was the first time I'd held a senior post in a working environment and what an eye-opener it was to the differences between elite sport and the working world. I was used to working in a group of thirty highly functioning women who all wanted the same thing and who always gave 110 per cent. They were all smart and independent.

In the gym I found life difficult because people there just didn't have the same drive – and I couldn't understand it. I would ask people to do something but more often than not they wouldn't do it if they thought they could get away with it. If I left things for the weekend staff to do, they would never get done. I didn't make any commission from gym memberships but the other staff could. In an effort to drum up new members, I scripted a phone conversation that employees could use when ringing prospective customers. I ran through it with one lad.

'I'll pretend to be the customer and you pretend to call me and go through the script, okay?' I said.

He nodded.

'Okay, let's go.' I pretended to pick up a call. 'Hello?'

'Hello NAME,' he said, 'this is NAME.'

Oh my God. It was very frustrating. I had written 'NAME' thinking he would realise that was where he was supposed to say firstly the customer's name and then his name.

Flyer drops had proven quite a successful way to attract new clients to our prices and seasonal offers. However, one day I was tipped off that someone had just dumped them in a Tesco paper bank. I went down, opened the bank and saw them all in there. I couldn't believe someone would care so little they'd just dump them.

That was the general attitude. They couldn't be arsed. It made me realise how lucky I was to be in an environment where everyone was so self-motivated. When you're trying to become one of the best hockey players in the country – and hopefully the world – you have to be on it every single day.

I took my job seriously and expected that if I was working hard to make the business a success, everyone else should be, too. I could understand people on low wages being reluctant to take on extra work that was outside their pay grade. People should be rewarded for the work they do. But in the gym employees could earn commission but even when I laid customers on a plate for them, they wouldn't follow it up. If doing a good job didn't motivate them and the lure of more money couldn't, then what could I do?

In the six months I was there I had to commute to Reading to play my club hockey and travel to Bisham for the training camps.

The big change at the start of 2013 was that Danny Kerry had moved to become performance director and we had a new coach, Jason Lee, a former Olympic and World Cup veteran with England and Great Britain, who had worked with the men's team for nearly ten years.

Truth being told, I celebrated Danny being gone quite a lot. I felt he had strung me along for years and given me false hope at times. He didn't like me as a player, he didn't appreciate my style of play and, ultimately, he was the face that I could attribute my non-selection to. Seeing the back of him really did motivate me to kick on.

'Right,' I thought, 'this is a new opportunity. The slate's clean. Jason knows nothing about me, nothing about how I play.'

At the turn of the year into 2013 I'd already been welcomed back into the fold when Karen Brown took an England side to Cape Town, South Africa, for an Investec Challenge tournament. England finished with a bronze and it was great to be involved again.

The new beginning I had hoped for soon came. Jason had a different style to Danny and a different mentality. His philosophy was, 'Let's work it out as we go along. You can learn and develop youselves.' For example, on corners, if a standard move wasn't on he'd expect us to adapt to the situation and do something different. There wasn't a structured plan, we were to be more fluid in our play, and learn from our experiences as opposed to being taught. A lot of the older players liked the very precise, black and white instruction favoured by the previous regime. Danny was very much, 'If the ball's here, there's a player there, this is what you do with the ball', whereas Jason was more, 'Figure it out'.

He liked flare players, problem solvers, and wanted people to think on their feet. I think he liked the way I played and I warmed to him quickly. He just let me play quite freely and encouraged me to go up and join the attacking side of the game.

It helped to be playing again and I didn't have the same fear of making a mistake as I'd had under Danny. Previously, when I'd been doing all the video analysis to pinpoint my weaknesses, I'd felt it had a detrimental effect. Different players prefer different systems. I also felt that the more expansive role I was being asked to perform from defence was showing my skill set off, having played in midfield for so many years prior.

Playing with greater freedom helped me get my confidence back. Not only was I getting selected but I was a regular in the starting line-up. I began to relax and enjoyed my hockey once more.

In June I was part of the England team that finished runners-up to Australia in the Hockey World League semi-finals in London. Our results ensured our qualification for the World Cup the following year.

Two months later, we entered the EuroHockey Nations Championship in Boom, Belgium in good spirits. We were in a pool with Germany, Spain and Scotland. We opened with a comfortable 3–0 win over Spain but slipped to a 2–1 defeat at the hands of Germany in our next match. When we faced Scotland we were tying 1–1 before I stepped up to hit the winner – my first senior international goal!

In the semis we faced the Dutch but held them to a 1–1 draw. In the subsequent shoot-out we won 3–2 to set up a final against Germany. To emphasise the significance of a victory over Holland, that was the first time Alex Danson had tasted victory over them in a competitive fixture in twelve years of tournaments, and this win was only after penalties.

The final against Germany was an astonishing game – for the neutrals certainly. In a match that swung from end to end, the Germans held a 4–3 lead at half-time. Susie Gilbert equalised to force it into penalties, but in time-honoured sporting fashion, an England team lost to Germany in a shoot-out.

We came away with a silver medal, which was a remarkable achievement, the first time we'd won better than a bronze at the Europeans since 1991. The fast-paced attacking game we'd adopted under Jason seemed to be working.

By the time we played in the Hockey World League Finals in December 2013, Kate and Helen were now both Richardson-Walsh, following their civil partnership in September. I was invited to their celebration and it was a great occasion. I was so happy for them both.

We ended the year with a bronze medal at the League Finals, beating the hosts Argentina on penalties.

After the disappointment of 2012, my England career felt back on track. I looked ahead to 2014 with renewed optimism. It promised to be another bumper year, with the World Cup and Commonwealth Games in Glasgow.

I was 100 per cent focused on hockey – my eyes on the prize. The last thing I wanted or needed was any kind of distraction.

So the last thing I expected was one to show up – in a garish-looking, bright yellow Lamborghini!

Chapter 13

Meeting My Match

If it was meant as a chat-up line it was a bit lame. I was waiting for my sister Maxine to come back with our drinks. We'd come into Alma de Cuba in Liverpool for a late night drink after dinner on a Saturday in February 2014.

A guy approached me and said, 'Do you mind taking a picture of me and my two mates?'

I got the impression immediately that he was quite confident, almost bordering on cocky. I wasn't really looking for attention. Saturday nights are always big nights in Liverpool but I was dressed pretty casually in black jeans and a leather jacket. While Maxine had gone to the bar, I stood and held our place on a raised step overlooking the dance floor.

The guy handed me his phone. I took a picture and noticed he had Snapchat open. I wrote on top of the image I'd just taken, 'The three ugliest guys in this bar,' and sent it to everyone in his contacts book. I must have been feeling mischievous and he seemed the type of guy who would benefit from being brought down a peg or two.

He didn't realise what I'd done until he saw his phone and started replying saying, 'Ha ha. Very true.'

I guess it was an icebreaker. We got chatting about that and then he started asking me all sorts, like what school I went to, and he was giving me a bit of grief about going to a private school. I gave as good as I got, saying, 'Well, you obviously weren't clever enough to get into a private school.' It was flirty, but it wasn't going to go anywhere.

He said I might know his sister because she also went to Birkenhead. I couldn't believe it. There he was, giving me grief over private schools and his sister went to my school! His name was Tom Mairs and as it turned out, I did know his sister, Rachel. The link was that Rachel used to date one of my brother Shaun's mates, whom I was really friendly with. It is a small world indeed.

He proceeded to ring Rachel in front of me to ask her what I was like. I thought, 'What an idiot. Why are you ringing your sister now, from the bar?'

His sister told him, 'Sam Quek? Yeah I know her, she's not your type – she's too sensible for you. I've never even seen her kiss a guy. She's known to be quite frigid.'

She was right. I was never one to be going around kissing Shaun's mates and stuff.

Anyway, we got chatting. He asked me what I did for a living. I said I was a hockey player. 'Oh, so you're unemployed,' he said. He didn't think it was a proper job and was trying to wind me up, probably because I was showing very little interest in him.

He asked me my surname. I said Quek and asked how he thought you spelt it. Strange question, I thought. I told him to guess and to this day he is the only person who's ever spelt Quek properly off the bat. I don't know why, but I was impressed.

So that was that. I left him, went back to my sister and cracked on with the night.

Later it transpired just why he had wanted to know how my name was spelt, as he added me on Twitter. However, it wasn't until April that he sent me a message through the social media site. We exchanged a few messages and he asked me on a date. I wasn't attracted to Tom at first. While he is a good-looking guy, he just wasn't my type. That said, he made me laugh in the messages we exchanged and we had the same 'take the Mick out of each other' sense of humor. So I thought, 'Why not see if he is as funny in person?'

He arranged to pick me up but beforehand he texted me to say, 'Make sure you wear flat shoes.'

Was he saying that because we were going to do something active or was it because he was really short? I couldn't remember how tall he was at all.

Me being me, and trying to be funny, I took a 'don't tell me what to wear' attitude, so I took flat shoes in my handbag but wore heels. It made the statement that 'I'm my own woman, I'll make my own decisions.'

I was at my parents' house and Tom rocked up. He texted me to say he was parked outside. I looked out of a window upstairs and there was a bright yellow Lamborghini with a black soft top and big silver wheels. I thought 'Oh my God.' I cringe at anything garish. I don't mind the classic look. I might not have minded a black one – something a little bit subtler. Inside there were black leather seats with yellow ticking.

I thought I would play this down. I got in the car and I didn't say anything. I said, 'How are you?' and we exchanged small talk before he fired the engine up. It was loud. It was at that point I said, 'Do you realise how much of a dick you look in this car?' – I wish I had a picture of his face.

I think I left him a little bit speechless. I said a Lamborghini is a gorgeous car but you don't need it in yellow for people to look at it. I gave him a bit of grief all the way over to Liverpool. As you can imagine, the car turned heads.

The date he had planned was mini golf in a place called Jungle Rumble. Tom was decent, but I won by one shot. I think he quite enjoyed my competitiveness. I remember having a Kopparberg cider to soothe the nerves, which I thought he had bought me. I remember saying 'thank you' and him saying he got it free with the golf deal. It was like that throughout the date – each of us determined to show no interest or attraction to the other. For me it was genuine; I didn't want him thinking I fancied him. But for him I think it was his way of flirting. It was a double-edged sword, I thought, and he knew what he was doing. By paying me no compliments and making out he wasn't at all interested, he was making me laugh a lot. He was doing stuff like opening a door, slipping himself through it and letting it shut right in front of me, then turning around and pretending it was a complete accident, and opening it for me. Cheeky bastard – it wasn't going to work on me.

We went on to Sapporo Teppanyaki for a bite to eat and chatted all night. He was asking all sorts of questions. In fact, it felt like an interview at times because he talked so fast, but we hit it off. We got on. When he gave me a bit of agro, I gave it back.

At the end of the meal we were walking back to the car and he said, 'Let me know when you are next free and we will see each other again if you like.'

'I don't know,' I said. 'It was okay, but it felt like an interview at times. And if we ever go on another date,' I added, 'don't pick me up in that car again.'

He went to get in the car. I think he expected me to follow him. 'What are you doing?' he said.

'I think I'm going to meet my brother and stay out for a few drinks,' I said.

The look on his face! I was trying to wind him up, but I think he thought his joking that he didn't like me had gone too far and I now didn't want to see him at all.

That wasn't the case, and we stayed in contact. It was very platonic, polite and fun. I was down in Bisham Abbey full-time, back on the programme, but whenever I was home I'd drop him a text saying, 'Hi, just wondering how you are.' Whenever we met up, we would always fall about laughing. It was a great release from hockey, but we never went past a polite peck on the cheek when we parted ways.

I had been living with Maddie Hinch, Laura Unsworth and Susie Townsend in High Wycombe. Just before the World Cup in June, Maddie bought a house in Maidenhead, which we moved to. Over time, Susie's South African girlfriend Dirkie Chamberlain moved in. Eventually, those two moved out to their own place and Lily Owsley took the spare bedroom. It was a convenient setup and fun to be sharing with teammates.

As I neared the end of the club season that year I felt I had outgrown Reading. A few of the players had moved on and the coaches had changed. I had played indoor hockey and wasn't enjoying it. I wanted a new challenge and to go to a club where I'd be one of the most experienced players.

Maddie and Unsy were at Holcombe, a Kent club that had been newly promoted to the top league. Moving there would certainly be a new challenge. They might not have been established in the top flight but they had ambitions to do bigger and better things. A significant incentive was that they had cash to pay players, and when I spoke to their coach Kevin Johnson about paying Maddie and Unsy the year before, they offered to pay me, too.

At first it caused a bit of an uproar with other players and clubs that we were getting paid. The system was changing and if you wanted the best you had to pay. That's why the club scene in Holland is so massive because they pay to attract the best players; they even give them accommodation and cars.

Moving to Holcombe meant a lot of travelling. From Bisham, sitting on the M25 was the last thing you wanted to do, but in terms of the money I got from there it helped me so much, so it was well worth the journey.

Anyway, all of this was going on when Tom came on the scene. It was all still very early days. I liked Tom's company but we hadn't even kissed yet. But by the time the World Cup was looming on the horizon we had been on quite a few dates and were now texting on a daily basis.

My concentration needed to be on England, though, because after a promising year with Jason Lee as coach, the wheels were threatening to come off in spectacular fashion.

Chapter 14

My Hunger Games

'Sam, you're the most determined, most aggressive in tackle. You give 100 per cent. I can always rely on you ...'

'Without a doubt my favourite person to play with in the defensive line, you bring energy to the game and I can see the trust you have in me when you pass me the ball.'

'Defensive last-ditch tackles are class as well as your attacking game which lights up the match. You are world class and you make the difference. Have the tournament of your life.'

Imagine some of the best things you dare to think about yourself – your strengths, what you bring to the team – and then imagine them being said by the people whose opinions you value the most ... your teammates.

What a boost it gives you.

I'd seen it done at club level and we adopted it in the international setup before a major tournament. It's a simple but clever and effective way of improving morale.

You start off with a sheet of A3 paper. You put the name of the player at the top of each sheet. Everyone called me Beyoncé, because I was a massive fan of hers. Everyone else had their usual names, like Ashleigh and Kirsty. You start at the very bottom and write down something about the qualities of that player. Then you fold it up, so no one can see it. And it's passed on. Someone else writes a bit, folds it over, passes it on. So when you're writing on it, you can't see what other people have done. And it's an unwritten rule that you don't read what people put before you, because it's quite personal.

I still have mine ahead of the World Cup.

It's all kept anonymous so you don't know who's saying what, but you can sometimes tell from the handwriting or by some of their expressions. For example, one of my mates always says 'Babes'.

From the first one to the last it makes for nice reading:

'Sam, I feel confident when you're on the pitch because I know that you will value the ball and work extremely hard in both your attacking and defending. You have great skills on the ball and when distributing you're always 100 per cent committed to yourself and you'll be awesome.'

'I love playing alongside you; I always know that you will be there for me to pass to. You're a solid defender and I know you will always give it everything. I think you're going to have a great tournament and going to be someone I will look forward to playing with. Let's smash it.'

'Sammy, on top of being a wonderful person to have in this team, you are fucking world class. The fight, the determination and 100 per cent commitment you bring to this team is invaluable. You're so strong on the ball and in tackles. We all know you will always put your body on the line for us, keep doing what you do pal and you'll have an awesome game.'

Everyone more or less had the same theme. It's heartening to know your teammates think of you as determined, courageous, aggressive, and always willing to put your body on the line. Granted, it would be nice if one or two said skilful or creative once in a while but, hey, you can't have everything!

It's nice to try to work out who said what, like, for example, 'Is that what Kate thinks of me?' One said, 'Top class bird. You're calm in possession and a great influence off the pitch.'

I came away feeling on top of the world.

And of course I wrote similar for everyone else on the team.

Ahead of the World Cup in The Hague in May 2014 we needed anything to help bring us together as a team. There was a lot going on behind the scenes, a lot of frustration from some quarters.

Cracks had started to appear in the test matches we had against Germany a few weeks before the tournament started. There were some frank words said on that trip and we needed to clear the air before the World Cup. Unfortunately, it wasn't enough. Cliques had started to form where there had been none before. Some of the more senior players were unhappy with the selections.

In the build-up to the World Cup there had been far greater media attention than normal. After London 2012, we'd built up a bit of momentum. Sky Sports were covering all the games. Their coverage was almost like what you'd expect with football, with a studio and guests. All the talk was about how we were going into the tournament ranked third in the world. We were expected to podium.

Everyone was asking, 'Can you go one better than bronze?'

I don't know whether we started to believe our own hype or got distracted by the increased attention.

I had one distraction to contend with. A boy I had dated for around five months and had broken up with a few weeks before I met Tom came to The Hague to visit me, literally sat down and asked if we could get back together. He was quite emotional. I explained I had moved on and I hoped he could, too.

There was still nothing romantically going on with Tom – and I wasn't even sure where he was in his life and his career. Besides, I was still very selfish about what I wanted to achieve with the upcoming tournaments and I wasn't really ready for a full-blown relationship.

That said, I was seeing now Tom more frequently. Before the tournament, we'd meet up if I was back home. I remember that just before the tournament got under way, he texted me asking how I rated our chances against opponents USA.

'We should beat them,' I said cockily.

But one of our assistant coaches, Craig Parnham, had gone over to be coach of the Americans after 2012, and our strength and conditioning expert Dave Hamilton had also made the switch, so they knew us inside out. They caught us cold with two penalty corners and although Kate Richardson-Walsh pulled us one back and we pulled Maddie Hinch off late on to give us an extra outfield player, we never looked like pulling it back. We seemed nervous and unsure of ourselves, and not on the front foot, as we like to be.

It should have been a wake-up call for our next match against China. Again, I said to Tom, 'We should beat them; they're eighth in the world.'

We lost 3–0. Two games in and our World Cup hopes were hanging by a thread. We had to beat South Africa, Argentina and Germany to stand a chance of qualifying. After the match Jason Lee said our situation was 'as bad as I've known things to be'.

If that was as bad as he'd known it, things were about to get even worse. South Africa thrashed us 4–1. They were something like eleventh in the world.

We started better against Argentina, taking the lead, but they came back to win 2–1. We eventually rallied against Germany, winning 3–1, but it was far too little, too late. We suffered the ignominy of finishing bottom of our group. That meant an eleventh-twelfth play-off against Belgium to see who could avoid finishing last out of the whole tournament. We didn't even win that. We had to go to a shoot-out. It was so embarrassing. It was England's worst World Cup finish ever.

We were shite, frankly.

After an abject performance like that there was a major review. A few people in the squad grumbled about Jason Lee's squad selection. For example, Helen Richardson-Walsh hadn't been selected after undergoing back surgery. It could have been argued that she wasn't yet back to her best, which was why she was left out, but she had been such a big player for us over the years that her absence became one of the issues.

It was hard to put your finger on what had gone wrong. Maybe, by giving us more freedom to play, we didn't have the same bite. It was perhaps easier for some people to coast through games. We seemed to have lost that edge, which when you think we were playing for England, wasn't acceptable. Sadly, splits were appearing in the team, people had issues with other people, they weren't getting spoken about and there was just deep underlying tension.

Senior staff held internal interviews with players to talk about our experience of the World Cup and why it was that we didn't perform as well as we should have. They wanted to know whether player selections had been justified.

I always maintained I had no issues with the selections. I was always for Jason because he was very much my kind of coach.

But that different mentality he had just didn't go down well with players who had been used to a rigid system for years. When things went wrong it was possibly the easy option to look at Jason and think the issues stemmed from his introduction.

Under Jason my confidence was restored. I became a natural leader in team meetings. I'd stand up and be counted, give my point of view, put forward my ideas and, if I didn't agree with something, wasn't afraid to say so. There were times when it felt I was the only one in the room with a certain viewpoint but then other people would come round to my way of thinking: 'Oh, actually, Sam's got a point.'

I'd never really done that before because I hadn't had the confidence as there were so many people ahead of me in the pecking order.

For me it had all been going well, up until that horrendous World Cup.

It was inevitable that Jason wouldn't last in the position. It was sad because he was a good coach. He had coached England's men to a first European Championships title in 2009 and also led Team GB at three consecutive

Olympics. He just didn't fit with some of the stronger characters in the group.

When the announcement came from England Hockey that Jason was stepping down – they said it was by mutual agreement – I was disappointed. Then I saw who was going to replace him. You have to be fucking kidding me. Danny Kerry was going to take temporary charge of the team and I couldn't believe it.

After my history with him as coach it was the worst news I could have received. He was going to continue as performance director and hold the two jobs until they worked out a permanent replacement.

I was mortified. It brought back memories of those times when I'd questioned why I was playing hockey; when I'd felt like he never really wanted to select me; when he was just dragging me along and granting me one pity selection; playing me for three games out of seven.

'Here we go again,' I thought.

As it turned out, my fears were misplaced. A week later they announced the squad for the Commonwealth Games, and I was in. Phew!

Our final warm-up was the Investec London Cup at Lee Valley, one of the legacy venues after 2012. We were up against Scotland, Wales and South Africa. We rediscovered some form and lifted the title, exacting a bit of revenge along the way on South Africa for the doing we'd suffered at the World Cup. In the final I scored what proved to be the winning goal from a penalty corner to secure the gold medal in front of a noisy home support.

I was super excited about the Commonwealth Games. Not only was it my first multi-sport tournament but it was just up the road in Glasgow, so for the first time all my family and friends would be able to come and watch. After the sort of mock events I'd experienced, I got to sample my first proper kitting out day, getting all the England gear for Glasgow.

Being able to stay in the athletes' village for the first time was a big deal. I know I'd had the opportunity to see what it was like in Beijing, but this was different because I was there on merit, not some meaningless legacy programme.

At the back of my mind I was still worried about Danny Kerry. Did he still harbour doubts about my ability?

When we arrived in Glasgow the team voted on who they wanted as captain and who they wanted in the leadership team – three other people behind the captain. We didn't have a single vice captain, but three players who people could obviously see as one of the leaders and who they felt comfortable to talk to. They also had to be confident enough to be able to say to the coach, 'No, we, as a group, disagree.' Kate was voted captain, by a mile, and Georgie Twig, Sophie Bray and I were voted as the leadership group. To be honest, I was surprised for the recognition from my teammates. They clearly could see how committed I was and I felt honoured. I thought it also sent a big signal to Danny that I had the respect of my peers.

We were in Pool B with hosts Scotland, along with Wales, Australia and Malaysia. We had fairly comfortable wins over Wales and Malaysia but the first real test would come against Australia. We slumped to a 3–0 defeat and although we beat Scotland in our final pool match, we finished second to set up a semi-final against New Zealand. In a tense match we took the lead through Lily Owsley but couldn't hold on, and a late Kiwi equaliser meant we were heading for penalties. We held our nerve to win 3–1. That set up a gold medal match against Australia, the defending champions.

I had been exchanging messages with Tom through the tournament, but somewhat out of the blue he texted me, saying, 'I know this will seem a little strange, but I am going to come up and watch your final. I know I am not your boyfriend, but I am hoping one day that will change and if we do have a future together, I don't want to regret not seeing you win your first proper senior medal.'

In honesty, I felt it was still a little soon for him to come to watch me, especially as I had never invited another guy to come to watch me play before. I didn't want the distraction of having to explain who he was, especially as my family were also going to be there for the finals.

I was very non-committal. We'd continued to be in daily contact but there was still nothing going on romantically. We were just enjoying each other's company. I have since found out his friends were taking the Mick out of him calling him a stalker, as he had been relaying to them how things were progressing.

Unbeknownst to me at this time, Tom got to Glasgow, checked into his hotel and went shopping for a gift. I had told him my favourite films were the *The Hunger Games* series and I liked the main character Katniss Everdeen, who was fiercely independent. He saw a bracelet that had wings like the Mockingjay motif from the film.

He got it and wanted to present it to me before the match. As he didn't have an accreditation to get through the road closures, he had to walk quite a distance in very heavy rain to get to the stadium.

I came off the bus with the whole team and management. In those hours and minutes before a big game you have to be 100 per cent focused. I had my game face on. He was standing there drenched and wearing a Glasgow

Council branded bin bag that he had somehow fashioned into a poncho. He was holding a bunch of flowers and a bag, which contained a card and a gift.

As soon as I saw him I thought, 'Oh my God, he's actually turned up. Danny is going to be fuming that this fella who I'm dating is here giving me presents.'

I was mortified and also a little angry that he hadn't appreciated this was a professional occasion. Perhaps he still hadn't realised that hockey was a proper sport.

I walked towards him. He said, 'Hi', with a smile, but I just took the things from him and walked in. I didn't say anything; I didn't want to draw attention to him or the situation.

He probably felt very embarrassed – but that was exactly how I was feeling.

I think I had mentioned to Laura Unsworth that Tom might turn up. Some of the girls saw him and must have thought, 'Who is this weirdo?'

I took his gifts into the changing room and opened them on the sly. My embarrassment and anger switched to a little warm fuzzy feeling inside, because he had been so thoughtful. There was a Thorntons block of chocolate saying 'Good luck' and he had also bought a good luck card. But what was really impressive was my little Katniss bracelet with the Mockingjay. I'd mentioned my love for *The Hunger Games* only once or twice, but he had remembered.

All of my family were there for the final. It was sometimes tough getting them all to come to games because we were often playing abroad and there were so many of them, so I was really happy they were there.

Lily Owsley's strike put us 1–0 up midway through the second half and we defended as if our lives depended on it in the face of mounting pressure from the Aussies. I believed we could hold on but with three minutes left I heard Danny shouting down from the stands to Karen Brown, the assistant coach, 'Karen, Karen, make the sub!'

He sounded quite panicky, because we were under the pump. They'd been peppering our goal for quite some time. To my dismay it was me they were taking off. 'Here we go again,' I thought, 'Danny ultimately doesn't trust me.' I had already questioned my selection and wondered if he had only taken me because we were competing as England and he couldn't take Scottish Emily Maguire.

There were only a few minutes left on the clock. Why wouldn't he just leave me on in defence? It was obviously his call to make but I was still so sensitive to the thinking behind every decision.

Then, with eleven seconds remaining and with practically the final play of the game, Jodie Kenny fired home from a penalty corner to send the game to a shoot-out where the Aussies held their nerve to seal a 3–1 win.

To say we were devastated doesn't come close. There were tears and a major sense of frustration because we were so close. We could almost touch the gold medal.

I looked into the stands and saw Tom. He mouthed, 'Stop crying! When you look at photos in the future, you won't feel like crying, you'll be proud!'

I remember talking to the girls, putting my arm around Alex Danson, saying stuff like, 'I can't be believe we did that. It was in our hands.' But then when I calmed down a bit and we had the medal ceremony I began to realise that actually what we achieved was brilliant considering what had happened at the World Cup.

After the formalities we were all lined up for a photo. My family were all there and I could see Tom behind them but they still hadn't been formally introduced. We were looking for someone to take a photo and my nephew Samuel, who had met Tom because he worked at one of the bars we went to, shouted across. Tom and I looked at each other with a look that said 'Oh no'. He hasn't met any of the others and the first thing he is called upon to do is to take a family picture. My mum was saying, 'Who's this? Who's he?'

I brushed it off, saying, 'It's just a friend.'

After all our duties were over we went back to the village to drop off our bags. We were heading out into the town and I organised taxis to take everybody because we were allowed to go out and let our hair down.

Tom's hotel was somewhere in the city centre. The original plan was that we would go out and meet my brothers, who were also out having a drink.

I said to Tom, 'I'll meet you at your hotel, or the club, or whatever.'

So back at the village we all got some food, got changed and got ready to go out. I was shouting to everyone, 'Who's coming out? I need to know numbers for a taxi.'

Strangely, this seemed to rub some of the girls up the wrong way. There seemed to be some underlying tension. Was it because of the manner of how we lost – in the dying seconds? I wasn't sure. Whatever it was I couldn't put my finger on it.

Eventually it seemed too much to try to organise everyone so I just jumped in a taxi with three of the others and dropped them off at the Bamboo nightclub, where we were all meeting. Then I met Tom at his hotel, which was just around the corner. I was still a bit upset by some of the team's hostility towards me, so I wasn't in the mood for going out. Tom said we could just stay in his hotel room, have a drink and watch a movie.

I turned the telly on and the Nicki Minaj song *Starships* came on, which I loved. All of a sudden I said, 'No, I'm going out.' So Tom and I headed round to the club. By then quite a few of the hockey players were there. Shaun and Mike, my brothers, were there, plus Shaun's girlfriend. My brothers had got their drinks and walked away from the bar towards the dance floor. Tom had got me my drink and as I walked away he grabbed my hand and pulled me towards him, and that was when we had our first kiss … in a sweaty Glasgow club called Bamboo.

It ended up being a really fun night.

In the wee small hours it was me, Lily and Unsy, four Scottish lads and Tom who were squeezing into one massive taxi and heading to the casino – the only place that was open. The Scottish lads weren't allowed in because they'd all apparently got kicked out the night before. The rest of us went in, drinking a bit more, playing some roulette, but just messing about.

Our Games passes got us to the front of the taxi queue so we jumped in a cab, dropped Tom off at his hotel and headed back to the village. As we were walking in, Unsy and I were still a bit drunk and said, 'Let's go straight for breakfast.'

So we walked into breakfast and the England men's hockey team were there getting breakfast. They all turned around, looking at us as if to say, 'Dirty stop-outs.'

They had a bronze medal match to play that day. We thought, 'Sod it; we need to get some food.' We knew we were all going as a squad to watch the men's medal match anyway. By the time we got into bed we could only sleep for about an hour, get up, shower, put some shades on and head out again.

The men won the bronze medal to cap a decent tournament for the England hockey squads. Team England topped the medal table overall, so on the whole it was a successful Games.

During the closing ceremony, I texted Tom to say, 'Kylie Minogue is singing and they've announced that the next Commonwealth Games are going to be in the Gold Coast of Australia. How unbelievable is that going to be?'

At that point I was thinking that would be an amazing experience, going to Australia for the next Games. In the aftermath of a good tournament I just wanted to taste more like it.

He texted me to say, 'You kissed me the other night. I don't know if you were drunk or not but if we can go on one more date and you kiss me again, great. If not, then we can just be friends. But after so long, I just need some clarity.'

He then said, 'When are you next free?'

I had no hockey commitments until training resumed so he had my undivided attention. I replied, 'Thursday, Friday, Saturday, take your pick.'

He said, 'I pick all three.'

In echoes of our first date he organised all the planning for our weekend together. And he didn't half raise his game – because this time it was a trip to Paris.

I had never seen planning like it. He had a folder with every ticket, booking reference and printout organised in event order. So there was the car parking reservation and then the boarding pass. The weather report was in there as well so he could plan whether we'd be doing an indoor or outdoor activity.

Even given the number of times I'd been away with hockey squads, I'd never quite seen a trip planned like it. I actually secretly liked it, because I was the complete opposite and a bit of a scatterbrain.

We eventually had our second kiss on a horse and carriage ride around Paris. It was the perfect trip. I realised I did have romantic feelings for him after all and I was pleased he had feelings for me, too.

Chapter 15

Fighting Back from Rock Bottom

Only when we returned to training did I discover the reason for the underlying tension back in the athletes' village after the Commonwealth Games gold medal match in Glasgow.

I could feel some people were talking behind my back. Others seemed to be avoiding me. Laura Unsworth – Unsy – seemed to be getting it, too. As we were living together we always used to get a lift together.

I'd seen cliques form in the group before but this was my first experience of being on the receiving end of some gossip in a team.

Finally I found out what was going on – and it explained why a few of the girls, including Maddie Hinch, Giselle Ansley and some others, were being a bit funny with me. Apparently, while we were waiting to get our medals someone heard me say to Unsy that it was Giselle's fault that we lost because it hit her foot in the circle, which gave away the corner to win the goal. It was petty hearsay nonsense. It was not true.

I was quite upset, especially given that they all knew how much of a team player I was and that would be completely out of character. I was also sad that no one had thought to come to me sooner to straighten things out.

Now it was out in the open, I said to them, 'I'm so disappointed. We talk about our culture, our team. Why is it that no one has come to me with this sooner to eradicate it? Why is it now getting built up where everyone is talking behind our backs? People are getting dead arsy; people don't even look at me anymore.'

We managed to clear the air, particularly with Giselle. I always liked Giselle, despite her being competition for a place on the back line. She was a good player, a lovely person, and I respected her a lot. Some of the other girls apologised to me. However, it was an unpleasant experience. There's often someone on the receiving end of some gossip. Maybe I hadn't just noticed it that much before because I wasn't the subject.

For the most part, we were able to draw a line under it. Although where one player was concerned, I was convinced relations with me were never quite the same again.

Our next tournament was the Champions Trophy in Mendoza, in November 2014. Kate Richardson-Walsh had decided to take a sabbatical. After the World Cup she had considered her future but after how well we'd played at the Commonwealth Games she decided to continue to the Rio Olympics in 2016. She felt she needed an extended break, however. Her partner Helen was still recovering from her back issue. In Kate's absence, Alex Danson took over the captaincy, as the next most senior player. Danny Kerry continued as coach, even though when he first returned it was only to be on a temporary basis.

Once the dust had settled from the Commonwealth Games, one thing that still rankled with me was my substitution at the end of the final against Australia with minutes to go.

It niggled away at me. All of my old insecurities returned: 'Am I going to be wasting my time now Danny's coach? Are we back to square one, where he doesn't want to select me?'

I couldn't risk potentially wasting the next two years of my life being a bit part figure and praying for someone else's misfortune to get my chance.

So this time I did something about it.

I went into his office. Even just doing that indicated how much more confident and grown-up I felt. I said to him, 'Danny, I really need this answering because I don't want to be wasting your time. I don't want to be wasting my time. And I don't want to be wasting space if you're not going to pick me.

'But I need to know, during the Commonwealth Games final, do you have a problem with me? Do you not trust me? Do you not rate me as a player? Because, when there's minutes to go and you pull me off the pitch, is that because you don't trust me?'

Danny sat there and listened until I'd got out what I wanted to say. Then he shook his head. 'Sam,' he said, 'I rate you as one of the best tacklers in the team, if not the world. I radioed down to Karen to get someone else off the pitch, to put you over to the left, and then Unsy on the right.'

I was stunned. 'What do you mean?'

'Clearly, Karen got the message wrong,' Danny went on, 'because I wanted to shore up that back four and make sure we were solid, just to make sure we had the game together.'

It put my mind at rest, but I was still wary that I had felt this way before after speaking to Danny and the aftermath of the last meeting with him hadn't turned out how I had hoped.

For the Champions Trophy we were facing Australia, Germany and Argentina, with New Zealand, Japan, Holland and China in the other pool. It was possibly fated that our first match would be against Australia. Our game plan was severely disrupted when Alex, now our captain, took a big hit in the first five minutes. I could tell from the way she fell it was a bad one. She went off and was out of the rest of the tournament with concussion.

I also took a heavy hit in that match, which left me reeling in agony in my side. I was still in a lot of pain after the match. My main concern was for Alex, though. With her out the team needed another captain. We put it out to vote.

To my astonishment, I was voted captain for the remainder of the tournament. I could scarcely believe it. I felt I was up to the task but hadn't realised my teammates thought as much. It was later told to me that I had won the vote by a significant margin, which gave me even more confidence that I had a clear mandate.

I was by no means the next most senior, but clearly the team had seen something in me that they liked. It was a big deal and one of the proudest moments of my life. I would have preferred it to come about in any other circumstance but what an incredible honour it is to captain your country at senior level. Plenty can say they have played, but not many can say they have captained the team.

I think the elation of being made captain had made me forget about the pain in my ribs. I went for a scan in the dodgiest hospital I had ever seen in my life and they concluded it was nothing serious, so I was cleared to play. I would lead out my team, albeit still suffering from a very strange, undiagnosed pain.

In truth, I was in agony. At times I couldn't catch my breath, but I was so wary that I didn't want to look soft, especially as nothing had been flagged up. In hockey tournaments, it is not uncommon to play four games in a week. At an Olympics you play eight games across thirteen days, therefore it was important for me not have anyone questioning my durability and I wanted to lead by example as captain, so I soldiered on.

We faced another tough test against Germany but our young side battled to a credible 1–1 draw. Again, there were some big hits in that game, with two Germans receiving yellow cards. Frustratingly, we weren't able to find the winner.

Against Argentina in our third match we started well, with Sophie Bray scoring on just seven minutes. Argentina equalised and we were matching them until the loss of Susie Townsend and a late flurry of goals turned the match in the Argentines' favour 4–1.

A quarter-final defeat to New Zealand sealed our fate and left us needing to beat Japan and then China to finish fifth.

I didn't play my best throughout the tournament due to the crippling pain, and it was only when we returned home that I discovered I'd actually broken two of my ribs in that opening match and it had gone undetected for whatever reason.

For the first time in my career I had a significant injury from which to recover. From the high of captaining my country, I now had to not only prove my fitness but also show I could recapture the form that was actually starting to win me praise from Danny.

Being injured really affected me. Returning to fitness proved more difficult than I anticipated. I came back in the following February, but I was not as strong or as fit as I had been. I was training for a good two months before the selection for the Rio qualifying tournament, yet I didn't even make it into the friendly matches before. I couldn't believe it. I was available but not selected. I wasn't even in the reserves, let alone the squad.

It brought all of the feelings of the 2012 rejection back again. I was scared, really scared, because everything was going so right and all of a sudden it had all gone wrong again. The Olympics were the following year and I began to question everything. I was becoming that person again – the one that overthought every move; the person my tattoo was supposed to remind me not to become. I was consumed by doubt and worry all over again.

How had I gone from captaining my country to not even being in the top seven defenders in the coach's eyes? I knew Danny didn't rate me. I always knew, and now my injury had served him up the perfect excuse to drop me again.

A few months back I was apparently one of the 'best tacklers in the world' but now, not even in the top seven in the team. It was all lies. My Olympic dreams were in tatters all over again and there was nothing I could do but sit back and watch it play out in front of me ... again.

I drove back up to the Wirral to spend the next fortnight with Tom. I didn't have to train, so I watched the World League tournament with him. As soon as I came in the door he could tell I was a different person. I was so negative, so sad, so angry and bitter.

One afternoon before the tournament had even started, I shed a tear and Tom asked me if I was okay. I bet he wished he hadn't, because it all came out. I spoke for hours and hours, about everything. I told him all about 2008 through to 2012, how I felt, and why I felt that way. I explained why it was so important for me to go to Rio and what it meant to me if I didn't. His reaction wasn't what I expected at all. He didn't pander to me, he didn't try to convince me I was being stupid feeling that way and that I should be proud of what I achieved. He said, 'My word, that's exactly how I would have felt had I been you. I cannot imagine how embarrassed and lonely you must have been. I can't imagine anyone could have made you feel better. That must have been terrible for you.'

He got it completely and I felt so relieved to have shared it with someone, especially someone whose first reaction was that I was being stupid and that I should be proud of what I had achieved so far. Our relationship was much stronger from that day forward.

We sat on his sofa and watched the tournament together – every minute of every game. The team played superbly. They won the entire tournament and went undefeated while playing some of the world's top teams, such as Spain, China and Argentina. The defence, in particular, looked rock solid. They hardly conceded a goal. With every game I watched I slipped deeper and deeper into my misery. It was almost worse than 2012 because I knew exactly what was in store for me; the crippling self-doubt would soon come.

Was I still the same player I was before?

If I wasn't, could I even get back to the level I was at?

If the answer to that was no, should I give up?

If the answer was yes, would the coach even care?

I sank lower and lower. It's one thing to go through the worst heartache in your life and persevere; it's a completely different thing to have come through it on the other side and then see the same thing coming for you all over again. It is so frightening and I was reaching breaking point.

I returned back to training at Bisham Abbey after the tournament and a few weeks passed. I was miserable again and my head was rammed with the same doubts, the same questions.

I Skyped Tom one evening and when we ended the conversation I decided to drive back home. I just didn't want to be in Marlow anymore.

When I arrived at his house, it must have been midnight but Tom sat me in the kitchen and dished out some firm words. Here I was, miserable, constantly on the edge of tears, and my boyfriend was bollocking me. I couldn't believe it. We had a major argument and were screaming at each other well into the early hours. He was sick of me being so defeatist and feeling so sorry for myself, while I was convinced he just didn't understand.

As I started to cry, I couldn't get my words out and I was forced to listen to him rather than shout back.

He told me how everything I was moaning about and everything that was worrying me was completely out of my control: Danny not liking how I played; the team captain being a defender and taking one of the spots away for the back line; Emily being Scottish and the pressures there may be to select her to have a GB squad than wasn't wholly English; Giselle being the team's penalty corner specialist and also a defender, so she was nailed on for a spot in Rio; how I felt Hollie Webb was the best defender, better than me and likely to be the other spot; how all that meant there was no place for me. He said that despite me playing in the reserve team and thinking I looked bad, that was just tough and I would have to get on with it and prove a point and stop wallowing.

He said I was reading into everything with a tainted view. When Danny criticised me, it was because he hated me, yet when he praised me he was only trying to keep me sweet. He also said that while he didn't know much about hockey, he had seen me play and thought my passing wasn't as good as some of the other girls, but that my tackling and work rate was far superior. He revealed that he agreed with Danny that I should play a simpler game with shorter passing and just concentrate on my strong points. He said I was needlessly rebelling against the coach's game plan as opposed to adapting to it.

I couldn't believe it. I trusted Tom at this point. He was completely out of order. He was a disgrace to be speaking to me that way. He was being a dickhead. And worse than all of this – he was completely right.

He finished by reminding me that I didn't become a shit player overnight and that I had to concentrate on the things I could control, and I needed to remember what had got me to and kept me at this level. If that still wasn't good enough, then so be it. But I should never let my mindset stop me from being the best player I could be, like it had in 2012. If I had really given my all and still fell short, at least I could live my life knowing I had done everything I possibly could have and it just wasn't to be.

More tears came from me. He gave it a minute and then I think he panicked. He started to hug me and apologise over and over. I told him that he was completely right. I knew he was completely right, because after 2012 this was the same conversation I had with myself on a beach in Thailand. I had forgotten who I was. I had forgotten the promises I made myself and he had reminded me of that.

That was the turning point. From that day forward I was so determined. Not determined to get to an Olympics, not obsessed by that idea, I was determined to be the best me I could be, so that on the day selection came, I could have absolutely no regrets.

The team were given two weeks off following their successful Rio qualification, so Tom and I booked a last-minute holiday to Croatia to give me the space and time to really sort out my head. The fight back was on, and whilst my family had always been in my corner whenever I needed them, in Tom I felt I had someone in the ring fighting with me. That said, while I was putting myself through a punishing fitness programme in the hotel gym, he spent his days drinking beer and lounging on the beach soaking up the rays. Tom is good at a variety of sports, but working out and fitness wasn't something he enjoyed.

By the time I got back to Bisham I was stronger, fitter and faster. I had more confidence in my ability because my strength was back, not just physically, but mentally.

Playing for my club and rediscovering my swagger in training, I slowly rediscovered some form; I was playing high-quality, carefree hockey again. When the squad for the European Championships in summer 2015 was announced my rehabilitation was complete. I was back in the frame and I felt I was playing the best hockey of my life.

The championship saw us return to the Riverbank Arena in the now named Queen Elizabeth Olympic Park, the scene of the girls' heartbreak in 2012 before securing the bronze medal.

We were in a tricky pool with Germany, Scotland and Italy but several of our most experienced players were back, like Kate and Helen Richardson-Walsh and Alex Danson. In our opener against Scotland we fell behind to an early goal from an excellent penalty corner routine, but rallied and a goal apiece from Kate and Helen secured the win. Helen was on the score sheet again, along with Nicola White in a 2–0 win over Italy. We then thrashed Germany 4–1, with Alex bagging a hat trick.

That saw us through to a semi-final against Spain, where goals from Alex and Lily Owsley were enough to see us edge it 2–1.

Waiting for us in the final were the Netherlands, who'd defeated Germany in their semi 1–0.

My parents and Tom came to watch the entire tournament, staying in the apartments above our team hotel. After every game, I would break curfew and visit Tom in his apartment. We would talk about the game and often have a late dinner together. Old Sam would never have dared break the rules, but I felt free and visiting him gave me a release from the hockey cauldron and cleared my head. I always made sure, though, that I went to bed in the room I was sharing with Kirsty.

Being with Tom was a constant reminder that there was a life outside of hockey and no matter what would happen the following summer, even without hockey I had a future.

Nobody gave us a chance against the Dutch but we were quietly confident that we could pull off a shock. It was a tight game but in the third period they nicked two rapid-fire penalty corner goals, leaving us with a mountain to climb. The Dutch continued to pile forward but we stood firm and tried to provide the platform for the forwards to create the opening that might give us a way back into the match.

With just eight minutes to go, Sophie Bray gave us a lifeline. The Lee Valley crowd could sense we were capable of pulling back and they willed us on. Incredibly, Lily Owsley netted two minutes later to level the match. Replays have since shown that she actually kicked the ball in and the goal should never have been allowed to stand.

Again, the Dutch came back at us, but we held out to force the penalty shuttles.

As if the shoot-out wasn't tense or dramatic enough, when Helen went up to take our first, the Dutch keeper Joyce Sombroek was ruled to have fouled her, resulting in a penalty stroke. Helen duly tucked it away. Further strikes from Sophie and Alex put us in command. The Dutch missed three of theirs and it ended 3–1. We'd done it!

I looked up at my parents, who were celebrating like mad. I then looked over to Tom, who was wearing England flag facepaint and a replica Quek England shirt he had asked me to get for him. He mouthed to me that I had been named BBC player of the match. After the year I'd had I couldn't believe it. I felt on top of the world. Given how low we'd felt after our World Cup disaster in 2014, it had been a remarkable turnaround. I hugged my parents and they were so happy for me and so proud. It was the highlight of my career up until then and I was so happy they were there to see it. I hugged Tom and he said he was proud of me and this was my reward for all I had been through. I could feel a tear of his that he had shed running down my back.

The result showed the level of belief within the team, that even at two goals down to the reigning Olympic champions, we all thought, 'We're not giving up on this.'

After finally triumphing over the Dutch we feared no one.

The team celebrated hard that night. We didn't even get changed out of our kits until the next morning. I was so happy. I hadn't drunk in so long and after the comedown of adrenalin I felt quite sick. In the middle of the night, mid sleep, I ran to the toilet to throw up. Clink … Clink … Clink … What the hell was that noise? I looked down and there my medal was swaying away tapping the toilet pan. I'd fallen asleep wearing it. As the bright bathroom lights beamed on down, it looked as shiny as ever. Despite feeling very rough, I couldn't help but smile.

With the Olympics just over a year away, we were hitting form at the right time.

Maybe, just maybe, we could start dreaming.

Chapter 16

'Quek, Sam'

Beryl Road, Wirral, 3 June 2016.

This was it – squad announcement day.

I decided to come home for it. In the last year I'd moved my things into Tom's house in Heswall, just fifteen minutes' drive from my parents' house.

All day I'd been quiet and quite snappy if spoken to. Initially, I'd wanted it just to be Tom and me, but my mum said it would be nice if we could come round to theirs so they could share in the moment.

I had been off the grid a little since my serious talk with Tom. We had created a little bubble of our own to ensure my mind was always in the right place and I was always focused and ready to compete. He took away a lot of life's little stresses. He helped me move into a flat of my own where I could have some time to myself and not be surrounded by my teammates both at work and home. Hockey was to be my only concern for twelve months. If I didn't have any outside influences nothing could distract me or take me off course. It had been working too. My family always meant well and they meant so much to me but any bad news or struggles they were having would take my full attention. It was a completely selfish mentality, but I knew it would only be for twelve months and I would pay them back as much as I could after this was all over.

Selection day was the same. I didn't want Mum to make a fuss. I didn't want her to get too stressed if it wasn't good news – or too excited if it was. But Mum was right. She and my dad had been on the whole journey with me; of course they should be there for this moment.

I was more confident than with any other selection that my name would be on the list, but there was still a significant element of doubt there.

Six months ago, our coach Danny had called in Crista Cullen, who had retired after London 2012. She was a very good player, whose drag flick goals ultimately helped the girls win the bronze medal because she was so effective from short corners. She could produce massive aerials – when you lift the ball long distances across the field over the heads of the opposing team or to get yourself out of trouble very quickly. Her recall caused a bit of unrest in the group, initially because people were thinking, 'We've all been training; how can she just rock up six months before?'

We needed a drag flicker and her aerial threat. Giselle could do it as well but Crista, with her record and power, was someone Danny invited back so that the team could deliver more consistently. Her inclusion indicated that she was going to be selected for Rio because otherwise, why would you bring her back?

When I weighed up the competition for the other defence positions, she was another name I could add to the list, so I couldn't take it for granted I'd be on that plane to Brazil.

There was the aforementioned Giselle, who also had that skill set; we had Kate, who was the captain, Hollie Webb, who was a fabulous player, and Emily Maguire, who had the experience of a bronze from London. We were pretty evenly matched but I still had that niggling feeling that Danny might go with Emily, the Scot, to satisfy any critics who claimed we were just the English team under a GB banner.

We were likely to take five defenders, maximum, so nothing was guaranteed. All I knew was that I couldn't have given more, so I wasn't as nervous as previously. I wanted it just as much, if not more than ever, but I knew I had given everything.

The email announcing the squad was due to drop at 6.00 pm. I remember arriving at my parents' house ten minutes before it was due because I didn't want to spend longer than I needed to talking about what I was thinking or feeling.

Even though I knew the email would land pretty much bang on six, I kept refreshing my messages just in case. It was a warm, sunny day and Mum and Dad opened their patio doors so we could sit outside. Tom was quiet. I'm sure he was thinking in his head, 'How will I pick her up from this if she is not selected?'

He had already arranged a Plan B. On his laptop he had flights and a hotel bookmarked and ready to purchase in the event of bad news. This would form part of a month-long trip to Italy that he had planned for while the Olympics were going on. It would mean I didn't have to see it unfold on the TV or read it in the newspapers all over again.

Then it arrived.

It got straight to the point: 'The following athletes have been selected for the Olympics in Rio de Janeiro …'

The squads are usually listed by first name, which means my name is normally down the bottom alphabetically, if it's there.

I glanced and had a mini panic. I couldn't see my name. Oh God! Please not again!

I scanned. And scanned again.

Finally. There it was – a bit higher than usual as it was listed on a surname basis. Our squad had two Richardson-Walshes, a Townsend, a Twigg, an Unsworth, a Webb and a White, so I was actually up near the middle. That's maybe how I missed it. Or maybe I just couldn't believe what I was seeing.

It was definitely there: Quek, Sam.

I looked up, expressionless. Tom and my parents were looking at me. Their faces all said, 'Well, come on. Have you been selected or not?'

'Yes!' I screamed out. 'YEEEEESSSS!!!' The neighbours must have wondered what the hell was going on. My face was red, my eyes were bulging and the veins were popping out the side of my head.

It was a scream that I had bottled up for so long, the intensity of which had grown over ten years due to my perseverance, physical exertion and mental torment. It was a scream that with every day that passed, the pressure was turned up another notch, but I could never release it until now. It was a scream to the skies to let everyone know I hadn't let them down. Every selfish action – every time there was an empty chair where I should have been sat, every text I had to send that started 'I would love to be there but …' – had all been for this moment. It was a moment that had never been promised to me, but I had hoped and dreamt for so long would come. It was relief – at last.

'Oh, Sam.' My mum was in bits. She was so happy.

I burst into tears.

Big hugs all round. My mum and dad were overjoyed. I was so proud for them. They had invested years of their lives in me solely for my happiness and right now I couldn't be happier. I think all the lows of 2012 made this high seem so much greater.

Tom was just relieved at first. This had been his life, too, day in, day out, for the last few years. Not one day had gone by when I didn't speak to him and there were plenty of days where I would start to doubt myself, or feel shitty and exhausted. He was always there to pick me up. He used to write me little motivational notes and hide them in my kitbag, or in my coat pocket or around my car. When I was away training and missing home, I would find them every so often and they would remind me what I was working for. He even stole my tactics book that I used to make my notes in and he skipped forward forty pages or so to write me a note saying, 'I know you are working so hard right now. We are all very proud of you, keep it up! P.S. Whatever game you are making notes for, you are going to win 2–0, Lily and Alex will score.' My favourite thing, though, was when I rang him in tears after a really hard training week, telling him my body was exhausted and I wanted to come home because I felt like I was running at 1 per cent. When I opened the door, he had bought ninety-nine of my favourite things, from my favourite crisps to my favourite movie and my favourite CD. He said if each one could perk me up 1 per cent then I could go back at 100 per cent. He really did love me and was putting his own life on hold too. It was therefore understandable that he was as nervous as I was before the email dropped.

My mum got out a banner she had had printed with photos of me throughout the years and 'Congratulations' written on it. It was lovely and a real reminder of the years gone by. I couldn't help but wonder if there was a banner somewhere in the loft gathering dust that read something like, 'Congratulations Sam, London 2012 awaits'.

Either way, who cared now? I'd made it. I was going to Rio to compete for Great Britain in an Olympic Games.

My first call was to my nana to tell her, then to my sister and my brothers.

One of the first people I would have called was Peter Cartmel. Sadly, he became ill in the years after London 2012. My mum had kept in touch with him and often met up for a coffee. On one occasion when they had met he revealed he'd found a lump on his collarbone. Mum urged him to get it looked at and tragically it was lung cancer. My mum used to take him for his appointments twice a week but the prognosis was that it was terminal. When he was admitted to hospital Mum would go round and take him food because he could only eat gluten-free. She was very close to him by the time he passed away. I spoke at his funeral, which was incredibly tough because I was so emotional. The church was packed with people he'd coached and members of the community he'd served. It was so moving to see the number of lives he'd touched. I spoke about how integral he was in terms of me growing as a player. Those little cards and notes he'd send he would also send to countless others, just constantly motivating and reassuring them. Those cards are something I'll always miss and remember.

When we knew he was passing away he left me a little gesture – a little card and a decent amount of money. It was so thoughtful and touching of him. He said, 'I want you to have something which will remind you of me when I pass.'

Sadly, his own family didn't have much to do with him in his latter years. Mum was one of those closest to him. He meant so much to us. He was very much a mentor to me and it was a very sad day when he died. So when I was finally selected for an Olympics I thought about him and how thrilled he would have been.

After I'd rung my family, I called some close friends. There was a strict embargo so everyone was sworn to secrecy. That night, my parents, Tom and I went out to Tai Pan in Liverpool and my dad was so proud but had to rein it in because we couldn't tell anyone. In fact, it was a weird feeling because you want to have this massive celebration but you have to go into business mode. Getting to Rio was only part of the story. We now had to go there and do the job.

It was amazing to think I would soon be an Olympian. For so long that had been my dream. Now it was a reality. With the squad we had and what we had achieved in 2015, I knew we had a chance to do something special.

It was so strange but in an instant my mind set a new target. Maybe it's an athlete thing. There was little more than a few hours of celebration before I had decided that I wasn't going to settle for just being an Olympian. It was no longer just the taking part, despite all I had ever worked for and wanted in my life was to be known as an Olympian. I wanted to go and become a medallist, an Olympic medallist, and after missing out on the bronze of 2012, I only wanted one colour … gold.

When I had time to properly look at the squad I have to say it was pretty much the one I expected. I knew, though, that for each of the sixteen names, there were players, who, like me four years earlier, would be gutted they'd missed out. My heart went out to them all.

The squad was announced a week before the Champions Trophy in the Olympic Park, London. The Rio squad would be the same one, understandably. Emily Maguire was listed as one of the reserves. She had been the defensive casualty.

It was a clever move by Danny to name the squad before the tournament. It actually wasn't a great event for us. We finished fifth. Our performances made a few people worried. Even Tom said to me, 'When you get to Rio, is it going to be an embarrassment?' Maybe the World Cup debacle was still in people's memories.

We might not have been great at the Champions Trophy but when you look back it was tactical genius from Danny, because we didn't give anything away with regard to our short corners or how we would press. It probably helped just to dampen down expectations but we knew in our own minds that we were ready.

When it finally sunk in that I was going to Rio, I couldn't believe the stress I'd been under worrying about it. It had become an obsession and especially where Danny Kerry was concerned. Once the voices of self-doubt in my head had finally been put to rest, I began to think clearly. I had got something so fundamentally wrong throughout my career and it still haunts me to this day.

Danny never hated me, he never lied to me and he never wanted anything but the best for the team. All those times in the lead-up to 2012 and from his reintroduction in 2014, I had made him the face of all my worries, just because he had the power to fix them. I could finally accept that in 2008 and 2012, I wasn't in the squad, not because I was too young, or because he didn't like me, or because he was playing politics, it was because he honestly believed that was best for the team. Who was I to question him? Danny is no doubt in my mind the most gifted tactical coach of hockey on the planet. His strategic knowledge and meticulous planning were extraordinary. This was a man who hadn't hindered my progress to an Olympic Games, but who had in fact kept me on course to achieve that dream. My frustration that he didn't respect me as a player was completely unfounded and stemmed from the fact that I refused to adapt my game to his preferred style of play. He had told me as much countless times, but I had chosen to process what he said completely differently. I had let my mind hear something that wasn't being said. He wasn't saying I wasn't the player for him and then not selecting me; he saw my talents, identified my weaknesses and adopted a system to make me a better player. That's what I had refused to see. Instead, my paranoia had created a world of make-believe where he had a personal vendetta against me. A world where if he sat on a different table to me at breakfast it was because he didn't like me, or if he put me in a hotel room away from his when we stayed away, it was so he didn't have to face me. Had it been the opposite, well, of course he was eating with me at breakfast, he was trying to keep me sweet, wasn't he, trying to make me feel I was going to be part of the team. And of course, my hotel room was close to his. He wanted to keep tabs on me because he didn't trust me. I was so negative, so stupid, so pathetic and so wrong. To think of all that emotional energy I had needlessly expended. I wanted to go to see him and apologise profusely, but it's kind of hard to apologise to someone when you have only ever hated them in the constraints of a make-believe world in your own head. Instead, I would repay him by being the player he always wanted me to be at the Olympics. I was determined to repay his faith in me, all the while still being chronically embarrassed that it had taken me so long to come to my senses.

To top it off, a week after the selection had been announced, I took part, along with Danny and some other members of the squad, in a programme for BT Sport that was looking ahead to Rio. If I ever thought about my place in the squad I'd always assume I was number sixteen out of sixteen – that there would be fifteen girls ahead of me when it came to putting names down. In this programme, Danny was asked to speak about three or four key members of the team. He chose to speak about Maddie, our goalie, Kate, our captain, Lily, the reigning world young player of the year, and me.

I couldn't believe what I was hearing. 'I am really pleased for Sam; she has worked so hard for this and the improvement in her game in the last few years has been remarkable. For me she is one of the best tacklers in the world, if not the best tackler. I am so, so pleased for her.' He was smiling as he said it and I knew he really meant it.

I was watching it with Tom and he said, 'We've spent two years of our lives shitting ourselves about this crap and you were one of the first names on his list!'

I still believe I would have been a better player had Danny said to me two years out, 'You're definitely in my plans for the next Olympics.' I wasn't a player who thrived under the competition for places; I was a player who thrived with my manager's backing. But I understand that it wouldn't have been fair to do this, not to the other girls and also not to me, especially if my form began to dip and ultimately he couldn't select me after all.

It could, of course, also be argued that having that fear of missing out forced me to work harder and he was right all along.

Whatever, it paid off.

I was going to play for Great Britain at the Olympics – the pinnacle for any hockey player.

Now all my energy needed to be focused on bringing home that gold medal.

Chapter 17

Village People

'Yo girls.'

We were about to board. Bound for Rio de Janeiro, trying to kid ourselves this was just any normal flight to a tournament.

We turned around. It was Usain Bolt. He was catching the same flight from Heathrow. It was all so casual. And that's when it truly hit home. We are going to the Olympics! We were the Great British women's hockey team: focused, determined, eyes on the prize.

Usain Bolt says hello and suddenly we're all like, 'Hi!'

I didn't reach for the camera. If it was Serena Williams, maybe, but some of the girls were taking pictures, savouring the moment. Usain was loving it. This was his domain. He'd been there and done it. It was very cool to see him breezing about so relaxed. As if it hadn't been surreal enough.

Up until that moment I'd been trying to contain the excitement. However, after the kitting out ceremony, it really hit home that I was on my way. Team GB had hired out a massive building, bigger than an aircraft hanger, at the NEC in Birmingham and invited companies from every sector you could possibly imagine to be there. From sofa manufacturers and yoghurt companies to utilities firms and electrical suppliers, they were all there, and most were giving away freebies. I think it was either because they had signed up to be an official Olympic partner or were hoping we would be seen using their things during either the Olympic coverage or on social media. The best freebie for me wasn't the designer headphones or any of the expensive stuff; it was a golden personalised spoon that Kellogg's gave us. It was really cool! Getting that and also receiving a special edition Olympic Blue Peter badge were my highlights. Amongst all the stuff they were handing out, you could have been forgiven for forgetting that we were primarily there to pick up our kit!

The kit was designed by Stella McCartney – my first set of designer-made clothes ever – and I loved the style and fit of it all. Putting it on gave me butterflies of excitement.

At the airport, we had our own dedicated terminal to check in. I felt like a VIP. Every time we used to go to a tournament, we'd always fly economy, but for the Olympics we saved a little bit of the budget to go premium economy. Trust me, those extra inches of legroom made such a difference. We had been told to wear a white GB T-shirt and I was petrified of spilling something on it. Whenever we flew we sat in alphabetical order, so I was usually next to Kate or Helen Richardson-Walsh, Lily Owsley or Shona McCallin. This flight was no exception, so I was next to Helen.

Although there was added excitement with this trip I tried to stick to my usual routine for Atlantic flights – just getting the headphones on, chilling and keeping myself to myself.

The only difference from this and our usual journeys to South America was that on this flight we had Usain Bolt kicking about and food prepared by gourmet chef Gordon Ramsay.

Normally we travelled underneath the radar but because everyone was so aware of the Olympics and it was coming up, the extra buzz of the recognition and the number of people wishing us good luck was incredible.

We'd been told how to prepare for the added interest. We worked a lot on developing the right mindset. Our position was, 'We're just training.' Nearly every eventuality we prepared for – whether the flight was delayed, the bus broke down, or something's happened at home. We all knew what our go-to state was. Hopefully it would stand us in good stead when the competition began.

As soon as we got on the plane, we put our body clock into Rio time. So if it was night-time in Rio, we would be putting our eye masks on. If it was daytime in Rio, we'd have the reading light on if the cabin lights were dimmed.

Although we were one of the first squads to go out to Rio we arrived to long queues for passport checks and accreditation. It took quite a while trying to get everyone through. South Americans are very laissez-faire when it comes to all that type of stuff. But for me, to have that accreditation finally around my neck and my Olympic pass, it was what I had longed for.

In the baggage reclaim we acted as a well-drilled unit, forming a line. The bags were instantly recognizable as Team GB and we passed them along, me-to-you, until we had them all. We then passed our bags to the army, who put them on a big lorry, and we jumped on the waiting bus with our backpacks.

We had been to South American countries before but we were warned about the poverty in Rio and the stark contrast between the haves and the have-nots. We arrived in the early hours of the morning and our ninety-minute trip through the city to the Olympic village took us past some of the infamous favela slum ghettos.

Then we caught sight of the big tourist attractions like the stadium and the Christ the Redeemer statue, which was all lit up. That was the first moment everyone stood up to take photos.

We arrived at the village at around 3.00 am. Tom had booked an apartment close by and I was excited to see it was pretty close to the village. Walking through to find our apartments it was deadly quiet. The only sounds were the 'oohs' and 'ahs' from the girls as they pointed things out. We got to our massive high-rise, which was obvious to spot because it was festooned with lots of GB flags.

We'd been given our key fobs, which were our access to all the village facilities. Arriving at our apartments, we knew roughly who we'd be rooming with. We were asked to name our preferences or stipulations. For instance, some people preferred not to sleep next to someone who would sleep talk or snore, or have a different bedtime routine to them. It was just another one of those things we thought of that might give us a strategic edge as opposed to leaving it to be randomly determined.

I like to stay up watching telly until about eleven because I can't sleep before midnight, but another one of my teammates could like silence and the room to be pitch-black and be in bed by ten.

I put Unsy as one of my preferences because I'd lived with her so I knew her routine. I also put Hollie and Shona, because I'd shared with them on a previous trip to Australia. When you're spending that much time with someone you need to be in the right company.

I actually ended up in a flat of seven. I was lucky enough to get the one single room with an en suite because I love a little bit of my own space. Within that apartment, Hollie shared a room with Shona, whilst Unsy shared with Georgie Twigg and Hannah Macleod roomed with Alex Danson. I used to share with Kirsty MacKay, our reserve goalie, as we were good friends and had been for a while. However, she was selected as a reserve and wouldn't be staying with us in the athletes' village. I think that's why I got the single room. Either that or no one listed me as a preference!

I started to get pretty excited again when I saw our Rio quilt and our Team GB posters, teddy bear, bathrobe – all essential items, of course!

As a team we'd made a pact that the first three days would be the excitement time to get all the non-hockey things out of our system. That first night we didn't get much sleep after the time it took people to get unpacked, get their bearings and have a chat. I unpacked my stuff and tried to make the room seem homely by putting up cards from my family and good luck messages from friends. In addition to the cards we'd brought from home, every player had another one, given to us when we arrived by Danny. He'd written individual cards to us all, which were so personal to each of us. Mine read:

> Dear Sam,
>
> Well here you are, ready for the Rio Olympic Games. I think many people forget you have been part of this squad since the Beijing cycle. Of all the squad I know you are a fighter and a winner and will do what it takes to get the job done. It is for these reasons Sam I have always loved working with you. Knowing you I am sure you will be enjoying the uniqueness of this experience, but come game time you will be focused. Keep your game simple and you will be brilliant. I wish you Sam, all the very best of luck in the world. You have earnt your right to be on this stage and your selection bought me great happiness. I have the strongest feeling you will be brilliant.
>
> Go well Sam,
>
> Yours, Danny.

It was perfect and it bought me to tears. It felt even more than the selection email like I had completed a journey with Danny. It confirmed everything I had realised far too late – that he had my back, he had always had my back. He understood how long and hard I had worked to be at an Olympic Games. He knew I was a fighter. He reminded me to keep my game simple, which confirmed my suspicions that he was trying to make me a better player as opposed to not appreciating other aspects of my game. I was so happy, but equally felt terrible that I had doubted him. All along I thought he was fighting against me, when instead he'd been fighting along with me.

Among my other personal items were my own pillow, a speaker and my room tidy as well, because I can't stand clutter.

Tom had been so sweet before I left. He had given me a digital photo frame and filled a memory stick with pictures of me, him and our Yorkshire terriers Max and Ollie, and our loveliest memories. I went down to Marlow before I flew out and forgot to pack the memory stick. I literally just had the frame. Tom said, 'For God's sake, Sam, that is just so you.' I'm a bit ditzy sometimes like that.

Our alarm was set for 8.00 am so we could quickly get used to Rio time. We immediately began our daily health tests, which was a regime introduced long before Rio where we logged the time we woke up, our heart rate, the colour of our urine and how many hours we had slept. We peed in a pot that would go to the physio's room to check if we were properly hydrated.

Everything was monitored: how fatigued you were feeling; if you had any muscle soreness; the mood you were in; whether it was the first day of your period. Before you even got ill or showed any sign of illness or fatigue it would be flagged up and they'd tell you to either rest or miss a session.

The issue of periods is a very important one for female athletes. Studies show that if you are on day one, you're more likely to get an injury, so you had to notify the team's medical staff if that was the case. I was lucky because I had mine not long after we arrived. Being in a tight squad where people know you inside out, talking about periods is second nature. We were so close, and had almost no taboo subjects. We used to call it the Red Sash. If someone hit a crap pass, made a terrible tackle, or was generally a little over emotional we'd say, 'Red Sash everyone! It's okay, she's on her period.'

Joking aside, it was important to be open about the issues around periods. There were members of the squad who, if they suddenly got really teary on the pitch and we knew they were having theirs, would get our sympathy. If we didn't know that about that individual, we'd be like, 'Wow, something must be seriously wrong', because it's not often that someone gets that upset when they're being shouted at on the pitch because it's part and parcel of the game. And there were some people who got really bad cramps. So if they missed a session you would know that they were not skiving.

It was important, therefore, to keep on top of the health monitoring.

On that first morning when we headed out for breakfast for 9.00 am it was then we realised our building was in a good spot – not too far from the transport hub and not too far from the dining hall, but not too close either, as the noise must have been an issue for those right next to it.

It was also then that we got a sense of what we were part of. That was when we saw athletes from other countries, representing almost every single different culture from all over the world. We could see the flags on the other buildings telling where each country was staying.

The dining hall itself was a sight to behold. It was huge. We were told it was the size of three football pitches but when you actually stood in it, it seemed even bigger. The choice of food was on another level. There was Asian, Halal, British and Spanish, every cereal, every bread, every drink, every milk and every fruit. Every taste and diet was catered for at any time of the day.

The temptation was to try different foods but we were on strict instructions to maintain the regime we'd have at home. If we were in the UK we wouldn't have a curry for breakfast, so why have one here? In those first three days our bodies would be adjusting to the new climate and cuisine, so we just had to be strict. We were also warned there was a high chance of food poisoning, so we had to be careful what we ate.

Another huge health consideration at the time we travelled to Rio was the threat of the Zika virus. Spread by certain mosquitoes, if contracted by a pregnant woman it could pass on brain malformations to her baby. Team GB and the British Olympic Association were absolutely excellent in terms of providing us with up-to-date information. They even had their own researchers trying different insect repellents to the particular mosquito that was carrying the virus. It turned out to be Boots' own, and they provided us with loads of it. We also had meetings with a doctor. What a lot of people didn't realise is that the Zika virus was a threat not just in Brazil but in the Caribbean and other parts of South America. They provided us with information on contraception and whether we were thinking of starting a family after the Olympics. Measures were in place if we ever got bitten. There was not one point when I was overly worried. A lot of top tier golfers had pulled out of competing, citing Zika as their concern. With the advice we had been given coupled with the fact this was the first time golf had been an Olympic event since 1904, I thought they would take a calculated risk. I wondered whether that was the real reason or they just couldn't be bothered to go to Rio as the Olympics didn't hold nearly as much prestige as one of the golfing Grand Slams, and there was no prize or sponsorship money involved. It will be interesting for me to see whether they decide to compete in Tokyo 2020 as their true intentions should be revealed. Ultimately for me, the Zika mosquitoes could have been dragons; it still wouldn't have stopped me going to Brazil.

We were all mindful of the dangers – particularly Unsy and me. We certainly didn't want to risk it. I don't like being bitten at the best of times and there was always that little bit of fear at the back of your mind.

The biggest risk from Zika came if you were already pregnant, so to make sure we definitely were not, one of the other girls and I took a pregnancy test before we went out. There was no way we were but, being athletes, we wanted to make sure every eventuality was covered. We had a good giggle going into Marlow Boots and buying a twin pack. And once in Rio we went around stinking of the repellant. Danny Kerry joked that he was convinced Unsy and I must have been thinking of getting pregnant right after the Olympics because we had so much repellant on!

I didn't have any plans on that front. The only thought I'd had about what I would do after the Olympics was that it would be nice to take six months off, whether we won a medal or not, to further my relationship with Tom. Our time together was always in short bursts – three days here, four days there – not for a whole week. We'd then maybe have a month off and then it was back to the routine.

That was all in the future, though. Back in the present, after that first breakfast we went to explore. We checked out the medical centre, and the entertainment zone, where there were pool tables, PlayStations, X boxes, dance machines – all the fun stuff, basically.

The number of freebies was unbelievable, like Powerade bottles with your name printed on, limited edition Coke bottles with Rio on them. You could have lost yourself in the number of amusements laid on – but we had more health monitoring to do. Every morning we'd have what we would call Basic Morning Monitoring. We'd do five minutes of a very slow jogging and take our heart rate immediately after, then rest for a minute and take it again. Then we'd do stretching or any exercises you had to do on a regular basis to just make sure that you were keeping injury free.

Team GB had set up our own fitness centre, with a lovely reception area – flat screens everywhere, fake grass, deckchairs and a table tennis table. And downstairs there was a multi-use gym, with water bikes and a big area with a soft floor where you could stretch, with medicine balls, stretch bands and foam rollers. Team GB had installed lots of extras for the athletes. There were TVs with satellite sports channels, ice machines – everything that you could possibly need as an athlete. For those first three days we relaxed, scoped out the village and, aside from some initial light training, we did fun stuff, like going for walks and hiring bikes.

It was also strange in those early days getting used to being in such a place. I bumped into Novak Djokovic, and on that occasion I did turn into a fan girl. I grabbed a quick selfie and posted it on Facebook. He was just passing so there was no time for a conversation, but he was pretty relaxed. Then the next morning there was a palaver going on and we realised it was Usain Bolt once more. The Jamaicans' flats were opposite the entrance to the dining hall. He was out on his balcony wearing tiny budgie smugglers with 'Jamaica' on the rear. He was posing and all the Koreans were taking pictures of him. He was there with a speaker. It was quite funny. It was refreshing, too, that there were no press around, but he was just messing about on his balcony, shouting to his mates. He knew everyone was watching him but he is a showman and enjoys it. Stuff like that was quite cool.

On the flipside, I felt sorry for the likes of Rafa Nadal because as soon as he got up from his table people would swarm around him. Jo-Wilfried Tsonga, the French tennis player, was also mobbed. People would respect them when they were eating but as soon as they stood up to take their tray back, they'd be swamped.

On the whole, however, it was awesome to see so many different sportsmen and women. You'd call the lift and golfers Justin Rose and Danny Willet would be in there and you're like, 'Alright?' It was a bit weird for hockey players because we're not used to that kind of thing, but actually it's really nice to see that they're on a level playing field with us. Then there were the cyclists like Sir Bradley Wiggins and athletes like Sir Mo Farah, and it was cool to see people who had done so much for their respective sports. The beauty of living in an apartment block was that our paths crossed with these household names.

Our floor was taken up with our team and the hockey boys were below us. The swimmers were at the top because they finished early, so they let them go up there and make some noise. We got to know the rugby sevens girls quite well, and Jamie Murray, brother of Andy, was lovely, always chatty, as were the judo girls. The athletics lot largely turned up in the second week quite late and kept to themselves. You could have got swept up in the whole spectacle but we took some measures to ensure we stayed focused.

We agreed to some pacts before the competition started. We came off social media the day before the opening ceremony. This was Danny Kerry's idea and we had a bit of debate at first about it because, while some girls thought reading negative comments could put them off their game, I thought we had an opportunity to promote hockey as individuals and give the public back home a glimpse of the Olympic experience. The outcome was we agreed to come off Twitter and Instagram, but Facebook was allowed because on that you can control who sees your posts.

We all stuck to it and it was actually a great idea – and quite nice not to be on it because it can suck you in.

We did have situations in the past where girls have been criticised on social media for the way they played or looked, and if that impacts on their form it hurts the whole team.

One of the differences between playing at a normal hockey tournament and the Olympics is that for a standard tournament you only get hockey fans watching. At the Olympics you get the whole world watching. If you're on BBC1 at five o'clock you're going to get everyone tuning in. And it's all very well to say, 'Don't read the comments,' but it's impossible not to want to.

One of the freebies we had was the new Samsung Galaxy 7, which was one of the best phones of the time and also came with a sim card. To avoid temptation, everyone pretty much used that phone, as it had no apps on it. I still had my iPhone in case people wanted to contact me, but I pretty much ignored it or put it on my Facebook status that I wasn't going to be available. But like the other girls, I decided to have this new sim card in my new phone, have numbers in it for my mum and Tom. In addition, I was in a WhatsApp family group and one with all the girls with their Brazilian numbers.

Our other agreement was not to watch or talk about any of the other women's hockey matches. This came from previous experience when the girls had felt a lot of energy had been expended on what was happening in the other group and trying to work out the permutations of the draw. We could only control what was in front of us, so we agreed not to watch the games together. You were allowed to watch games in your own time, just not as a group.

We could watch and see how the men were doing because that didn't involve us. One or two of the girls were dating the guys so they wanted to support them, but in terms of watching sport, we didn't really watch any hockey.

Our prime focus was on the other teams in our section, Group B – Australia, America, India, Japan and Argentina. The group held a lot of danger: Argentina were the world number two; Australia were world number three and we always struggled against them; USA had already shown they could do us damage since our ex-coaches moved there; Japan and India we played before we went to the Olympics and beat them comfortably, but we knew that when you get to a tournament it's a completely different kettle of fish.

We felt our preparation was second to none.

The reason we had headed to Rio early – and based ourselves at the village straight away, while some teams stayed in holding camps away from the hub – was because there was a shortage of top-class hockey pitches elsewhere in Brazil.

In order to prepare us for the pitch we'd be using at the Games, an exact replica had been installed at Bisham Abbey, so we'd been getting used to playing on the vivid blue and green surface. There would be far more elements to contend with now we were in Rio, of course, such as the weather, but at least GB Hockey tried to prepare us as much as possible.

On our second day we travelled to Deodoro, in the western side of Rio, to practise on the pitch for the first time. Jumping aboard the bus, where you sit on that morning is important because as soon as you establish your seat on the bus, nothing changes for the duration of the tournament. If you were more of a quiet and focused person you would want to sit with a fellow quiet person away from the louder people. The louder people found it easier to prepare by not concentrating so much on the game ahead, preferring to chat or relax while listening to music.

Some people were also quite superstitious. I wasn't that bothered but I respected that people were. I sat next to Georgie – Twiggy – and to my left were Unsy and Nic White, who always sat next to each other, shared headphones and always listened to the same playlist. They were so drilled that the playlist would tell them if they were running a little bit early or a little bit late because they'd always get to a certain point in a song.

The same went for the changing room. Once you established a seat in the changing room everyone would sit in that same place for every match.

On the way to that first training session – and for every trip – our bus had an armed escort. We'd been briefed on the potential terror threat because sadly it is the reality of the times we live in and we talked about what we'd do should something happen. It didn't really faze us, though, because escorts were relatively common, particularly in South America.

However, we had been warned about potential hijacking situations. On that first trip to the stadium we travelled through quite a deprived area, as a highway that was being specially built was not yet completed. We never felt under threat but the potential dangers were at the back of your mind, and it was a bit of a relief when the highway and tunnel through a mountainside were eventually completed.

Whenever we went away, it didn't matter if it was just up to Scotland or to the other side of the world, the first training session was always terrible. We called it a 'shitty-get-it-out-of-your-system session'. After the warm-up and stretches we do a lot of mobility to get our bodies moving. Then we get in pairs and pass the ball from left to right, up and down, to learn the grain of the pitch, how it's rolling, and the distribution of the water. Normally, it always feels like you've lost all your coordination. You can't trap a ball or find a pass.

Anyway, for this first session we split up into two groups. The front five – the midfielders and attackers – did shooting practice with the goalies; the back five – the defenders and two of the centre halves – started fizzing the ball around, transferring it around the back. We'd only been doing this for five minutes when Danny called, 'Right, okay, time.'

Silence. Everyone looked at each other, like, 'What the hell was that?' And we all just burst into laughter. Even Danny joked, 'Right, let's go home, shall we?' It was one of the best sessions we had ever done. We were fizzing it fast, trapping, net passing … we had three balls going at once. And I just remember feeling that we were in the groove.

We hadn't trained for days, we'd been on a fourteen-hour flight, but we didn't feel tired. It was strange. The pitch helped. It was lovely – fast, smooth. I thought, 'This is going to be good. The pitch is going to work in our favour because we're a team that likes to fizz the ball around and we like to play it fast.'

I think that session probably gave us a massive confidence boost, especially as a back four when you have to get it right because if you don't, one interception leads to a goal. Subconsciously, that session was crucial. We only gave it an hour because we didn't want to overdo it. Feeling physically sound was one thing, but such a huge part of modern sport is the psychology.

For about a year leading up to Rio we all had to write things down about our personalities – what you were like on a good day and what you were like on a bad day as a person. Then on the pitch: if things are going really downhill, what do you need from your teammate to make you get back to where you need to be? It was stuff like how you should talk to a person, the words you would say or you wouldn't say. Or if someone in the apartment is being quite sulky, you know when to go up to them and say, 'Right, snap out of it' or when to go up to them and put an arm around them. It was letting out teammates know what we needed as individuals. We started to know each other inside out. It was the same in the changing room: everyone knew how the others prepared for a game and respected their routine.

Andrea Furst, the psychologist for Team England and Team GB, would prepare a profile on each of us. For example, it would say, 'How do we know what Sam Quek's going to act like when she's going to have a good game? What does Sam Quek act like when she's not going to have a good game?'

So if I was quiet people would know there was something up and then it would be a case of my teammates knowing how to get me back to where I needed to be to perform. It covered every aspect – off the field, in the changing room, on the bus, on the field. Every single bit of time we spent together, people would know how to manage each other.

And obviously, as well as knowing everything about each other, it was crucial that we also knew our opposition inside out.

Our first match was against Australia, rivals who always gave us a tough game. We'd been over there in February 2016 for a series of tests so both teams held few surprises for the other. We'd been through a spell of not winning against them so we understood how hard it would be. We knew their strengths, their weaknesses and how we were going to exploit them. It was just a case of whether we could implement our game plan. Could we do the basics right? Could we score our corners when we got them and defend our corners when we had to?

We knew this game was going to be crucial. If we could get three points it would put us in a very good spot for going through to the next stage.

We all sat down with the coach to talk about our goals, anything we wanted to go through last minute, how we were feeling and to discuss what position we'd be playing and what our pitch time was going to be. The match was going to be on 6 August, and it would be the second hockey match to take place on the very first day of Olympic competition.

The opening ceremony was going to be the night before. We'd decided as a team that it would be favourable from a performance point of view not to attend the festivities. When we weighed it up, we were going to be on our feet for several hours, which meant we'd be dehydrated, and by the time we got back it would be very late and we'd likely struggle to get into our sleeping patterns as we would still be buzzing from the energy of the spectacle.

It was gutting to miss such a showcase. Part of my dreams of being an Olympian was featuring in the opening parade. I imagined my family, friends, and even some casual acquaintance who may have thought, 'I wonder what happened to that hockey girl', seeing me on the TV in my kit, walking behind our nation's flag, representing Great Britain. But it wasn't to be – and for sound reasoning.

When we had gone to the kitting out we'd all been given our opening ceremony outfit – a little dress and white jacket.

On the night of the ceremony, all the GB athletes who were not attending were camped out on the artificial turf outside our high-rise apartment block sitting on the Team GB deckchairs, watching it all unfold on a big screen. Mostly they were lounging in their tracksuits. We hockey girls decided to put on our opening ceremony gear. We weren't going to let them go to waste, and we found it funny.

Some other teams went to the ceremony. Argentina and the USA both went and they were playing each other first the next day. I think not going gave us a mental edge. We thought, 'Bloody hell, they're going to be knackered.'

It was 100 per cent the right decision not to attend.

I couldn't wait for the day of our first match to arrive. I was filled with nervous excitement. I was desperate to get my GB Rio kit on the first time. I remember standing on my balcony with the gear on, hair done, ready to go. I made some last-minute phone calls to make sure Tom and my parents had made it to the stadium. They were going there in plenty of time to take in the earlier match. It was a relief to know they were inside. I couldn't really settle otherwise.

We arrived at the stadium and I was surprised at how empty it was. We'd heard how expensive the tickets were and how they were going to corporate people who might not turn up, but it was still disappointing to see the reality of the situation. It wouldn't affect us on the pitch but it would have been nicer if it was busier, if only for the television audiences to see people did actually turn up to watch hockey.

Once I saw where my parents were I could relax a little more. Tom made it easy for me. He had brought a different outfit for every single game and, whereas my mum and dad were quite low-key with just 'Sam' T-shirts, he was there in his Union Jack suit banging his drum to get the atmosphere going. He yelled 'Sam!' and I gave him a little wave. We warmed up on a little quarter-sized pitch behind the changing room that no onlookers could see, but both teams were there at the same time.

We'd played some practice matches in the run-up to the Olympics but this was different. We were sizing each other up, seeing how the warm-up was going, how they were looking.

I looked across to the Australian girls and thought, 'Game on.'

We were minutes away now. Our Olympic adventure was about to begin.

Chapter 18

When Hope Becomes Reality

I smoothed down the pillar-box red vest. The anthems were about to begin. 'I'm here now,' I thought. 'I'm so proud to be part of Great Britain's Olympic team.'

I made eye contact with Tom briefly during *God Save the Queen*. He had tears streaming down his face. To this day he says that was the proudest moment of his life. He didn't care how the tournament had transpired. He told me afterwards, 'Nothing after that mattered, you had done it. Singing that anthem in the middle of that Rio pitch, you were now officially an Olympian. No one could take that away from you. You had achieved your dream.'

I had another dream – an even bigger dream, and once the anthem had finished, I had 100 per cent focus on the game.

I'd be starting on the bench. That had been the preferred strategy and as much as I'd have loved to have been starting on the pitch, I accepted the game plan and knew that due to rotations I would be on in five minutes or so anyway.

The match started at a frantic pace. There were some crunching challenges very early on. It set the tone; this was going to be a battle. The first few minutes flew by and I soon got the signal from our assistant coach, Karen Brown. I was on. I did have some butterflies but as soon as I got my first touch and made my first pass, the nerves disappeared. I remember thinking, 'This is the Olympic Games, your first match.'

When I'd thought of the Olympic Games I'd always imagined everything being much harder than any other tournament I had been to. The Olympic motto of '*Citus, Altius, Fortius*' translated to 'Faster, Higher, Stronger', so it would have been easy to get overwhelmed. But the more I thought about it, it was the same pitch, the same dimensions, and we were playing a team I had played many times before with all the same faces. So I actually relaxed quite easily and managed to treat it like any other game.

The first goal was going to be important and we managed to get it in the second quarter, Lily Owsley doing superbly well to slide in and finish a nice move involving Hollie Webb, Shona McCallin and Sophie Bray. It was the perfect start to our campaign.

Australia came back at us and equalised in the third quarter. They were only on level terms for ten minutes, however, as Alex Danson produced a sensational finish after being squeezed wide of goal. The Aussies put us under a lot of pressure in the final quarter but we held firm to win 2–1. At the final whistle everyone was buzzing but there was no sense of celebration. It felt like any other game. Whether that was down to the crowd size or our preparation I don't know. It was just a case of 'Right, job done. Get in the ice bath.'

We came off the pitch, did our warm-down and then it was into the ice bath, which was basically one big paddling pool. That's how technical it gets. Half the team got in, had a soak and then it was the turn of the rest. When we win the ice bath can be one of the most sociable areas to be because it turns into a mini debrief of the game.

Before Rio I'd been in baths where it was dead silent and people were just staring, reflecting, whispering to each other because it's quite quiet and you don't want to interrupt people's quiet time. But after the Australia game it was a bustling dressing room, players going through our post-game routine. We also get weighed because in a match you can lose a kilogram in weight, so you have to replace your fluids. Our whole life there was routine, routine, routine, so once we'd all completed everything we needed to do, it was back to the village.

Team GB hired out a school – the British School – where we went for recovery between matches. They had a gym on site and that's where friends and family would meet us. I only actually sat down with my mum and dad and Tom twice during the whole Olympics. Obviously they were keen to see me and talk about the game but I wasn't interested. It sounds harsh and my mum used to get quite upset, but I was there to stay focused, not be distracted.

Maybe only those who are in an Olympic squad will understand but it was hard to meet their expectations. I just didn't want to meet up and talk about the match. If you didn't have a pass, you weren't getting in the village. And I didn't want to go out because it was a bit dodgy. Tom thought I didn't make enough effort but, as selfish as it sounds, when I'm in hockey mode it's all about me, my performance, the team and what I've got on. He didn't really share my new medal mission. He felt that just getting there was mission complete, and I understood why. I love Tom to bits and I would spend every minute with him if I could, but at the Olympics it was about me. And he was very good, to be fair, but I remember the first few days he found it difficult to accept. It's tough to tell someone who has travelled halfway around the world to see you and support you that actually you don't want to see them, but it was for all the right reasons.

It sounds terrible and if you're not in that elite sports mindset it's hard to comprehend but you are so focused that you don't want anything else to interfere. If I nipped out to see someone I wouldn't want to risk being late for a team meeting.

You have to have that selfishness, and it wasn't only in Rio. At a tournament in Stratford I fell out with my mum once because I said to her, 'I've got a meeting,' when she asked me to go for lunch. Then she spotted me out for lunch with Kirsty, my friend since the days of England under-16s. I look back now and I think, 'Sam, that's so selfish and so disrespectful, you lied to her.' But when I was in that zone and I only had limited time, I wanted to spend it with my best mate who knew what was going on in our hockey world.

Actually, in Rio, I was gutted for Kirsty because even though she was the number two goalkeeper, she was staying outside the village. She was normally my go-to confidante. On every trip we used to share a room but for Rio they only allowed two additional players to stay in the village and a nineteenth could stay off site. Naturally, the rates of injury in outfield players are far higher than the goalkeeper, so it made more sense for the two reserves in the village to be outfielders. Kirsty only got told three weeks before the Olympics and straight away she was gutted because she felt even more detached from the team. She could come in with a pass but was only allowed to stay for a certain number of hours. She didn't have a bed there, or a sofa to relax on. She had to lie on a beanbag in our living room when we had two hours off and I shared my room with her.

So there was quite a lot to contend with but while I appreciated massively the support from my family and Tom, I preferred to be in the village with the team.

After our strong start we needed to make sure there were no slip-ups against India.

Before we left the apartment I texted Tom: 'What outfit are you wearing today?' As was becoming customary, he sent me a photo of what he'd be wearing.

On each game day we'd have our usual morning monitoring and then match SWOT – Strengths, Weaknesses, Opportunities and Threats. And that would normally be about forty-five minutes to an hour. We'd get all the information on the opposition, what we were going to do and how we were going to overcome them, and what we were going to take advantage of.

Then we'd have a bit of down time for treatment if we needed it. We'd then break for lunch and have a little bit more time off, and then snacks, followed by the actual debrief, which was a punchy ten-minute reminder with bullet points. We'd then have half an hour to get ready, get on the bus and head to the ground.

After a cagey opening period, we finally made the breakthrough late in the first half when Giselle Ansley fired in from a penalty corner. Two minutes later, an Alex Danson shot was parried to Nic White to flick home. Lily Owsley then set up Alex for her second and we made it two wins out of two.

We'd got off to a brilliant start but our next match against Argentina was massive. We'd prepared for it to feel like an Argentinean home game and it was exactly that. They had their mass drums and trumpets, whereas we just had our small contingent, who nevertheless made themselves heard. The atmosphere was incredible – one of the best I've played in. We were on pitch two, which was the smaller stadium, and it felt like a full house.

My mum had told Tom not to wear his Union Jack suit to the game, but just to put it on in the stadium in case he got into trouble. We didn't know how hostile the crowd might be.

Our matches against Argentina might not be ferocious but there's a rivalry in terms of big tackles, big hits, controversial decisions. It promised to be a feisty encounter and it lived up to the billing.

Carla Rebecchi, their captain, was the playmaker. I had the job of marking her when she came forward. I thought, 'I'm just going to man-mark her. If she's in my zone, just stay with her the whole way. As soon as you give her a little bit of space, she'll punish you.'

They had a corner and I was on the left-hand side going out to the player running in. Another player, Delfina Merino, ran into me and fell on the floor. All the Argentina girls started making a big hoo-ha as if I'd pushed her or body checked her. I knew for a fact I hadn't so I stood my ground. Each team has one referral per game and they used theirs for this. It was still really early on in the first half.

Play stops and the umpire refers to an official who watches the video replay.

They were all saying, 'She took her out, she body checked her.' I protested my innocence but, as they referred it, I just started laughing as they remonstrated to me and the umpire. I knew I had done nothing wrong and they were about to lose a vital referral early in the game.

Tom said to me after, 'I can't believe you just stood there and laughed.'

The incident came up on the big screen, so everyone in the stadium could see it. And the replay again is me running out, holding my ground and Merino just running into me.

They lost their referral. I think it showed we were already getting into their heads a little. We then hit them with two rapid-fire goals, both scored by Helen Richardson-Walsh. We added a third through Sophie Bray on thirty-eight minutes. We didn't even have a chance to consolidate the healthy lead we'd built when they hit back with two quick goals of their own.

It was probably one of the most high tempo games I've played in. Then they really put us under the pump. We defended like our life depended on it. Maddie Hinch pulled off some great saves and we held out to win 3–2.

That win was enough to see us into the quarter-finals but we had to make sure we finished top of our group to avoid the likelihood of meeting the favourites Holland in the next round. While we didn't fear the Netherlands, they were considered the best team in the world by a distance. If you made up a world XI, it would be fair to say at least half would be Dutch. They had won gold at the previous two Olympics and the bookmakers had made them 8/15 odds-on favourite to take the gold again in Rio.

We knew every win was important. We were looking at each other as if to say, 'That's a result.' Another of the conversations we'd had was not to pre-empt anything but I remember Unsy saying to me, 'We could do this.'

I agreed: 'We're going to win it.'

We just had that feeling. Unsy and I talked about how we felt on the pitch. 'Did you ever feel that you were going to lose?'

Sometimes you do think, 'Oh God, this is a slog.'

There was never a point in the Olympics where I thought that. Sure, there had been moments when we'd been up against it, but I always thought we'd come through it.

We were unbeaten – three wins out of three. Next up was Japan. On paper we should beat them but we had to make sure we did our jobs properly. There were going to be no easy games.

Unfortunately for me, I chose that game to have a shocker. It seemed that I couldn't pass, was giving the ball away and didn't play a good game at all. It was probably the first time in a while where I started to doubt myself. As teammates you demand more of each other and after one terrible pass, Unsy looked at me and said, 'Come on, it's not good enough.'

Normally that's exactly what I need and I thrive off it but I remember thinking, 'Come on Sam, this is shit.' I could feel myself getting a bit uptight and tense.

Thankfully, we scored early, Lily Owsley after five minutes, but Japan proved stubborn to break down after that and it wasn't until the second half that Nic White scored to give us a bit more breathing space.

The important thing was we won. It was another victory and our momentum was building. None of the girls said anything to me about my performance. But Tom, who's my biggest critic as well as my biggest fan, said, 'Yeah, it wasn't great.' We had an agreement years ago, where he promised never to try to manage my expectations. If he never misled me into how well I played, then I could always believe him when he said I did well and take confidence from that.

I'd probably built it up in my head that it was a lot worse than it was. Everyone in the team had so far been operating at such a consistently solid level I was sensitive to any dip on my part. I had an average game, but average wasn't good enough at this level.

The focus was now on our last group game against the USA. They were enjoying an equally good tournament and had four wins out of four, just like us. Our clash would determine who topped the group – the reward being a potentially easier route to the final.

It would not be easy. USA had been a bit of a bogey team; they always caused us problems. The coaches knew key elements of our play like our tactics at corners, which added an extra dimension. While it wasn't going to be a make-or-break match, we wanted to maintain our winning streak.

Right from the push back we were on the front foot, putting the Americans under pressure, and they had their goalie Jackie Briggs to thank for some fine saves to keep us out. We suffered a setback when they took the lead in the fortieth minute. We didn't panic, and kept our composure. Our pressure finally paid off when Sophie Bray slotted home after a corner with seven minutes remaining. We could have settled for the draw but we were determined to push for the win.

With just four minutes left, I got the ball on the 25 metre line and, looking up, saw a gap through to Alex Danson up front.

I knew Danny drilled us to play from the back but this was a chance. The card he had written for me at the start of the tournament explicitly said, 'Keep your game simple' and I didn't want to let him down, yet here I was, contemplating a champagne pass. If I could just thread it through to her … I put it in as hard and as fast as I could to the back post. When you've got Alex on the back post, on the end of a long hard ball, she's going to put it in. She saw the pass, put her hand down on the floor and swept it home. We'd won 2–1.

I felt amazing. As a defender you don't score many goals unless it's from a set piece but to set up a goal was a great feeling. Straight away I said to Unsy and Kate, 'That pass will be in the debrief.' It may have won the game, but I knew I was going to be in trouble.

Sure enough, the first clip shown the next day in the debrief was the clip of that pass. Danny's opening line was, 'God Sam, you're a pain in the arse!'

Everyone just started laughing. He went on: 'God, it's tough being a coach!' He spoke it in a non-aggressive but reluctantly jovial tone. It was kind of a signal to me of 'Okay, that worked on this occasion, but don't you dare make a habit of doing that pass'. Fair enough.

He'd trained us to build it up and round the corner, but actually on that 1 percentage time it paid off because that was the right decision as the pass was on. Thank goodness he had understood the situation on the pitch at the time. I believed I had made the right play. I wasn't trying to make a point to him or rebel. I was doing what I honestly thought was best for the team, regardless of how it panned out.

That win meant we topped the group and in the quarter-finals would face the fourth-placed team in Group A, which was Spain. If we came through that match we'd have two shots at a medal. Because there was so much at stake, Tom said that for everyone in the stands this was the most nerve-racking match.

We got off to the best start with Georgie Twigg, Helen Richardson-Walsh and Lily Owsley all scoring to put us 3–0 up at half-time. The shine was taken off the scoreline when Gigi Olivia, their main player, came into the side of the 'D' and scored an absolute worldy – an unstoppable shot and a great bit of hockey – but it ended up just being a consolation goal.

We were into the semi-finals where we faced New Zealand. The Kiwis were also having a great tournament. They beat their arch-rivals Australia to reach the semis so we knew it was going to be a hard match. But we also knew we would have two more games and so long as we won one, we would be guaranteed a medal, although everyone was solely focused on one medal in particular. I can honestly say that throughout the Olympics I can't remember myself or any of my teammates at any point even referring to the silver or bronze as either an option or a consolation.

Semi-finals are such crucial games. Win and we were guaranteed at least silver. Lose and we'd have to pick ourselves up from the crushing disappointment to fight it out for bronze.

As well as that it was also the most important game for the future of hockey in terms of funding. That was something we were very aware of.

The blood, sweat and tears, putting our bodies on the line, it's because we were playing for the future of our sport. If we didn't medal, it was likely the funding for the next cycle would be cut and those who came after us wouldn't have the opportunities we had. We were all very conscious of this. The future of hockey in Britain was quite literally in our hands. This was not going to be just another game.

On a personal level, it was a landmark game and a very proud moment – my fiftieth cap for Great Britain. What a time to win it.

Since we'd arrived in Rio the temperature had risen, and by the knockouts it was scorching hot. We were fortunate to draw the later evening semi-final. In the earlier matches players had to come off for water breaks and the pitch had dried because it was so warm. By the time our games started it was still hot but by the second quarter the sun had dipped behind the stand and the conditions were perfect.

Before the match started we knew it would be the Netherlands waiting for us in the final after they'd come through their semi-final against Germany on penalties.

New Zealand started the strongest, putting us under a lot of pressure and creating good chances. They didn't take them, though, and we punished them, Alex Danson scoring when they failed to clear a penalty corner. In the final quarter we stretched our lead when we were awarded two penalty flicks after Helen and Lily were taken out.

We looked like we were cruising but then we lost Crista Cullen and Twiggy to head injuries. I'd just come off for a break and Karen, who was organising the subs on the bench, came up and said, 'Sam, you're going to go on left forward.' 'Left forward?' I said. Ordinarily I don't get any further forward than the back line. I had no idea how to play up front.

The Kiwis' key player, Stacey Michelsen, was renowned for playing right wing and cutting inside, dribbling past everyone and scoring. She'd scored a goal like that in the previous tournament at Lee Valley.

Karen said, 'Don't let her cut inside, make her go back.'

Well, I had newfound respect for forwards that day.

As a defender your running is long, you sprint over long distance and it's more aerobic, whereas forwards are on for five minutes and then go off for a rest. It's just sprint, shuttle, shuttle, sprint, sprint, sprint, sprint, shuttle – because you've got to get across as they transfer it to cover the lines.

All I heard was, 'Sam, step right! No left! Sam!'

I was just basically trying to cut off the direct line to goal. I didn't know the actual running lanes. I had a rough idea how to do it because you listen to it in the team talk. But in terms of actually running the correct patterns and how to cut the ball off, I didn't have a clue. It must have worked because we closed them out to win 3–0.

I came off completely knackered. Again, post-match everyone was taking the Mick: 'Alright there Sam? Found yourself at left wing?'

The team were all still buzzing despite an intense match. We were surviving on a cocktail of adrenaline and excitement. We knew that by holding on to this result we were guaranteed the best finish a women's team had ever achieved at the Olympics – the previous bests being the bronze medals in 1992 and 2012. We had also pretty much guaranteed our sport funding for the future.

After the match, Maddie Hinch, who was also celebrating her fiftieth cap, and I were presented with flowers to mark the milestone in our careers.

The celebrations were muted, however. We'd achieved our basic goal – to win a medal. We'd maintained our unbeaten record but there was still a job to be done.

The gold medal awaited us.

Standing in our way was only the best team in the world.

Chapter 19

A Golden Moment

This was a blow. We'd come this far and on the day before an Olympic final one of our key players was an injury doubt.

Helen Richardson-Walsh had picked up a hamstring injury in the semi-final. The morning after, we were in the British School doing our recovery and Helen was getting treatment. A few whispers started go round that she wasn't going to make it. No one is indispensible in any team but Helen was such a key player for us. She's not just a big personality, someone who's got that bite – and the twinkle in her eye that she's going to step up and do something magical – but she's also Kate's wife. Our worry spread to our captain. Would it be affecting her? We'd be gutted for Helen if she didn't make it – seventeen years chasing an Olympic dream, battling back from two back surgeries, thinking she might never play again, and to make it this far …

I saw her that morning. 'Come on Helen, just neck some painkillers, you'll get through it, strap it up,' I said, being deliberately flippant. 'Come on, one more game.' Helen was so much more than an average squad member. She was our penalty flick taker due to her cool head and she had already popped up with some vital goals in this tournament. She was in a rich vein of form. Added to that, the Richardson-Walsh name had become a hockey institution, such was Kate and her international standing in the game. I honestly believed that if the Dutch read our team sheet they would instantly recognise that one of us was missing and they would glean extra confidence from that.

Everyone had their fingers crossed.

To the outside world we remained positive – and kept shtum. No one would be texting outside the group because the last thing we wanted was the opposition getting any indication we were weakened. So we went to the British School, did our rehab, had lunch and just chilled. It was the normal routine. Just because it was an Olympic final didn't mean we'd do things any differently.

The morning of the final on 19 August, Helen had a final fitness test. She disappeared and everyone was just waiting to see when she came back.

When she returned the whispers this time were that she was okay. It was good news.

Helen being fit to line up meant a little bit of history would be made. She and Kate were going to be the first same-sex married couple to make it to an Olympic final together.

Normal service now resumed, we could get on with our preparation.

Every morning daily schedules were printed out and pinned on the doors in our corridor. For every other game they listed details on what would happen 'should we win'. Today they had information for 'when we win'. No one wanted to get hung up on it but it did say what attire we had to wear to the medal ceremony. Obviously we knew we were winning a medal of some sort, so we needed our leggings, our tops, stuff like that. It also told us what colour the day was – either white, red or blue.

For the final, we were told: 'Today is a white day.'

That meant, white T-shirt, white top.

The other boost we got was being told we'd be wearing red for the final. The Dutch would be in their change strip of charcoal grey and orange. Our officials successfully appealed that their usual orange would clash with our favourite strip.

We'd won in both white and red during these games but for some reason the red made us more confident. We were all superstitious to some degree – Sophie Bray didn't wash her kit for the whole tournament because she was so convinced it might hex it. I thought this was taking it bit far, but luckily for Soph, or maybe the squad, she had a relatively pleasant natural odour, so no one minded too much.

In the build-up to the game we obviously talked about Holland and pored over videos. We were used to playing them – and Danny had always made us aware that when we play the Netherlands it's going to feel like you are under the cosh. Looking through footage, especially from the Champions Trophy in London in June, when we'd lost 2–0, it felt like we were getting absolutely battered.

However, we'd had our opportunities. Danny made us feel very comfortable with the idea that when you play the best in the world, you will be defending for long periods, but that was where we were most solid. We had some of the best defenders in the world and if we took our opportunities we had a chance. Games against the Dutch were always tough because they were such a class outfit. It was just a case of knowing our job and expecting that was how it would feel.

Arriving at the stadium, I did my usual checks – where was Tom, where were my parents? Tom, you couldn't miss. He was in full Union Jack

Morphsuit and hat, beating the drum. He'd had some journey, too, since he'd arrived in Rio. After the first couple of games his persistent drumming seemed to annoy some of the parents who wanted him to give it a rest once in a while. By the final, everyone was onside and he'd become a leading cheerleader. Against the raucous Dutch support we were going to need him – and the growing number of GB fans who had followed our progress. Team GB was on course to have its most successful games for over a century, eclipsing even London 2012. We hoped to add to the gold rush.

Everything had been normal. Everything routine. It was just another game. One more match to get through. Standing for the anthems, however, the nerves began to build. That was when I knew something was getting to me. In those seven minutes after the game started and I was watching from the bench, I was desperate to get involved.

My introduction into the fray hadn't calmed me down. Giving away that penalty flick just seconds after coming on hadn't done wonders for my confidence.

All eyes were on Maartje Paumen as she stepped up to face Maddie Hinch. She meticulously researched all her opponents' favourite shots. Did she have any more up her sleeve? We were expecting Paumen to roof it. She flicked it – and Maddie palmed it away to safety! Maartje didn't get hold of it, which meant it was at a nice height for a goalie. It was a save you would have expected Maddie to make, and thankfully she did!

My whole body seemed to drop from pure relief. I gave her the thumbs up. Thank goodness!

It was a huge let-off but back the Dutch came at us again. Their movement is second to none and they were enjoying the lion's share of possession. They broke again and another shot was deflected wide. Ten minutes in and we hadn't laid a glove on them. It was still 0–0.

Finally we managed to generate a quick break of our own. Sophie Bray weaved forward, skipping past three Dutch defenders. She fed Lily Owsley, who squeezed it in from close range. 1–0!

I'd never known happiness like it – not only from my own point of view, but from the team's, especially after the start I had. 'Right Sam, settle down,' I thought. 'Make your tackles, cut out the mistakes. Focus.' We'd been up against it but we had our noses in front. Maybe, just maybe …

Back the Dutch came. Another short corner. Another chance missed for them.

We made it to the end of the first quarter with our slender lead intact. The game plan was working – so far.

Second quarter. The Dutch continued to press. They hadn't won the last two Olympic finals by giving up easily. We looked liked we'd weathered another mini storm. Kate had possession and I was on the left looking to receive the pass. The Dutch overturned it and I could just see Kitty van Male bearing down on goal.

Shit.

We were in trouble. I ran full pelt but there was no way I could catch her. Maddie came out. Van Male went wide. Hollie Web looked as though she'd got there but then – no way – van Male just smashed a world-class shot into the roof of the net. 1–1.

The pressure was relentless. Crista Cullen received a green card for using an elbow but the Dutch didn't capitalise. A few minutes later, there was another penalty corner to the Dutch. This time, Paumen smashed it in. 2–1 to the Netherlands.

Straight away, it was our turn to break forward. Crista Cullen suddenly found herself in space in the Dutch 'D'. She drag hit the ball and it looped it over the goalie. A world-class strike! 2–2!

Half-time. What a match it was shaping up to be. The Dutch had so far been everything we expected – fast, determined and were ahead on every measurable statistic, except the one that mattered, the scoreline. We'd been under pressure but we'd taken our chances, just like our coach had predicted. It was anyone's to win.

When the whistle went we ran to the changing room, as we're drilled to do. It doesn't matter how tired you are, you run. Not only do we want to make full use of the time we have with the coaches but it also sends a signal – we're not tired, we're raring to go again. By contrast, the Dutch walked off, possibly wondering how they weren't ahead. Their body language suggested they were in need of the breather.

Inside the changing room we sat down – in the same positions we'd been in since the very first match. Everyone had their wet towels because it was so hot. We had a minute to compose ourselves. We were sat on benches running down each side of the changing room and Danny Kerry was standing in the middle. Some girls were opening gels or having a banana. I just wanted water as any food or the powders made my mouth sticky.

Danny was very calm. There was no, 'Come on, it's an Olympic final' – none of that. It was just very much, 'Right, okay. That's the first half done. Nerves are out the way, we're back on. It's 2–2, we're level. You've got all that crap out of the way.'

I'd made a mistake. Kate had made a mistake. There had been silly mistakes from the Dutch as well. That was the point he was making. 'That's the Olympic final nerves out of the way. You've got thirty minutes. This is what we're going to do.'

We talked about the game plan – nothing really that different. It was very calm, very measured. No one brought up my error – or anyone else's. There was no point because we all know when we mess up. The defenders equally wouldn't mention any sitters the strikers may have missed. There was nothing to be gained by bringing up the negative energy. The only discussions were of a technical nature. 'On that press, can you just make sure you do this?' or, 'Kate, keep up that ball pace, it's bloody brilliant', or 'Crista, keep doing the aerials. We're really under the pump here.'

Third quarter. It was the same pattern as before. More Dutch pressure. Their corners seemed to be relentless, but the defence held firm. I was off the field when the Dutch had another penalty corner, expertly executed. It looked very similar to the move Scotland had pulled on us at the Euros. We weren't the only team to study videos and they had clearly identified a weak point in our corner routines. 3–2 to the Dutch.

It was not where we wanted to be, behind in an Olympic final, with the clock ticking down, but we'd come back from two down against them in the Europeans. We could do it again.

It was the Dutch who continued to carve out the chances. Throughout the second half I was trying to outlet the ball but they kept coming back to us. Despite the pressure we tried to remain calm and accepting of it. It was tough. There were moments we thought, 'Oh God, that could have gone in', and 'Wow, that just fizzed past the post'. When Danny said to us, 'Listen, we're playing Holland; expect to have long periods of time when you're under pressure and them pummelling the goal, because that's what Holland are like.'

We just had to hang in there and keep trying to create an opportunity.

Eight and a half minutes left. We had a short corner. The play went on and I saw the ball running in and hit a Dutch foot but the umpire hadn't blown the whistle. I put my arm up to appeal, shouting, 'Corner! Corner!' But the umpire played on. It popped out to Nic White on a reverse stick. She just bunted it towards goal. I watched it, almost in slow motion, cross the line. 3–3!

'Oh my God!' I grabbed Nic in a headlock type hold and her chin smashed my elbow. Thank goodness they didn't accept my appeal!

The tension was off the scale. In the closing minutes both teams did everything to win it but we were heading to penalty shuttles. When the final whistle went we all ran in to the bench and to the coach because, like half-time, the game was not over. By contrast the Dutch girls just stood still initially. They put their sticks down, took their gum shields out and walked back to the bench. It looked for them like the game was over. Our mindset was that there was still a job to be done – not just for Maddie in goal or the girls who were taking the shuttles but for all of us who were going to be supporting them. We were all in a huddle just making eye contact and everyone was nodding, 'Yeah, come on, we've got this.'

We were so pumped and so focused.

I glanced over to the Dutch and thought, 'They've lost this.' You could see in their faces. We'd beaten them before on penalties. We'd been through this. We knew we had one hand over them; we knew we had Maddie in goal; we knew that every single one of the girls taking our shuttles had sat down and watched what their goalkeeper did. We were so prepared.

In football, penalties are considered a lottery; in hockey, less so. In fact, recent results had shown that they heavily favour the keeper. The night before, about ten of the girls had their name on the list and watched footage of the Dutch team. Maddie sat down with Kirsty, as our reserve goalie, and went through the Dutch girls and what their preferred move was, because ultimately, under pressure, people go to their strengths and habits. Number nine might go reverse stick, for example.

We had to assume that the Dutch keeper, Joyce Sombroek, had done the same with our girls, especially as she had saved four penalties in their semi-final against Germany.

I wasn't on the list of takers. I stood next to Unsy and Twiggy and watched the drama unfold.

Back home, the BBC *News at Ten* had been delayed so the millions who had tuned in could watch the conclusion.

Helen Richardson-Walsh was up first but Sombroek stood firm and blocked her effort. Maddie also made a save to keep the score 0–0. Another save from Sombroek denied Alex Danson, and then Ellen Hoog also missed her shuttle. Sophie Bray stepped forward but was brought down as she tried to take it round the goalie. Penalty stroke! Helen had nerves of steel to sweep it low into the corner. 1–0! She had broken the deadlock. Thank God she had been fit for the game!

Maddie made a great stop to deny Laurien Leurink, tracking her run and leaping to save. Unsy was up next. Her first shot was blocked and her rebound missed the target. It was almost too tense to watch. I wasn't aware of any noise from the crowd or noticing anyone in the stands, nothing.

The Dutch looked to have finally got on the score sheet with their fourth effort but Maddie just managed to get enough on the goalbound shot to deflect it onto the post. Was it going to be our night? None of the shuttles from the first eight attempts had been scored. Only Helen's flick was the difference.

When Hollie Webb stood up, I remember being at the back, asking, 'What's the score?' In all the drama I'd lost track. 'If we score, do we win?' I watched the ball so closely. I could make out the dimples on it. I didn't watch the goalkeeper, I didn't watch Hollie; I just focused on that florescent yellow ball.

We were all in a line; I was sandwiched between Unsy and Twiggy. I was willing the ball over the line. Hollie twisted and turned. The goalie committed and she saw a chance. When she hit it, there didn't seem to be any way it could squeeze in. But then, in an instant, it passed the goalie. As soon as I saw it get over the line and hit that backboard, I broke the line. I was off. Just running to Hollie. That was probably the fastest I've ever run in my entire life. I said nothing, just stared and sprinted towards Hollie thinking, 'Oh my God.'

Then comes all the emotion. 'We've done it. We've actually bloody done it.'

All sorts of tears – crying, screaming, disbelief.

We were in a huddle and I remember that I made eye contact with all of my teammates, just going, 'Oh my God!' It was our moment as a team. We were all there in that moment of time and we realised we had achieved something great together, but we just didn't know how to react to it. Every single emotion came out … and then once you've had that initial jumping on top of each other, screaming in each other's faces, that's when you kind of step back and you hug the coaches and look at the crowd. You see your mum, you see your dad, you see Tom dumbfounded. You get a fleeting sensation of what it all means. And it's just … surreal. It was absolutely nuts.

The crowd threw us Union Jacks and we were jumping all over the place. They were trying to get us off the pitch to get back into the changing room to put our outfits on for the medal ceremony but I don't think we really cared. The party had started.

Eventually we went to the changing room and it was strangely calm. I was next to Unsy, Georgie Twigg, Lily Owsley and a few other girls, putting our eyebrows on and a little bit of eyeliner along with a bit of blusher to de-sweat. I remember thinking, 'These photos are going to go viral.' I didn't want to look a sweaty mess, but it was unavoidable. We had to get changed into our podium wear, which was Team GB stipulated leggings and tracksuit top and trainers.

One of the delegates kept coming in shouting, 'Come on! Stop messing around with make-up. Come on, we're running out of time here for the telly!'

I was trying to process it all. 'This is the moment,' I thought. 'This is going to go down in history.' It was just disbelief. We were lined up, just underneath the stand. Everybody was there – the Germans, who had picked up the bronze, to our left and the Dutch to our right. I could see the Dutch girls crying, mortified, and the Germans were probably just as excited as we were that we'd beaten the Dutch because their rivalry is pretty hostile. They were all cheering and clapping us and giving us high-fives, which again was really nice.

We were all remarkably calm, just lined up getting ready to walk back into the stadium. Over the public address system we could hear them introducing the bronze medallists. Germany walked out. Then they announced the silver, on went Holland, and then it was the gold and we left the tunnel.

There was the podium all set up. I felt calm, trying to take everything in. I hadn't cried up until that moment. I felt quite composed. And then they brought the medals out on the trays. I could see the gold. And that's when I burst into tears because I could actually see a gold Olympic medal.

They presented Germany and the Netherlands with theirs. Then they went down the list in number order. I was standing next to Kate, with Alex Danson on my other side. For our captain Kate, it was twenty years of chasing a dream, almost retiring. She was just in tears and I wept them for her. I was so pleased for her. Once Kate received her medal, the announcer said, 'Number 13, Samantha Queek.'

They couldn't even get it right then, when you were getting a gold medal! But I didn't care.

They put it over my neck and there were more tears. I kissed the medal. I kept looking at it, mesmerised by its beauty. It was quite heavy, with Nike, the goddess of victory, and the words 'XXXI Olympiad'.

I turned around and looked to where Mum and Dad and Tom were. It was all just so surreal. 'Can you actually believe this?' I thought. 'We did it. It's been worth it, it's actually happened and all the crap we've had to do beforehand, the emotions, the sad times, the non-selections – and this has just happened. Oh my God, I've got an Olympic gold medal.'

And before I knew it, came the announcement: 'Please stand for the national anthem of Great Britain.'

Normally the anthem goes so quickly. But this was the slowest, most reflective, emotional anthem. I was blubbing all the way through but singing really loud, while also trying to breathe.

All the times I'd watched athletes on TV over the years and thought, 'That's a dream come true, to be stood there with an Olympic medal and your anthem blaring out.' It genuinely was the best feeling ever. I was crying the happiest of tears the whole time and embracing every second of it.

We did a lap of honour and shuttle runs, jumping the podium stand like hurdles. We held hands and went, 'Waaaaaay!' towards the crowd.

It seemed like no time but after everything was done we retreated back to the changing rooms. It was only then I checked my phone. I had loads of text messages and dozens of WhatsApps.

But one message jumped out. It was from my sister Maxine. 'Can you ring me?'

I immediately knew something was up.

She was back home and I rang her immediately. She was saying a lot of words including congratulations, but the only ones that hit home were about my nana. I couldn't believe it. I came crashing back into the real world.

She's had a stroke.

Chapter 20

Nana

I burst into tears and quickly ran out of the changing room. I couldn't believe what I was hearing but I knew I didn't want to bring anyone else down. They were all so happy and celebrating.

My nana means the world to me. When I was a teenager and argued with my parents, as adolescents often do, she would listen to my problems, never judge and always offer sound advice. Even when my time was at its most limited, I always made some to go to see her. She is an amazing woman, so nice, friendly, sharp as a tack, and she has seen it all. She was pushing one hundred, had lived through two world wars and raised eight children – one with Down's syndrome, and she remained her primary caregiver until she was ninety years old. She is one of the most inspirational women you could hope to meet and the head of our family. I love her so, so much.

Once I heard Maxine utter the word 'stroke' everything else just paled into insignificance. The rest of the conversation I couldn't recall. Later, when I spoke to Tom, he asked me what my sister had said and all I could remember was, 'She had a stroke.'

What Maxine had been telling me was that she was doing fine, but I still didn't really have a sense of how bad it had been. I just kept thinking, 'She's ninety-four.' And when you hear the word 'stroke' you just think, 'Bloody hell.'

I had already been crying. My emotions were all over the place. I had gone from this incredible high to suddenly worrying about my dear nan and whether she was going to be okay. It had been touch and go. The doctors had thought she wouldn't make it, but miraculously she regained her speech, got back on her Zimmer frame and being the ledge she is, even managed to make it to the local pub with around forty of my family and friends to watch the final. When I finally understood she was going to be okay I was so elated once more.

I went back into the dressing room where the party was still going off. I had a sudden thought of how I could mark these two momentous moments – winning gold and my nan battling back from a stroke to witness it happen. 'Sod it,' I thought, 'the social media ban doesn't apply now. We've won gold.'

I grabbed my phone and almost instinctively knew who I should dedicate the triumph to.

At 1.02 am I tweeted, 'Yes that's an OLYMPIC GOLD MEDAL!!!! Nana, that was for you, thank you for holding on xxxxx.'

I didn't really think much more of it, because we were still being swept along by the occasion, but later I would find out the full story of what had happened to her.

It was between our matches against Japan and Argentina that my nan, Doris Higgins – known as Dolly – suffered a major stroke and brain haemorrhage. Everyone thought there was a real danger she could die. The doctor said she would probably pass away if she didn't improve rapidly within twenty-four hours. Nana is my mum's mother and I have five uncles on that side, so they made a decision at first not to tell my mum because she was in Rio. They wanted to see how Nana's situation developed. When the specialists told them their worst fears, they decided that they had to tell my mum. A decision was then taken not to tell me. So behind the scenes, discussions were taking place about how best to handle it.

Before the Argentina game, which was tense anyway because of the rival factions with the fans, Mum told Tom. She was getting ready to fly back in the next twenty-four hours if Nana didn't improve. Conversations were had with the squad's performance operations manager Michaela Smith, who was going to be the liaison and the one in the camp to tell me what was happening should the situation develop. If I had got that news earlier I would have been an emotional wreck, so it was the right decision not to tell me.

I've been at a tournament and at training before when one of the girls' relatives was rushed to hospital. Someone comes down and tells them and whisks them away. At the end of the day, hockey is hockey. Yes, we treat it like it's the most important thing in the world, but family always comes first. I'd never thought such a situation might happen to me.

My nan had had such a tough year. My Auntie Barbara, my mum's older sister, had died – she was only in her sixties – and Nana was obviously distraught. For any parent to lose their child is a tragedy. That had taken its toll. Even before that she'd had a fall and broken her hip. She had been the main carer for my Auntie Ann, who has Down's syndrome, and when she fell some people in the hospital weren't rating her chances of making a recovery. We had to fight a bit to make sure she continued to get the best care. She might have been partially sighted and struggled to hear but mentally she was all there. It took her six months but she made a full recovery.

Naturally, I have been very, very close to my nan. She's an inspiration to me. She embodies the don't-roll-over, don't-die attitude – just keep fighting. Before I left for Rio I visited my nan and said bye to her. I took a selfie with her and she said, 'Go on, bring that gold medal back.'

She went to the Kylemore Club, a community social group run by Help Link in Pensby, and told everyone, 'My granddaughter's going to the Olympics.' Every time I used to win a medal, like from the Commonwealth Games, I took it into her club. Nana used to go in every week and update them with, 'Oh Samantha won this, and she's been doing that.' The people there used to be so made up to see the medals, but I used to find it surreal because I'd be speaking to people who had fought in the Second World War and had won medals of their own for bravery. It was an experience I would always enjoy.

So unbeknownst to me, while Nana was very poorly, all these discussions were going on. I think my mum was beside herself, unsure of what to do. Over that twenty-four-hour period, my sister Maxine and my uncles sat with Nana the whole time. My sister was convinced Nana could still hear her, even though she was out of it. Before the Argentina game Maxine put headphones on and let her listen to the commentary on BBC Radio 5 Live. Maxine said to her, 'Come on, you want to see Samantha win the gold medal. You need to pull through. You're strong, you can do it, come on Nana.'

We don't know whether she was awake during that commentary or out of it but somehow she decided, 'I've got to fight through.' To be honest, I think it was probably the latter but I believe she had a choice to make that day, and fortunately she decided to fight on.

She regained consciousness, then her speech returned and finally enough movement so she could get up and about. Incredibly, she was fit enough to see us win the gold medal. It was miraculous, really.

She's done that a few times. After her hip operation she told me she had a choice whether to pass over or not, but she's always been worried about other people. When she did her hip she was worried about my Auntie Ann with Down's. 'Who will look after Ann?' Even as she was about to go into the operation, that's what she was saying, 'Who's going to look after Ann?'

I think when she was listening to the game she was probably thinking – as selfish as this sounds, but my brother even said it to me – that she wanted to see me win a gold medal. I like to think that's what got her through in the end.

What Maxine was telling me after the final, about Nana, was that she was okay and that they had her out in the Devon Doorway pub in Heswall with the rest of the family to watch the final. But all I heard was 'Nana' and 'stroke'.

When I posted the tweet dedicated to Nana on Twitter I meant it literally – thanks Nana, for holding on. It was a small gesture to a woman who meant the world to me. That tweet was my first post that went out after the Olympic final. As I joined the girls to head out for our celebratory party, I thought nothing of it. Why would I? Who else would be interested in my family drama?

Chapter 21

History Makers

*Y*ou and me got a whole lot of history ...
          Tom and I had originally adopted it as our song, but when the girls put me in charge of the team's playlist before we flew out, I played them the One Direction song *History* and it instantly became the squad's anthem for the Olympics.

In the rooftop restaurant of the hotel close to the village, as we celebrated our incredible triumph that night with those closest to us, someone must have asked the DJ to play it.

There we were, all in a circle, screaming out the words like we were 8-year-old super-fans: *We could be the greatest team that the world has ever seen ...*

We hadn't even had that much to drink. We were just so excited to be talking to the family and friends we had only seen twice over the whole tournament. I think I carried around the same glass of champagne all evening.

We'd first seen our families not long after the medal ceremony formalities were over. There was a temporary fence by the side of the pitch, which after each game we always used to go to. After the final, we thought, 'Right, we'll just move it and go and say a quick "Hi".'

There were lots of hugs and it was the first time our families had seen the gold medals.

We then caught the bus back to the village. I'm usually the instigator of any chant or singing on the bus and I instinctively launched into *We Are The Champions* by Queen. Everybody just roared and joined in, and that was us for the duration of the journey back. We had bottles of full fat Coke, which obviously we hadn't touched during the tournament, but then it was like our equivalent of beer because we didn't have any alcohol. So the party began with Coca-Cola and Gatorade!

At the Team GB flat a few athletes were waiting around having watched the drama unfold and they were all buzzing for us. My memory is hazy from that night but I think it was the likes of Jessica Ennis, Adam Peaty, the Brownlee brothers, who were big fans of ours, and Jamie Murray. They were all congratulating us. I think some of them tried to make us go for food but no one was having it. We were all like, 'Sack that, we're going straight to the bar.'

We dumped our stuff, didn't even get changed and went downstairs to the basement to have a quick two-minute meeting. We were shown a quick video of how rough Rio could be if we ventured out. Basically they tried to scare us from leaving the village, but good luck trying to scare a group of girls who've just defied the odds to win gold medals.

We walked out of the village, just over the road to a hotel where the bar foyer was full of GB friends and family. As we walked in everyone cheered. It was fantastic. The hotel staff moved us up to a roof terrace, which they'd kept private just for the team, the coaches and only the closest friends and family. There had been a few GB fans milling around but they were really tight about who they let in. It was great to have that private space, with no media or onlookers.

It was all very unrehearsed but Danny Kerry and the coaches, and Kate, our captain, made some speeches about how proud they were. It was really lovely.

Danny was actually really sweet. He went round all of us but when he came up to me he said, 'Sam! That tackle! You were brilliant today, you were brilliant.'

It was a wonderful night, but there was a crazy energy because we were bouncing off the walls celebrating and at the same time frantically trying to catch up with people we'd only exchanged text messages with all week.

It was like a mad information dump. I was firing all these questions at Tom, like, 'What have you been up to? What was this like? What did you do after the Spain game? What sports did you see today? Who did you meet?' It was almost like prison visiting hour. You're trying to catch up as fast as possible.

We took endless photos and a had bit of a boogie, then our sing-a-long to One Direction, Queen and the likes of Tina Turner's *Simply The Best* and S Club 7's *Reach* got a rendition.

The hotel staff started to get worried for the other guests because of the noise. We moved downstairs and at first they told the bar staff not to serve us, but then the manager said we could have some beer that they had over-ordered. None of us had ever heard of that type of beer, but no one seemed to care and everyone drank it anyway. After a while, we got taxis to take us to a club. We were all in separate cabs and when we turned up at the club they'd stopped letting people in. We didn't want to get the gold medals out and they didn't understand we had been competing. We tried two or three more clubs and got into one place but by then everyone was starting to disperse, and it was so busy and big that I decided to get into a taxi with Tom and his best mate Greg, whom he had flown out to keep him company. I had the urge for a McDonald's. I hadn't had one in ages and I do like a chicken nugget. So we went to a McDonald's drive-through. I got a cheeseburger, nuggets, a Diet Coke and some chips.

I stayed at Tom's apartment and just sat up chatting with him and Greg. It was around 5.00 am that I started to come down and think about sleep. I would only have a few hours' rest as I had to be up for media duties.

When I did wake up about five hours later, my first thought was, 'Wow, I am an Olympic gold medallist.' It felt surreal. I'd left the medal on the side table next to the bed and just stared at it, thinking, 'This is crazy.'

It was a forty-minute walk to the village from Tom's, but Kirsty, being the reserve keeper, was also based outside the village, so I picked her up and we walked back to the village together.

Some of the girls had media interviews from as early as 6.00 am for the breakfast news so they mustn't have had any sleep. By the time I got back I only had time to wash my face, brush my teeth, spray on some deodorant and change my underwear. We were required to still be in our podium wear so I had to remain in my tracksuit. We went to the public area of the village where those with accreditation could meet us. I did some interviews with my local papers, the *Wirral Globe* and the *Liverpool Echo*, as well as a handful of national media.

We hadn't appreciated just how our success had captured the nation's imagination back home. We knew the news had been delayed so millions would have been tuning in, but the dramatic nature of the victory made it compelling viewing. We didn't know that celebrities and fellow sportsmen and women were tweeting about it and commentators were predicting an upsurge in the interest in hockey. It was only later that we got a sense that we might have done wonders for our sport and added to the huge feel-good factor generated by the Games.

After the buzz of doing interviews, we had a precious moment to ourselves as the team and coaches met for a match debrief. There was no video this time; we just sat together and talked through the key elements of the game. It was actually a special thing to do because everyone in that room knew what we had been through.

That period of reflection was important because after that it was on to British House – Team GB's headquarters at Parque Lage, in the shadow of the Christ the Redeemer statue – and which was basically party central, with food and drink all provided for us. We did some more interviews, this time for sponsors, although Reggie Yates came in to film a fun chat with all of us. He was asking us all light-hearted questions, like 'Who's got the best dance moves?' The girls pointed to me and I leant over and did my signature high kick move. That was our last official engagement – we were then free to party!

We couldn't have hoped for a better location. British House was a stunning, ornate mansion with a massive dance floor in the middle of an open square flanked on three sides by columns, with views up to the statue on the hill.

Our friends and family started to arrive and as other athletes finished their events they also began to filter in. The rowing team was there, table tennis players, all the swimmers, the Brownlees, while a large screen showed the rest of the sporting action. A DJ then came on and ramped up the music and the dance floor lit up.

I tried a caipirinha, the Brazilian cocktail made from cachaça, a type of rum, but it was like rocket fuel. I switched to cider instead. It started to rain and although the weather failed to dampen anyone's spirits, they had to put a barrier around the dance floor because it was becoming a slip hazard. Undeterred, I ran on with some of the other girls and when the rather stressed-out bouncers tried to stop us I kicked off a conga. People were joining in whether they were athletes or not. Eventually the bouncers relented and they just let us on the dance floor. It quickly became carnage in terms of people getting drunk and slipping over.

At one point we heard an almighty 'dunk'. We had each been wearing our medals all night and we knew what had happened instantly. Georgie Twigg's had fallen off the ribbon. We were all saying, 'Oh my God.' The medal was dented but fortunately she was told any faulty medals could be replaced.

A bus was meant to take us back at a certain time but the majority of people missed it because they were having such a good time. I was one of a few people who got taxis into town to head to a nightclub but, as the night before, once it got to 4.00 am, I was ready to call it a night. Naturally, we couldn't get a cab and when we finally did it dropped us off a distance from Tom's flat because the streets had been cordoned off. Then Tom realised he'd left his wallet and keys in the taxi so we had to find an emergency locksmith, which in the middle of Rio at 5.00 am when you don't speak Portuguese isn't the easiest task in the world. It was daylight by the time the locksmith arrived. He got us inside in seconds but Tom had to cancel all his bank cards.

By the time we'd sorted all of that there wasn't any point me going to bed because I had a team meeting at 10.00 am back in the village. We were going to be leaving the following day, so we had to go through the logistics – what we'd need to pack, what we'd be wearing, what presentations we'd have for players who'd reached significant milestones, that kind of thing.

When I walked out with Tom on the way back to the village I spotted someone walking with one of the Rio Olympic torches. I hadn't seen one close up, let alone touched one, so I approached him and asked if I could get a picture. He said 'No!' quite assertively. No doubt he had been asked by every passerby if they could hold it and have a picture. Tom said, 'Get your medal out.' As soon as he caught sight of the gold he suddenly changed his tune. We did a trade-off with the photos.

Back in the village I returned to my room, effectively for the first time in two days. It was in a state. I had about half an hour so decided to lie down for a bit. I moved my pillow and there was a cheeseburger that had been lying there from the previous day. 'Sack it off,' I thought, 'I don't care. I want this cheeseburger. I'm eating it.' So I did.

That night was the closing ceremony. Kate was going to be flag bearer, which was not only an amazing honour for her on a personal level but for hockey it was great to get that recognition. It was still raining but people were still on a high and we could finally wear our cool flashing shoes that were part of our official kit, which we hadn't worn before because we had skipped the opening ceremony.

Hundreds of buses had been lined up to ferry the athletes to the stadium. There was a ring road around the village and they were nose to tail all the way around.

Once we arrived at the Maracanã stadium we were handed ponchos, bottles of water, and a little bag containing sandwiches and goodies in case we got hungry. We must have stood for about an hour and a half before they even started to usher us in. Then we had to wait again. The rain was on and off, although just as we walked out into the stadium it came on again. We had our ponchos, so we were all cheering and waving. The lights were so bright, though, it was hard to see the crowd.

I said to Unsy, 'Let's try and get a camera to wave at everyone at home.' I think we got on it once with Alex Danson. However, we all went and found Kate and got a photo with her and the flag. They provided us with little white plastic fold-up seats, but by the time we could sit down they were soaking wet and it had turned quite cold. Half the team left before the ceremony had even finished. I think there was only about six of us there at the end, and when it actually finished people immediately ran out and I was left with Shona and Nic White. It finished with the Rio carnival dancers and by this point they were up for anything. So when we went to dance with them they let us try their outfits on. At one point I had the full carnival gear on, next to a big float. We were just messing around, so happy.

We had such a laugh, trying things on and bumping into athletes from around the world. It actually worked out quite well because by the time we left there wasn't a queue for the buses. It was past midnight by the time we got back to the village and we were starving. We headed straight to the canteen to get some pizza.

Back at the Team GB high-rise, tables were set up with booze everywhere – cans of beer, bottles of wine, cider, everything. All the athletes were basically congregated around underneath, playing table tennis and chatting. A few were kissing each other. I saw Jade Jones, the taekwondo athlete, dancing on the ping pong table and her teammate Bianca Walkden catching her as she fell off. A lot of the athletes were drunk but for the most part it was just a great atmosphere. People were playing 'killer' on the table tennis table, where you have to bat it and run around. The table was actually looking the worse for wear after the amount of drink on it and the number of people that had fallen onto it. Most of the hockey girls had gone to their rooms but I stayed down speaking to people because it was the only time we'd really had to speak to the other athletes and it was a one-off occasion – our last night in Rio.

The party was still going strong when I called it a night at around 4.00 am to go to my room and pack the rest of my stuff.

I took a lot more stuff than I arrived with. I even managed to get my bed quilt into my suitcase, along with limited edition 'athlete's village' Coke bottles. I wanted every souvenir I could get my hands on.

There were other things left, though. With poverty rife in Rio, we were asked to leave any unwanted items of clothing or toiletries in a box outside our rooms. We left whatever we could – perfumes, some leftover Team GB kit, toothpaste, moisturizers – for the cleaners because they were so desperate for it. They were so grateful. It was a nice touch of Team GB to think of doing that.

When it was time to vacate the room, it was chaos trying to get all the bags down in the lift. We were on the seventh floor and I remember putting my bags in and then walking down to get them at the bottom. That was definitely when the comedown started to kick in. I was sweaty, hung-over, tired, hungry and thirsty. I realised just how exhausted I was and I began to well up.

Before we left for the airport, we held one final meeting, a last goodbye. Danny said to us all, 'Just take a moment to sit down and enjoy this particular meeting because it'll be the last time, I guarantee you, that every single athlete and every single member of staff will be in the same room together. Every person who achieved this gold medal is here now. This will never happen again, and this is a really special moment and I just want to thank you all for everything. Obviously we've got the team back at home, the doctors, the players, the staff, but to be here in Rio, everything that you've done, you've delivered, you couldn't have done it better and it's the gold standard and you've got us a gold medal.'

After those words, there were lots of tears because there were players who knew they were retiring. There were coaches who knew they were moving on. So, Danny was right, it was a really special moment.

And that was it. We boarded the bus and headed to the airport.

British Airways offered us first class seats for the journey home but only for sixteen of us. We flew out with nineteen players, which included Kirsty and the other two reserves who were outfield players.

I felt so much for the three girls who didn't have medals as I knew what that felt like from when the team won bronze in 2012 without me. I particularly felt for Kirsty, not just as my closest friend, but because she was an extraordinary goalkeeper. Maddie was arguably the best goalkeeper in the world at the time, but Kirsty was also generally rated in the top three in the world. She has won Women's Player of the Year for her heroics in the Premier League, which is no mean feat for a goalkeeper when rated against outfielders. She will without doubt go down as one of, if not *the* best goalkeeper never to play at an Olympic Games. How unfortunate for her that she and Maddie were not just the same nationality, but born in the same generation. She handled her role as a reserve with great dignity, as did the other reserves, Ellie Watton and Joie Leigh.

When we got back to England, Tom read a newspaper article about young athletes to watch out for in Tokyo 2020, which highlighted Joie Leigh. He cut it out for me to send it to her. I wanted Joie to know that her time would come and to also let her know that I knew what she had gone through watching us in Rio. Of the three reserves, I was most worried how Joie was holding up as she was quite quiet during the tournament. I think she was dealing with missing out on selection similar to how I did back in 2012 and I didn't want her feeling alone. Ellie was often inconsolable, especially after we won the gold medal. I remember her shedding a lot of tears. That outpouring of emotion will have helped her and it also told others in the squad that she was hurting, so they put an arm around her. As for Kirsty, as one of my best friends, I knew she was a strong character who had made her peace with the situation long before the selection email dropped.

At the check-in desk back in Brazil, we turned around to the airline staff and said, 'You need to give us nineteen seats.'

'No,' they said, 'we've only got sixteen.'

'Fine then,' we said. 'We're sitting together.'

So instead they put all nineteen of us in premium economy. There was no way we could have gone into first class without the other three. It was bad enough that we had medals and they didn't. Some other athletes were able to take advantage of first class: Adam Peaty, the Brownlee brothers, the double gold-winning gymnast Max Whitlock and some of the rowers.

We were among the last to get on board. The plane – named *VictoRIOus* in our honour – was quite quiet, with just a little bit of a buzz. We got on and were handed a glass of champagne. Then, just before takeoff, they put on the national anthem. Everyone else just sat there but the hockey girls all stood up and started singing. Asha Philip, the sprinter, filmed it and the video went viral.

Not long after we took off, they came round with more drink. Not many people were drinking, though. I slid over to where Kate and Helen were sitting.

'Girls, why aren't you drinking?' I said.

They shrugged.

'What do you want?' I said.

They both said wine. So I ran to the back where the galley was just behind us, and said to the flight attendants, 'Is there any chance I can have that?'

'Yeah,' they said.

I ran back and gave them the drinks. Then Twiggy, who was next to Unsy, said: 'What about me?'

'Right, okay. What do you want?'

'A G&T.'

I ran back, got her a gin.

Then the flight girls started joking. 'Why don't you just take the trolley down?'

Unsy was with me. More of the team were now firing their orders at us.

We went back to the British Airways girls and swapped uniforms with them. We both put the scarves on, the little waistcoats and put our hair into a bun. Then we took the trolley down and started serving drinks to all our teammates. It was such a laugh.

With that, Adam Peaty and the Brownlee brothers possibly realised that the party was going on behind them. They came down, and then the gymnasts appeared. I think we delayed dinner by two hours because we were serving so many drinks.

Eventually I nodded off. When I woke someone had a paper – I think it was *The Times*. Kate was on the front with the flag. It was then I thought, 'This is a big deal back home.'

Shortly before we were due to land they made an announcement saying we would be disembarking in a particular order. I think the boxer Nicola Adams was going first. Then they wanted the hockey girls up front, lined up.

I was so excited to be back in Britain, just to see what people's reaction was going to be and to continue the celebrations.

We landed and instead of going to a regular gate we had our own private one, in the middle of the tarmac. We rocked up and I didn't see anything at first, but as we turned into this sectioned-off area I looked out and saw a wall of hundreds of photographers. Dozens of British Airways crew were also lined up to acknowledge us all.

I stepped out, felt a gust of wind on my face and just thought, 'I'm home.'

I couldn't stop smiling but, seeing all those cameras, I kept saying to myself, 'Don't fall, Sam.'

The BA staff clapped us down the stairs and escorted us into the airport building. We were then coming past normal passengers. Everyone just stopped. Normally Heathrow Airport is manic with people running for their flights. It's chaos.

But everything stopped for us. It was like the sea parted. People just stood still down the side, taking pictures of us, clapping us. We heard a few people recognise us, not perhaps as individuals, but as the team: 'Here are the hockey girls.' It's a moment I'll always remember – people cheering, applauding. We knew we'd done something special.

Normally when we come back from a tournament no one knows if we've won a medal, let alone who we are or even what sport we play. So for people to actually recognise us, we thought, 'Wow, this is awesome.'

If that moment was sublime, our coming home experience quickly became ridiculous. We went down to get our luggage and the whole team's luggage was coming through on one belt. There were about 600 Team GB bags – all identical, with only the nametags to tell them apart. And each athlete had three bags, all red.

It took about two hours to find your bag because they were all coming off randomly. You had to look at each label. Eventually we sorted it by shouting, 'Right, any hockey labels, drag them over here.' We created a mini pile of bags, which made it slightly easier to sift through. It was still carnage.

For all the chaos in the baggage hall, it was nothing compared to what awaited us once we came through Arrivals.

I've never seen anything like it. We couldn't even see where we had to walk through because the press were grabbing everyone. Someone got hold of me: 'Sam, how does it feel? Did you expect this response?'

I gave a quick interview but amid the chaos only one thing was on my mind. Now I was back in the United Kingdom, I just wanted to go home and see my nan.

Chapter 22

An Outsider in Demand

In the cold light of day, when I thought about the tweet I'd posted after receiving the gold medal, it occurred to me that maybe I should have praised the hard work of the team or made reference to everything we'd been through – but I'd just instinctively thought of my nan.

Over the next few hours and days I'd started to amass followers on Twitter – 10,000 … 15,000 … 20,000. I was thinking, 'What's going on here?'

Some of the news media had picked up on the tweet and once the story came out it just went viral.

The BBC's *The One Show* wanted the whole hockey team to go on that night.

'I'm not going on *The One Show*,' I said, when the team's media officers told me about it. 'I'm going to go see my nan; she's not well.'

There was a bit of pressure put on me to do it, but I was determined. I wasn't staying in London; it just wasn't going to happen, come hell or high water. I was going to get the first available flight to Manchester and go straight to hospital to see Nana.

The rest of the girls went straight to a media party in a hotel next to Heathrow. I broke away from the group and snuck back up the escalators to Departures and said to the woman at the British Airways desk, 'Can you get me on a Manchester flight please?'

The staff acted strangely when I got to the desk. They were excited to see me. They knew the story of the Olympics. One of them, a Scottish lady, was lovely. 'Of course,' she said. 'I'll get you on the next flight out.'

I didn't have to pay, which I could scarcely believe, but was very thankful for. I walked through Departures with my medal still around my neck, full kit on. When I landed in Manchester all was quiet until I cleared the gate and exited Arrivals.

A bank of photographers were waiting for some other athletes. Tom was there to meet me and as we came out of the airport they saw the kit and someone shouted – 'There's that hockey girl!'

I wasn't expecting to be bombarded. I felt a bit sorry for whomever they were originally intending to see, but it wasn't for me as no one knew I was coming up. I gave a quick few words to the reporters as the photographers snapped away and Tom took the cases to the car.

On the way to Clatterbridge Hospital on the Wirral we stopped so I could buy some flowers for Nana. She can only see block colours so I got some in red, white and blue for obvious reasons. We arrived at the hospital and there was an ITV van with a huge satellite dish on it outside.

'I wonder what they're here for,' I said.

'Are you serious?' Tom said.

Then it hit me. Oh God!

My mum was already at the hospital. The nurses were aware the TV crew was there. A producer met me and was trying to tell me what he wanted me to do and where he wanted me to stand. I think I was a little rude to him. 'I'm sorry, but I really don't care, I am just going to see my nan and I am going in now.' As I walked off down the corridor, he ran after me and asked if he could at least put a microphone pack on me. 'Fine. Just please do it now because I really am not waiting any longer.'

I didn't have a clue they were going to be there. In fact I was a little annoyed, but I didn't have the energy to protest. I was getting quite impatient and upset at the prospect of seeing Nana in a hospital bed. We later found out that a journalist in Heathrow had been tipped off as to why I wasn't with the team.

'Where is she?'

The nurses pointed me to a ward on my left as I went down a corridor.

When I first saw her I got very emotional. It was so lovely to see her but I just thought about what she'd been through and how touch and go it had been and the tears welled up. All the fear I'd felt when I'd first heard about her stroke came flooding back. She was sitting up and when I asked her how she felt she said, 'Better for seeing you.'

We hugged and I showed her the medal and let her touch it. I told her she deserved one herself for what she had been through these last few weeks. I put it around her neck but warned her it was heavy. I told her we'd all had sore necks the morning after wearing them for the first night.

ITV filmed us talking for the first couple of minutes and we posed for some photos together. They then left us to be on our own. Nana looked a lot worse than she did before I had left for Brazil, but a lot better than I had feared, which was a relief. She was slurring her words and was a lot slower than my nana usually was, but she was still there.

When we got home I freshened up because I stank a bit from the flight. We then went to the Devon Doorway, where my sister Maxine had organised a surprise party for me with all the family there.

The strange thing was that while the girls were on *The One Show* that night, the national ITV news had my visit to my nan as one of their headline stories. Hockey was getting great exposure, just as we had hoped.

The media interest just snowballed after that. *Good Morning Britain* asked if I would go on. Previously, whenever a TV programme requested interviews with members of the hockey squad, England Hockey invariably put up the same three or four faces. Now, TV companies were asking, 'Can we have Sam Quek?'

They just wanted to talk about my nan.

I was caught up on a wave of interest in the story but it was the start of being seen as an individual rather than solely as part of the team. I didn't appreciate that it might lead to some of the squad wondering why I was being interviewed on my own – but that was the reason why and it was in no way planned.

It all stemmed from that one knee-jerk tweet when I was in a highly emotional state. One producer said they liked how I wore my heart on my sleeve. 'Don't change,' she said. 'Don't be one of these media trained, just say the right thing types.'

I wasn't like I was saying anything controversial. I didn't try to be anything other than my natural self. If someone said, 'What was it like?' I'd say, 'You know what, it was amazing, I cried every single minute I was on the podium. All the times in the past when I had been upset and was missing your best mate's birthday, your nan's birthday, your nephew's christening, it's all been worth it for this moment.'

Good Morning Britain wanted me to come on and talk about my nan's story and my Olympic experience. England Hockey would have preferred two or three of us on together, but they were insistent. They were so taken with my nan's story.

Slowly but surely I started doing more things. I went on the Channel Five breakfast show with Sophie Bray and they asked me to do a mini hockey class for Gaby Roslin. People started contacting me directly, so Tom and I set up an email address to handle commercial requests. Soon, the inbox became inundated with requests from the likes of *Hello!* magazine and *A Question of Sport*. It was quite exciting.

About a week after we came back from Rio, Team GB held a media day in London. It was the first time I'd get to see all the girls since we'd come back and chat about what we'd been up to, because it had been a crazy time. I was really excited to see them. I got the train down and then got a car across to where we were meeting. When I arrived everyone was getting their hair and make-up done and stylists brought out dresses for us to wear. The theme was *The Great Gatsby*, so it was all 1920s long dresses and sequins. The majority of the dresses were neutral colours but as I was one of the last people to get into wardrobe, the stylist had already selected mine – a red sparkly dress.

We all got changed and only then did I appreciate I was the only one in a red dress. Everyone said, 'You can't wear that.' I tried to explain that I hadn't realised, but they went on, 'Everybody else is in black, you can't wear red.'

'Sorry,' I said, 'if you really want me to change it, I'll change it.'

I went looking for other dresses but I figured, 'I shouldn't be made to feel bad here because I've been given this dress.'

Just then, Alex Danson arrived and she was also handed a red dress.

'Al,' I said, 'will you wear the red dress with me so I'm not the only one in red?'

I ended up staying in my red dress but by then I felt bad, like I'd messed up in some way.

I started to feel there was something bubbling under the surface. It was a strange atmosphere anyway, because everyone was buried in their phones doing different things, which was understandable, but when I wanted to chat to people, I wasn't getting much back. It seemed quite far removed from how it was before and during the Olympics, when we were all so together as a unit.

Usually when we met up it was a raucous wall of noise with everybody catching up, explaining what they'd been up to and everyone taking the Mick out of each other. This felt different. Everyone was polite enough but it all felt a little stilted.

I rang Tom quite upset and he said he would play devil's advocate. 'Imagine it from their naïve point of view. You land at Heathrow and you go to see your nan instead of going on *The One Show* with all of them. That's all perfectly fine; no doubt they understood that. But then all of a sudden you end up on ITV News on your own as a lead story, and they are a smallish segment of *The One Show*. Then, because you are now one of the most recognisable within the squad, the newest breakfast show in Britain wants you and you alone, whereas everyone else was going on smaller shows in groups. Then when you meet up, the stylist puts you in a bright colour and them in regular ones. Add in the fact that you are 1/16th of the team, yet seem to be getting the majority of the media requests – now can you see why they may be upset?'

'You know as well as I do it's not like that,' I said sharply. 'You make it sound like this was all planned out, as though in the moment after we won gold I thought, "I know what, I'll tweet about my nan and this may take off and set me apart!"'

'I know that's not how it's gone, and you know that's not how it's gone, but they don't. If it was the other way round, we would be suspicious and a bit jealous too,' he said.

'No, you may be suspicious, but I know my teammates and they should know me better than that! They've known me long enough.' I was now both upset and angry at the team.

Two days later, I was filming for *A Question of Sport*. It was an Olympic special, with the theme being 'Gold Rush – hockey verses cycling'. Jason Kenny and Laura Trott, as she was then before they married, were up against Maddie Hinch and me. We were filming in Manchester and I was beyond excited. I've always thought, as a sportsperson, if you're on *A Question of Sport* you've made it. I never thought I'd get the chance to be on it because even if they chose a hockey player I assumed it would be the captain or Hollie as the winning penalty scorer, or maybe Maddie as the heroic, penalty saving goalkeeper.

Besides being grateful for having been chosen, I'm a quiz geek anyway, so I was completely buzzing. Alex Danson had been on a few months before Rio and I remember watching her and she did very well. It was great to see a hockey player on such a well-established show, and she represented the team and the sport really well. Now there was another chance with Maddie and me. Tom came with me because he was equally excited to see how it was filmed. We were ushered through into a green room, where there were two sofas facing each other on the left and a mini putting green where Jason Kenny was hitting balls. Maddie was leaning on one of the sofas talking to someone. It was a very small room and I walked up to Maddie and said, 'Hi!'

Nothing. She didn't even look at me.

I looked at Tom and then at the woman she was talking to. She even looked at me as if to say, 'Why hasn't she answered you?'

As it was such a small room, everyone stopped and said, 'Oh, hi.'

I tried again. 'Hi, Maddie!'

Again, nothing.

I was mortified and so embarrassed. She must have heard me, and now people were picking up on the awkwardness.

I stood in front of her. 'Hi, Maddie!'

Finally she said, 'Oh, hi.'

I'm sure everyone else was thinking, 'That's a bit strange; aren't they teammates?'

As I went to get my hair done, I sat in the chair and wondered what the hell had just happened.

On screen, however, she was fine, high-fiving me and stuff like that. In the end we did okay as a team, with Phil Tufnell as our captain. We were pipped by just one point.

I hadn't expected Maddie to blank me so obviously in public. Our relationship had broken down some time ago and I honestly don't know the reason why. She just stopped talking to me all of a sudden. It was just after the 2014 Commonwealth Games when it started. Even during the Olympics, other than when competing on the pitch or when we won the gold, she never said a word to me. She's unfollowed me on Twitter and on Instagram, despite me continuing to follow her.

I have a shirt in my house that is framed and signed by the team. It is my match-worn one from the 2015 European final. I recently discovered the whole the squad have signed it for me, except one – Maddie.

Regardless of what TV show I went on to try to keep hockey in the public's consciousness, there would be no public or private message of support from her, no matter how big they were, or where in the world they were filmed. Bearing in mind I had lived with Maddie for a number of years and travelled the globe with her, I knew the shows she watched and spoke about on her social media, but it was almost like me being on them upset her so much that she wouldn't even mention them or me at all. We used to be so close. I genuinely have no idea what happened, but I hope one day we can be friends again. It seems so ridiculous that we shared so much of our lives together, achieved so much, and now it is like this.

The TV requests kept coming. I appeared with Unsy and Twiggy on *Soccer AM*, Sky Sports' football-based morning show. I was comfortable there because, being a Liverpool fan, I can talk about football all day long. We took part in the Top Bin challenge, which for us was to see if we could shoot a hockey ball into the bin in the top corner of the net. Unsy managed it with her first shot. The pressure was on then. I managed to bag one, too. Get in! The whole day was awesome. It was vintage GB girls having fun together. Unsy was always one of my closest friends in the squad and I rated her as one of the world's best players. Twiggy has always been lovely – just a really pleasant girl. Every time we see each other, whether at an event or when our club teams face each other, we always make time for a catch-up.

Twiggy later appeared with me in the *Hello!* spread, as did Maddie. We didn't get the full celebrity treatment. They just used stock images rather than a photo shoot but it was mad to be in *Hello!*

Tom and I were clueless to how this all worked because we were doing everything for free. It was only afterwards someone said we should be getting paid for articles like that.

It sounded as though I might benefit from having an agent. Tom contacted some on my behalf as I was too embarrassed to suggest that I might need an agent to someone on the other end of the phone. We had one person say, 'Sorry, we're too busy. We look after the likes of Ant and Dec, Holly Willoughby. You're probably not right for our books at the moment but we can recommend X, Y and Z.'

One name came up a few times – Luke Sutton of Activate Management – and a few people were speaking highly of him. He sounded like a good guy, as did some of the others. We went down to London and met a few of them.

One agent spoke to Tom the whole time and didn't really address me. Tom had been the point of contact but I was thinking, 'Hi, I'm just here.' As we sat over a table he was saying, 'We can do this, we can get that sponsorship. I look after golfers, they're sponsored by Rolex. We'll get Rolex for you.' He finished by saying, 'I've got a really good lingerie company lined up for you.'

That's when I thought, 'You haven't got a clue.' He just wanted to milk the cow for everything it was worth.

He believed he could make me a million in a few years and was so confident he said, 'I will pay you the first instalment, £250,000, upon signing, but you won't get anything more until I make back my fees and then we'll pay you in instalments after that.'

I think the underwear shoot alone would have been worth between £25,000 and £50,000 and might have been for a leading lingerie retailer because not long after, they launched a line with another sports girl. It was all about looks and nothing to do with talent. 'You are very aesthetically pleasing,' he said.

What we wanted was someone who might be able to help build me a career. The life of a sportsman or woman is not long in their chosen field and it would be nice to lay the foundations for some sort of life beyond my playing days.

When we met Luke he was the opposite of the 'do as much as you can now' approach. His philosophy was not to get sucked into signing up for the first deals that came my way. He said if I could afford financially to wait, it would be better for me in the long run. He talked a lot more calmly and sensibly. He cited as examples David Beckham and Steven Gerrard as two footballers who had different career paths. Both had achieved major honours but while Steven Gerrard remained in football, David Beckham transcended football and even sport in general. He was quick to stress that he wasn't saying I'd be the next David Beckham but he said, handled correctly, it might be possible to build a long-term career that wasn't solely focused on hockey, because that market simply wasn't big enough on its own.

I did hope that new opportunities would come out of our Olympic endeavours. It wasn't about making a fast buck or cashing in on our success. Since my relationship with Tom began, I'd moved out of the house with the girls in Marlow and moved in with him. He'd funded everything and now I wanted to stand on my own two feet and pay my own way. The money available through hockey, while moving in the right direction, was still very modest.

Since coming home I'd made the decision to take a break from hockey for six months. It had been a punishing cycle leading up to Rio and I felt like I'd lived my life in hotels and apartments for tours. I'd had ten years of pushing myself to achieve my ultimate ambition and I wanted to use this time to take stock. Plus, I owed it to Tom to devote some time to our relationship.

Tom had been helping me expand my knowledge across more sports besides hockey and football. He was really into American football and I got into it, too. I would always drive up to see him after club training in Kent on a Thursday night. I would arrive home in the early hours, where he had a bath run and a meal waiting for me. We would then sit down and eat while watching American football, because due to the time difference with the US, the games would begin at 1.00 am. I was hooked immediately and despite being knackered from training and the four-and-a-half-hour drive, I usually made it through to the end of the games. I wanted to see a game live, so we went to see the Kansas City Chiefs beat the Detroit Lions at Wembley. I knew enough about the game at that point that I was invited by the NFL to be a guest at one of their fans forums. I caught them off guard and they were really impressed at how much I knew. I wasn't just a casual fan now, I was pretty knowledgeable. In the end, this extra sporting knowledge proved to be a big help when we started having discussions about sports presenting. We were just waiting for the right sort of opportunity to come along.

I didn't have long to wait. Incredibly, Luke had managed to arrange an interview for me with the producers of *I'm A Celebrity*. I couldn't believe it. It wasn't sports based, although I was a huge fan of the show, but never in my wildest dreams imagined one day going on it. One problem though, the clue was in the name – you had to be a celebrity, and I certainly didn't think I was one. After the initial surprise had passed I obviously leapt at the chance to be interviewed.

The meeting was going to be at the ITV studios on the Southbank, in London. Travelling down the night before, I thought, 'What am I going to say if they ask me this and that?'

Luke was fairly new as my agent at this point. I met him for a coffee just outside the ITV studios. He was easy to get on with and was helping to reassure me, but at the same time I found the fact that I was sitting talking to an agent about a possible appearance on a reality TV show very surreal. 'Just be yourself,' Luke said. 'Don't try to be anything you're not because they'll see straight through it.' I couldn't be any other way.

We entered the ITV studios, checked in, and a runner took us up to a floor filled with desks, with people busy on laptops, on the phone, all sorts. We walked around the corner into a little goldfish office. I don't know what I was expecting, but it was tiny, not remotely glamorous, with just a wooden table with chrome legs and standard wooden IKEA-style chairs.

Meeting us were Daisy and Micky, who Luke told me were bookers for the series, but the reality was they were senior producers who run some of ITV's big shows. It was probably good that I didn't know that beforehand. We talked for nearly three hours about me, my Olympic experience, how I'd be in the jungle, what I'd do if there was a certain character in the camp.

They asked how I got into hockey. I told them about Mrs Concannon and I did a little impersonation of her Scottish accent.

Once they'd learned a bit about my background they went on to ask about the jungle. 'If you were to get into the jungle, how would you react if you were with someone like Helen Flanagan?' The *Coronation Street* actress had famously refused to take part in the gruelling bushtucker trials when she appeared in 2012.

'I haven't got a problem if people couldn't do the trial,' I said. 'What I'd have a problem with are people who wouldn't even try.'

Then they said, 'Well, what if she decided not to do it and she kept refusing?'

I said, 'To be honest, me being me, I'd probably let it go, but I'd probably then try and be encouraging towards her, like, "Have you tried this? Maybe zone out? Try a different technique?" After that though, to be honest, I would probably get a little bit arsy because people start getting hungry.'

'What would you do if there was someone who was so overbearing and wouldn't lift a finger?'

'I'm very straight,' I said. 'I don't like conflict but if there was any I'd tell it as it was and try to put out the flame before it gets too big.'

I thought the meeting went well but at that stage I was not expecting to get in.

Over the next couple of weeks, when Luke got in touch to ask if they knew what was happening, it went from, 'We don't know yet' to 'Yeah, there could be a good chance'. Then I started getting quite excited. However, a week later, it would change to, 'Oh, we don't know'.

It transpired that they devise a number of line-ups depending on who commits. I fell into two campmate categories: likely 'athlete' and, perhaps, 'young female'. They were speaking to several other athletes from the Games and a lot would depend on who else signed up. I was never under any illusions. I knew if someone like Jessica Ennis agreed to do it I'd be overlooked because, firstly, she was a proper celebrity and, secondly, they wouldn't want two female athletes of similar age in the same group. Obviously they have to pick people from different backgrounds and ages to get a nice mix of personalities.

Then it looked like they were cooling altogether. The feedback was that I wasn't quite fitting and they weren't quite sure.

The makers of *The Jump* – the Channel 4 series where people learn to ski jump – also invited me to meet with a view to joining its next series. I thought that would also be quite fun to do but I wasn't sure whether to accept because we still hadn't heard from ITV. When I met with its producers, they were much more positive and their language was, 'When you're on the show we think you'd be great … you're an athlete, you'll be strong, you'll be competitive,' and they were talking to me as if I was going to go on the show.

I started to think, 'Okay, wow.'

The fee they were offering was something I just wasn't used to. It was around four times my annual hockey salary. I was really tempted but we wanted to hear a definitive answer from ITV before deciding.

In the meantime, I was invited to the *TV Choice* Awards in September and Luke arranged it so I'd be presenting one of the awards. It was our first experience of a red carpet. I was so nervous. I went to town and splashed out on a stylist, because I didn't have anything to wear to such an event. Among the outfits she suggested was a black rubber mini corset with feathers around the bottom.

'You'll really stand out,' she said.

'Maybe – but for all the wrong reasons,' I said. It was awful, plus I didn't want to stand out as such, I just wanted to look nice.

Luckily she also had a more demure, floaty peach number that was more me. Although the awards are not televised they are a big deal in the industry and the great and the good from the TV world turn out in force.

I'm sure the vast majority of people there didn't have a clue who I was but I took along my medal and that was a massive ice-breaker. A lot of people were buzzing even to see what a gold medal looked like.

I was presenting the award for Best Lifestyle Programme. I didn't know who the winner was beforehand but I hoped it was *Gogglebox* because I had prepared a little quip. When it was my turn to take to the stage, I was so nervous. It's worse than playing at the Olympics. Luckily the winner was the one I'd hoped, so I said: 'The winner is … and I hope they sat and watched the Olympic Final … *Gogglebox*.'

As I came down from the stage, the one or two people who did know me were Ben Shephard and Kate Garraway from *Good Morning Britain*. Ben literally grabbed me and introduced me to all on the table, which was really nice of him, given that probably the rest of the room were thinking, 'Who's she?'

It was strange to be in that environment as a whole, because it seemed everybody was competing for the limelight. I didn't really like it, to be honest. It was fascinating to get a glimpse of the TV world though and when I thought about my ideal job, I had ambitions that one day I could make it as a presenter on daytime television and not be restricted to sport.

Since arriving back in Britain it felt like I was living in a dream. I loved every minute. Our achievements seemed to have made a real impact with everyone. People had been stopping me in the street saying they knew who I was and giving me loads of congratulations.

It seemed that everything was falling into place. I was excited about what was going to happen next. And so the last thing I expected was to have my name associated with a scandal. It was the smear every sportsperson fears most – the insinuation that you might be a drugs cheat.

Chapter 23

TUE to IAC

The first thing I knew was when Sally Munday, chief executive of England Hockey, rang me.

My name, she said, was about to be leaked as one of a number of athletes granted a TUE – Therapeutic Use Exemption. A Russian cyber espionage group called Fancy Bears had hacked into records held by the World Anti-Doping Agency and planned to release details of athletes' medical records.

My first response was, 'I haven't had a TUE.'

She said Dr Mike Rossiter, the chief medical officer for Great Britain and England Hockey, would call me to explain. When he did call he said I was on record for the inhaler I was given back in 2008. Then I remembered the test we'd undergone at Loughborough and the inhaler they'd given me in case I'd suffered shortage of breath from exercise-induced asthma. I couldn't believe it. Not only was it an invasion of my privacy and unethical to reveal details of my private medical records, but why would anyone seek to smear the name of an athlete for something they were given on health grounds eight years ago?

Then I started to see the reaction on social media when the names were leaked: 'Is Sam Quek a drugs cheat?'

'Will England's hockey team be stripped of their gold medals?'

When I saw how potentially damaging it was, I was furious. I wasn't the only athlete whose name was released in September 2016. There were eight British names leaked. Alex Danson and Crista Cullen were also named from the hockey squad. Four-time Olympic gold medalist Mo Farah was shown to have been granted two TUEs, once for the corticosteroid triamcinolone in October 2008 and another in July 2014, when he was placed on a morphine drip after he collapsed on a training run in the USA. Scots cyclist Callum Skinner, rower Helen Glover and golfer Justin Rose were also among those named. As with me, there was no suggestion of any wrongdoing on the part of any of the athletes.

However, that didn't stop people speculating on Twitter and sparking debates about the implications. The problem was that few people had an understanding of what a TUE was and the way they were being used in the headlines made people look like they were cheating. Few people, it seemed, even bothered to read the articles on the topic. People didn't seem to know it stood for therapeutic use exemption. They just assumed it must be a drug in its own right or something.

When I woke up in the morning and I saw all the comments it felt like my world had shattered.

The advice was to say nothing. Don't draw any more attention to it. It would blow over. But when you're in the middle of a storm it's hard to sit still.

What pushed me over the edge was when my Wikipedia page had been edited to include a mention of the World Anti-Doping Agency leaks. I knew anyone could go on there and edit it and there was nothing technically inaccurate, but it was the secondary thing you would learn about me after my Olympic triumph.

I just thought, 'I'm not having this.' Even aside from thoughts about my own reputation and any stigma, I thought of a young girl taking up the sport and relying on her inhaler. What message did this send out? I needed to do something.

I told Sally Munday I wanted to say something. She understood my reasons.

I wanted to have my say somewhere reputable, so chose *The Guardian*. Even then I was worried it might be slanted in some way, like, 'Athletes trying to justify why they use TUE', or something similar.

To my relief they presented my words fairly.

I said:

> I have nothing to hide. I was given permission to use an inhaler for asthma in 2008 until 2010, and, in my case, it was essential to have one to ensure I could perform and stay healthy.
>
> TUEs are not about cheating but a perception has been created by certain media outlets in the past few days to make it look that way. Being named in this fourth leak with seven other British athletes puts me in a category that, obviously, I would never ever want to be in. And my worry now is that the first thoughts of people when they hear our names are negative ones.
>
> I am quite concerned that myself and Team GB are going to be tarnished by this negativity despite the fact TUEs are completely legal. If people want to try and draw any sort of link from this instance eight years ago to me winning gold at Rio 2016, then good luck to them.

I went on:

> Now I am concerned that the next generation of athletes could turn
> away from using TUEs because they have been tarnished by these
> stories. It's worrying that in future Olympic cycles there could
> well be a hockey player like me, chasing her Olympic dream and
> pushing her body to its limit in search of success. What happens
> if she becomes out of breath and needs an inhaler? Not to get an
> unfair sporting advantage, but to breathe and make sure she does
> not die. Yet she may still think twice about using one, or at least
> feel guilty about doing so. That is wrong and we need to make sure
> people understand how important these exemptions are.

What seemed unfair was that I could not have been more anti-drugs in my
career. I was scared even to have a Lemsip. I was so paranoid that I wouldn't
want to touch the communal mixer we had at Bisham for an isotonic drink
in case it was spiked. And that was in Bisham, which was a safe environment.

I wasn't sure what impact the release of the leaked medical records would
have.

At the beginning of October, when I still hadn't heard from the producers
of *I'm A Celebrity*, I was starting to write off completely going to the jungle.
The Jump wanted a final confirmation from us, so we had to go to ITV and
say, 'This is the final day. We have to give *The Jump* an answer.'

We were expecting them to confirm I wouldn't be on *I'm A Celebrity*, but
instead they tantalizingly said I might still have a chance.

On 7 October, I was invited to Stamford Bridge, home of Chelsea Football
Club, for the Sport Business Summit, part of Leaders Week, a forum looking
at many aspects of sport. I was on a panel with Chelsea Ladies forward Eni
Aluko and sailor Libby Greenhalgh to discuss the growth of women's sport
from an athlete's perspective, chaired by BBC broadcaster Eleanor Oldroyd.

I was just about to go on stage when Luke ran in.

'Sam, Sam,' he said, 'I just heard. It's been confirmed ... *I'm a Celeb* ...
they're sending through the contract today.'

Oh ... My ... God!

Surrounded by these other top athletes, I tried to remain calm and keep
it all low key as I obviously couldn't give it away that I was going on the
programme because it was still very hush-hush.

The discussions were going on around me but all I was thinking about
was, '*I'm A Celebrity ... Get Me Out Of Here* ... oh my God, this is going

to be amazing.' It was like I was removed from the situation – I was there, talking, but not there. My mind was in Australia and the jungle, and what it would be like and how my life just seemed to be a crazy ride of experiences at the moment – from Rio and winning gold to being on iconic sports TV programmes, and now the biggest TV show in the country.

Before Australia, I had a trip to New York for my birthday with Tom that we had booked well before the Olympics. It was the holiday that we had decided would signal the start of our new lives together – a celebration of the end of the Olympic cycle. We could plan the rest of our lives together with no requirements to be anywhere or do anything at a certain time. Little did we know when we booked it before Rio what would transpire!

It all of a sudden dawned on me. New York was going to clash with Team GB going to Buckingham Palace for a reception with Her Majesty the Queen in honour of our sporting triumph, as well as the athletes' parade. It would be one of the most incredible honours in any sportsperson's life and I was set to miss it. What was I to do? Go to the palace and let Tom down again, despite all the promises I had made him that life would be different when I got back from Rio? He had been there for me for so long and never made me feel bad for being selfish. In my heart I knew that if I chose to go to the palace, then he would understand, but if I did decide to cancel the holiday of a lifetime and visit the palace, I would then also soon be leaving to go to Australia for a month and be separated from him again.

It was exciting and bewildering at the same time and I felt pulled in several different emotional directions.

Chapter 24

Welcome to the Jungle

O n that rooftop terrace in Rio – after we'd won gold and were celebrating with our families and friends – Karen Brown, our assistant coach, turned around to me and said, 'You're going to be famous after this.'

Karen had been there, done it and seen it all. She'd won bronze in 1992 with Great Britain.

'I can tell right now who is going to benefit from this and who's going to be famous,' she said. At the time I wasn't sure what she was meaning or why she thought I might be one of the squad that emerged from the group with a higher profile than some of the others, but those words stuck with me.

Being asked on *I'm A Celebrity … Get Me Out Of Here* was the surprise bonus from all the groundwork I'd done since Rio. It hadn't been handed to me on a plate. Building a profile, getting my face known across several sports and networks had taken a lot of effort and I'd spent more on train fares, hotels and clothes in those last few weeks than I had in my whole life up to that point. Until you stop being an athlete, you don't realise just how few clothes you actually own, because you are always in your kit or training tracksuits. I only had a handful of dresses, two pairs of jeans and a few tops, and a couple of pairs of trainers. Hearing about *I'm a Celebrity* made it all seem worthwhile. Not only did I hope the boost my profile would get from being in the jungle might help open some doors, I also hoped I could raise interest in hockey again. When I'd had conversations with the senior figures at Great Britain Hockey they acknowledged that we were experiencing a spike in interest after the Olympics but they expected it to only last until they end of the year. If that was the case we needed to do all we could to keep hockey in the public eye.

As soon as my panel discussion finished I said 'bye' to everyone and ran outside the stadium to ring Tom. He was equally as excited. I just stood outside Stamford Bridge brimming with excitement.

That weekend I went home and told my mum and dad. They were happy for me but my mum was worried. It's natural for your mum to think, 'What's the worst that could happen?' I'm sure she was wondering how I would cope being in front of the cameras, worrying whether I would be exposed in some way and fearing the worst about the press attention and the reaction from the public.

I was told not to tell anyone outside close family and I took that right to the letter because I'd never been in the situation before. I only told my mum, dad and nana, no one else.

There was lots of speculation around who had been chosen. I'd known they had been speaking to other athletes and at one stage it was rumoured Maddie was in the frame.

As early as the following day, my name was being mentioned and I panicked. How could my name have been leaked? It certainly wasn't from my camp. I was more paranoid than ever to keep it a secret as I didn't want to get kicked off the show. When my name came out a lot of friends got in touch to ask if it was true but I had to say, 'No'. I even told Tom's family that it wasn't true.

Luckily I was leaving for New York with Tom for my birthday on 18 October. We were there for a week. His NFL team, the Baltimore Ravens, were playing on the first Sunday against the New York Giants and then on the following Sunday against the New York Jets. We were taking in both games. We'd had it planned for ages and I was gutted when I saw that the parade in London for the Team GB Olympians and the reception at Buckingham Palace was falling while we were away. I wanted to be with the team and be there for the incredibly special occasion, but I owed it to Tom not to cancel the trip we had planned together as a celebration – especially as I would be jetting off to Australia soon.

That said, we did look at flights back to London or Manchester to see if it was possible to fly home, go to the parade and fly back to New York. However, when I looked at flights the prices were ridiculous. We tried everything, but British Airways were quoting £2,400. We even tweeted Air India, but their timings meant I would only make half an hour of the ceremony. It wasn't worth it. Besides, I didn't want to disrupt things and leave Tom in New York alone.

So I made my decision, for the first time in a long while, not to put hockey and my teammates first. It was a very foreign feeling and not a decision I took lightly.

I sat on my hotel bed watching the images of the parade and pictures of the girls at the palace fill my social media pages. I may as well have flown home, because all I did was cry that I was missing out. We didn't go out that afternoon or that evening, but just sat in our hotel, ordered room service and refreshed Twitter. I was gutted.

Unfortunately, my decision was taken the wrong way by some of my team. They believed I thought that I was now too big for the team, I was going off to New York and going into the jungle and doing what I wanted to do.

I could understand why some – certainly not all of them – felt that was the case, but I didn't feel I had a choice and there was the added complication of contractually not being able to talk about *I'm A Celebrity*, so I couldn't explain myself fully.

On my birthday, Tom surprised me by tracking down two hockey balls that had actually been used in the Olympics and might even have been used by us in the final. I think he had to pay an astronomical amount to get them at a specialist auction. It was a very thoughtful gift. It's funny, though, he's much more sentimental than me when it comes to souvenirs and mementos. While we were in Rio, he secretly arranged for his PA to buy almost every newspaper, every day, so I didn't miss out on any of the coverage. For Valentine's Day one year, he cut every one out, made a collage and had it framed. As you can imagine, there was a lot of press leading up to and after the final, so the final display is around 4 meters square, but it hangs proudly on our landing at home, a great memory of a special summer.

I arrived back from New York into a week of manic preparation for *I'm A Celebrity*. I travelled down to Holborn Studios in London, where they took me into one room to get my hair and make-up done before filming the sequence when you turn to the camera and the letters land. In the next room I put on my jungle gear for the press shots. Then I was ushered into a car and driven away. What I didn't realise was that each of the contestants were there at the same time, being shepherded from room to room at different times so we didn't bump into one another.

I just felt like a little deer in the headlights. I was too scared to say anything like 'I don't want my hair like that' or 'I don't want to blow a kiss to the camera'. I thought, 'I'll look a right dick if I do that,' because I was so new to it all and very self-conscious. I didn't want to come across as someone I wasn't.

In the lead-up to my departure to Australia, where *I'm A Celebrity* is filmed, I found myself having dilemmas and debates that I never thought I would. Do I get a spray tan, get my lashes permed, my eyebrows tinted? Do I put chicken fillets in my bikini, because I've not got no boobs at all? Am I best stopping people trolling me early before they start taking the piss out of me?

Naturally every woman has insecurities and for me, as an athlete, being exposed in a bikini in front of millions of people, was not something that happened every day.

I was nervous about showering in front of millions of people. Everyone remembered Myleene Klaas from 2006 when she showered in a white bikini and the images became iconic. I worried that I might be a headline. These were the sort of conversations that were happening during the preparation.

On 31 October, Tom and I were invited to the Pride of Britain Awards, at Grosvenor House in London. It's a prestigious event celebrating the ordinary people who do extraordinarily wonderful things to help the lives of others. As well as providing the chance to honour some remarkable people, the event is known for boasting a guest list that is like a *Who's Who* of British popular culture.

While we'd been waiting to get on the red carpet, in the queue we saw the late Stephen Hawking. He was wheeling up the pavement and I was smashing Tom on the arm. 'Tom! Tom! It's Stephen Hawking!' That was probably one of the very few times that I've been star-struck, but it was because at that time he was rarely going to events.

Team GB had received a special invite and Tom and I arrived to find we were at the same table as Maddie and Hollie Webb. Hollie and I were in the same dress but in different colours. Unbelievable, but we had a laugh about it. Maddie was still being frosty towards me.

During the night it was impossible not to be moved by the countless stories of courage. I was particularly touched by the story of Nikki Christou, a girl then twelve who was diagnosed with arteriovenous malformation (AVM), which caused her face to swell up. She was so inspiring. She set up her own YouTube channel and spoke about being yourself and being comfortable in your own skin. That's what had got her through her worst days. I sat there, welling up and thinking, 'Why am I getting so stressed about putting chicken fillets in my bikini and people pressurising me to get my eyelashes permed?' She inspired me to think, 'Sod it, be who you are.' And then the more I thought about it, the more I realised, 'Actually, if I go in with chicken fillets in my bikini, I'm not being true to myself and I'm not being true to all the other girls who have got a small chest.' I'm going in to represent me and anyone else like me. I thought, 'I'm just going to go in and be me.'

At the end of the event, everyone from Team GB got on stage for an acknowledgement – the final shot before the end titles ran and all the confetti came down over the winners. Carol Vorderman had been presenting the event. There had been rumours she was also going to be on *I'm A Celebrity*. She looked over to me and mouthed, 'I know you're going in the jungle!'

I mouthed back, 'Are you?'

'Yeah. I'll catch you for a drink. Meet in the Red Bar.'

We went through to the bar and it was like being in a sea of famous names. Tom offered his best wishes to Cliff Richard, which he seemed to appreciate, given the year he'd had with unfounded allegations made against him.

Carol came in and immediately took me over to a table in the corner. It was the first time I'd met her and straight away we hit it off. She's lovely and we're very much on the same wavelength. She was taking the Mick, a proper girls' girl. We were chatting about what we were going to do in the jungle and imagining what it would be like. We knew Scarlett Moffatt, from *Gogglebox*, was going in but we didn't really know her. We ended up chatting until 4.00 am and I don't know how we got round to it but I ended up throwing peanuts that were in a little bowl into Carol's mouth, as a game. We were merry from drinking and just larking about.

It had been such a surreal night.

A late party at my brother Shaun's bar, Chamber 36, back home was a final send-off before I prepared to depart for Australia. The relationship between Tom and I had become a little tense too. I think now it was on our doorstep, he was starting to worry about me going into the jungle. I wasn't going to see him for a month and I hoped he wouldn't get too much hassle from the press or be left cringing at the coverage. It was yet another step into the unknown for both of us.

When I arrived at the airport an *I'm a Celebrity* chaperone met me but I was so early that they took me to a lounge to get breakfast. In there was one of the press women whom I'd met before with the crew and a few of the make-up women. Their plan was to fly people out at different times and as I didn't have children, I was one of those that went out first.

We boarded the plane and I was excited to find we were in business class – my first time turning left as I boarded a plane. I sat down with my glass of champagne absolutely buzzing.

I had a check of my emails and saw one from Susie Townsend. It was a bit of a surprise to get one because since the girls had been to Buckingham Palace I hadn't heard from many of them.

Susie said she missed me and said if I was able to confirm I was going into the jungle I should send a message to the rest of the girls before they read about it in the papers. She was looking out for me because she could see some of them getting annoyed that it looked like I wasn't keeping the girls in the loop.

I appreciated her thinking of me but, while I couldn't confirm my participation on the TV show, I replied that to me it seemed that some of the team were already annoyed with me anyway.

I referred her to an interview that Hannah Macleod, one of my teammates in Rio, had given to the *Daily Telegraph* around the time I was confirmed on *I'm A Celebrity*.

While discussing how women were portrayed in the media, she said: 'If you look at the sixteen gold medallists from the women's GB hockey team, which ones have got higher profiles? Not the ones that contributed the most, or scored the winning goal, or had been captain for thirteen years. It's the ones that looked prettiest, and you can see the opportunities that come for them. So, it's blindingly obvious, still, there's a way to go.'

Up until that point I'd kept my views on those words to myself because I didn't want to publically tarnish what we had as a squad. I believed it had been the efforts of thirty-one players who had been in that squad over the cycle leading up to Rio that won the gold, not a select few.

I considered those words a public attack from one of my teammates, regardless of how wrong she might have been about how my opportunities had arisen. To question my, or anyone's, contribution to the team, was out of order, let alone damaging to our squad's togetherness. Reading that in a national newspaper killed me. I'd even had a journalist approach me to see if I wanted to respond but I'd declined.

I also told Susie that I'd felt I'd become a pariah on our WhatsApp group chat. Many of my comments or questions had passed without reply and no one seemed concerned for me either when I couldn't make the Team GB parade. Things had changed and become so sour with some of the team. Even those I was close to weren't speaking up for me in the groups.

I didn't believe the girls in the squad who had an issue with me wanted to know if I was going into the jungle to congratulate or support me, my efforts to promote hockey and the team. I think they just wanted to know out of curiosity.

I said to Susie: 'I find myself for the first time in ten years on the periphery of the squad and it's really quite sad. I really appreciate you keeping in touch, looking out for me, and I know I can be honest with you, hence the reply, but I really am at a loss and feel that regardless of what I do or say, opinions of me have already been made and I am being judged negatively for wanting to try to make a new career, whilst also promoting hockey.'

Susie said she was struggling to know what to say because she was hearing it from both sides. She didn't want me to become an outsider or feel like I was alone. She did say, however, that she didn't think anyone begrudged me making money.

That to me was the key issue though. Sadly, I suspected that people were worried about whatever money I was making, and were maybe a tad jealous.

The reality was, up until that moment I'd made £34 from my appearances so far, when you factored in all the costs I'd incurred. I was far from rolling in it.

Susie urged me to be upfront about my plans, not just about the jungle but my hockey future, too.

What crossed my mind, though, was firstly, I hadn't even told members of my family or Tom's family that I was going to Australia, so it wasn't as though I was deliberately leaving them out. Secondly, and more concerning, if my new career plans failed, how could I ever go back into the squad when several of them now thought so little about me? I couldn't believe it. These were my closest friends for years. Had they completely forgotten who I was as a person for the nine years prior, based on their perceptions of what had been going on for only a few weeks?

Once the flight got under way I was so tired from so little sleep the night before, partially due to worry, partially due to excitement, that I fell asleep for most of the journey. I cursed myself when we began our descent into Dubai – the end of the first leg. I could have just slept in economy! I hadn't taken advantage of the movie library, the free snacks or any other aspect of my first ever business class flight.

I went through immigration to get my bags and that's when I first saw Ant and Dec getting off the plane. I went up to Ant and said, 'Hiya!' He looked at me, like, 'Who is this creepy fan?'

It then occurred to me that he might not even know the line-up and because I wasn't that well known, he probably didn't have a clue who I was. He just nodded an acknowledgement and carried on walking. That wasn't a great start. I was mortified.

While I was waiting for my bags to come through, I rang my mum and Tom and sent some final WhatsApp messages because once I entered the programme setup I'd be banned from using all gadgets. I must have sat there for about forty-five minutes after my bag arrived before I went through the final immigration doors to meet the chaperone the other side.

As soon as I appeared, a blonde woman came up to me. 'Hi Sam, how was your flight? How are you feeling?' She was British.

'This must be the chaperone,' I thought.

So I replied, 'Yeah, it was alright, thanks.'

I felt quite nervous and a bit reserved but I thought, 'Thank God there's someone here to meet me.'

But then as we walked further, an Australian woman approached me and said, 'Hi Sam, I'm Jules, I'm your chaperone ...'

I thought, 'Oh my God, the first woman must be a journalist.'

Suddenly there were photographers taking pictures and questions were being fired at me: 'How are you feeling? How does your boyfriend feel about you going into the jungle? How will you feel when you've got kangaroo bollocks in your mouth?'

I just kept smiling away, trying not to give too much away.

Jules said she was worried they'd missed me because I was taking so long in baggage reclaim. I didn't want to admit I'd been doing my final round of family calls.

We finally got to the car and Jules said, 'Right, time to make your final phone call.' I thought, 'Go on, have another phone call.' So I rang Tom, just to say, 'This definitely is it. I'm getting rid of my phone and all contact devices.'

I told him I loved him and I'd be thinking of him constantly.

Then it was time to hand over my phone.

We arrived at the hotel on the Gold Coast and the rules were even stricter than the Olympic village. Jules said, 'This is as far as you can go. If you ever want to go out, you need to let us know so we can get Neil, the security guard, to chaperone you.'

She added, 'Have you got any more communication devices?'

'No,' I said.

I checked into my room, opened my case and completely forgot I had my iPad.

Oops!

I clicked onto the WiFi just to see if it would work and it did – but you had to use your room number and name.

I thought, 'I can't log on. They'll know it's me.'

I was so nervous. I checked the phone and outgoing calls were blocked. 'This is pretty serious,' I thought. I was too scared to risk it.

I checked out the room and it was amazing, with views out to sea. The room was massive with a large balcony and a bathroom that was so big it could have been a room in itself.

I arrived a week before filming was due to start so there wasn't a lot to do but sit by the pool and hang around in my room. In that time I got to know

Jules very well. She was an older woman with three teenage children. She was lovely. We became proper friends. We'd spend evenings watching TV programmes like *Say Yes to the Dress* and the *The Chase Australia* on my bed.

I'd been there for about three days and I was still deliberating over whether to use the WiFi. I didn't want to use my own details, for fear of being caught. One night I went for dinner with Jules and when she signed the receipt I happened to clock her room number and surname. I felt like a right detective.

When I went to bed I thought, 'Okay then,' and used her details to log on.

I was so paranoid, though, because I didn't know how strict they would be. I kept expecting Jules to bang on the door. Was there CCTV in the room? Could they detect radio waves or something? It probably wasn't that big a deal but I was just so nervous that I was doing something I shouldn't.

I logged on to my iPad and my notifications went ping, ping, ping – it was all the backlog since arriving in Australia. Twitter was nuts, Instagram – I'd been tagged in everything – WhatsApps, and text messages all came through on my iPad as well.

One of the text messages immediately stood out. It was from Tom. 'I know you can't answer me, and you've got no phone, but I just want to say this – all I want to do is ring you now.'

I started to get emotional. I could tell something was up. He would never send me a message like that, so something bad must have happened.

'Should I reply? Is he going to pick it up?'

Oh fuck it.

I hit Face Time. His face popped up on the screen and I'd never seen him so sad. I thought, 'Oh no. What has happened?'

It was terrible. He'd had an awful day. He was being hassled relentlessly by the media and one paper in particular was being horrible to him. It was really difficult for him. I told him everything was going to be okay, and no matter what was said or written, I loved him unconditionally.

I suddenly realised how big a show *I'm A Celebrity* was and the media attention around it was something off the scale, not just for me, but also for my whole family.

It was just so good to hear his voice and to reassure him that everything was going to be fine.

That was the last time we spoke before I went into the jungle. I never told anyone else I had access to my iPad because I was worried that if my mum knew I had it and didn't use it to contact her, then she'd be gutted.

I only used it once to Face Time Tom. And that was only because I got his message and knew I had to get in touch. Maybe he was right. Maybe it was fate that I logged on just at that time.

It sounds crazy now to think it was such a big deal but you are so conditioned to playing by the rules. However tough it was for me to be out of contact, it was far worse for Tom, being at home and having to deal with all these other issues.

After our conversation I felt like a whole weight had been lifted. 'Right,' I thought, 'I'm going to enjoy this now.'

The medic, Bob, gave me one last medical and they showed me a rough map of the camp, telling me what to expect. They showed me a picture of one spider. If I saw one of those I had to tell the camp immediately.

I was scared of spiders – I was scared of quite a lot of things. I was actually dreading it.

There was then a briefing on what was poisonous, and what wasn't. 'Don't eat the leaves; you don't know if they're poisonous.'

In all this time at the hotel I didn't see another contestant.

On the day before we went into camp, I was hit with a very nasty cold. It had come on two days earlier. I had a rasping cough and was spitting up balls of phlegm. Jules had to keep giving me tissues and throat lozenges.

On the Friday morning, I was led to believe this was the show starting. We had to select an outfit and get camera ready with our hair and make-up. I chose a long dress that I'd picked up in the sale in Primark for £5. It was a belter and fitted me perfectly. As we left the hotel for the first time, Jules blindfolded me and put on some earmuffs for a journey to a secret location. I thought I was going to be taken to the middle of nowhere but it was just a five-minute drive.

From peeking out the sides of my blindfold it seemed we had parked next to a massive field and what looked like a housing estate. There was a park on the left with lots of black jeeps. 'That must be the contestants,' I thought.

When it was my turn to get out, I felt the presence of a lot of people around me. I had to put two hands on someone's shoulders and they led me away. We were walking on gravel and then square flagstones. Someone said, 'Right, you're going to have to take big steps.' Jules was laughing her head off because I was taking the most over exaggerated big steps. But when you've got a blindfold on it's hard to know what to do! I was led around the back of what I soon saw was a villa, down some steps, next to a river, where I was sat on a chair.

There was a little slit at the bottom of my blindfold and I could see Larry Lamb, the *EastEnders* actor. The blindfold was then taken off. There weren't that many people around me now. I was directed to walk up some stairs, turned right and there was a pool and loads of cameras, crew and a big screen. I looked over and there was Ant and Dec and all the other celebrities. I thought, 'This is it,' we were starting and I was the last one in.

I made eye contact with Carol Vorderman and said, 'Hiya.' She waved back.

I saw some of the others. Ola Jordan, the former dancer from *Strictly Come Dancing*, and Lisa Snowdon, the model who is now a TV and radio presenter, were two I recognised initially, along with Larry. I wondered how I might get on with Ola and Lisa, because they looked so much more glamorous than me. Perhaps they weren't the types to get stuck in and get dirt under their fingernails like I was. It's funny how wrong first impressions can be. I imagine some of the contestants were also making their own assumptions about me – 'Here's an Olympian, I bet she will try to do all the physical trials and be non-stop active and working out all day.' If they were thinking that, they would be wrong with their first impressions, too!

I hadn't realised what was going on at the time, but what viewers would see was five of the celebs choosing a partner to see who they would save from the first trial. Unbeknownst to me we had been split into 'jungle celebs' and 'city celebs'. All the other celebs had been paired off so it was Ola and me remaining. Ola would have to do a challenge to save me from the first task, while I would have to do something else to save Ola. It was amazing how quickly you get wrapped up in it all. My competitive streak kicked in and immediately I wanted to make sure I completed the challenge and do well for Ola.

Once we'd paired off, however, our group of 'jungle celebs' were returning to the camp. The other group went straight off to do their city challenge. For the rest of us, the show would begin properly the following day.

I went back to the hotel in my own car with Jules. That night it was just the two of us for dinner again because they didn't want us mingling with the other celebs. They wanted our initial conversations to happen in the camp when we were on camera. We feasted on a lovely grill, with lots of my favourite things like buffalo wings and halloumi. I stuffed myself, knowing it was my last proper meal for a while. It was then early to bed because the alarm was set for 4.00 am as we had to be on set for filming to begin at half past five. I would be wearing the same £5 Primark dress because they wanted to make it look like it was filmed the same day.

I went to bed full of nerves, apprehension and excitement. Tomorrow we would be going into the jungle. I was itching to get started – but almost dreading it. What had I let myself in for?

Chapter 25

An Unexpected End to an Incredible Year

Ohhhh Myyyyyy Gooooooooddddd!!!

That was what was going through my head as we plummeted from 12,000 feet out of a helicopter.

This was my introduction to the 2016 series of *I'm A Celebrity … Get Me Out Of Here*, and I was terrified!

The challenge involved a skydive, but after freefalling for several thousand feet, a parachute was deployed and I had to count for sixty seconds and then light a flare. The celebrity closest to the sixty seconds when the flare was lit would spare their partner from doing the dreaded first bushtucker trial.

I had been in a helicopter only once before. That was scary enough, but this time the door would be opened mid-flight and I would be told to jump out of it. I don't mind admitting I was crapping myself! It went against every instinct I had.

The budget for the show must have been ridiculous because there was a helicopter for the footballer Wayne Bridge and me and our skydiving partners, and then another one for Lisa Snowdon. Plus, there were two other choppers flying around filming us. No expense had been spared.

I watched Lisa tumble out and just thought, 'No … no way will I be able to do that.'

Soon it was my turn. Before I had time to protest, the door was open, I was sitting on the edge and my instructor shouted, 'Go!'

He then lent on me until I fell out of the helicopter. I just felt the world flip upside down. I was feeling lousy anyway with the stinking cold that I couldn't shift and immediately I was hit with motion sickness.

Once the initial shock had worn off, the freefall was amazing – such a buzz. But when we came out of it I was dry retching and feeling really sick. We hadn't had a bite to eat since getting up at 4.00 am and it was past midday before we went up in the helicopters. At least I knew I wasn't going to embarrass myself by throwing up in mid-air. Despite feeling a little peaky, I was enjoying the views of the rainforest and mountains. They were so beautiful and made me think of *Jurassic Park*.

Then it hit me …

Oh shit!

I was supposed to be counting to sixty seconds! I knew I was well over, but I lit the flare immediately. I had totally forgotten the reason we were being thrown out of a helicopter, because I was too busy trying to come to terms with actually being thrown out of the bloody thing.

All of a sudden, I realised something wasn't quite right. We were getting further away from the landing target, not closer to it. A gust of wind had blown us off course.

The instructor behind me said, 'Right, we're going to have to abort landing and go somewhere else.'

'Sorry ... what?'

I couldn't believe it. I was scared already but this was a new type of fear. 'Where are you going to land?' I screamed.

All I could see were trees. Thankfully, though, he managed to find a random garden amongst the jungle beneath us and we ended up landing in the grounds of somebody's farmhouse. Thank you, God! We were safe, and we only had to wait for about fifteen minutes until someone came and found us.

I knew if I made a big deal or appeared shaken up and scared on landing it would be shown on the show. I was determined that the first impression of me wouldn't be me making a drama, so I just progressed as if everything was normal. Truth be told, my legs were like jelly and I was on the edge of tears. I was just so thankful we were down in one piece and it was over.

By the time we got back to the rendezvous point and Ant and Dec came to see us it was chucking it down. It was torrential rain, not like rain we get back in the UK. We had these big, thick jumpsuits on from the skydive – mine was bright yellow – and I still had my Primark dress on underneath. Everything was soaked through. We were all freezing cold, jelly legged and starting to get really hungry. Before we could ask for anything they told us, 'You're not allowed any food.' They wanted to see how we would react to being hungry. Would anyone be snappy? In the end they had to give us something because we were all on the edge of hypothermia, so they gave in and provided some tea and biscuits. We took shelter in a van and Jules, bless her, was trying to slip me a cereal bar because she was really worried. She was literally taking her job into her own hands because they are employed to stop us being snuck what they called 'contraband'. She understood this wasn't a normal situation, though, and she was really worried for me. She just kept saying, 'We need to get you dry.' She got me a towel and we ended up getting in the car to warm up. It was an hour's drive to the camp and I fell asleep because I was so tired and full of cold. I had to peel the wet clothes off myself, so I was sitting there in my bra and knickers with my soaking wet suit around my ankles. I must have looked like a drunk girl in the back of a taxi after a very late night out on the tiles.

We met up with Larry and Scarlett and made our way to the camp. I'd had a chance to meet Scarlett earlier. We instantly got on well. We were two northern girls, around the same age and with the same sense of humour. Neither of us took the experience too seriously. She had a Primark dress on as well, funnily enough, but she'd also had her tan done, all her hair blown, nails painted, the works. She looked fab. Scarlett and Larry had done a canoe challenge instead of the skydive for health or medical grounds. Scarlett apparently couldn't swim, so Larry had to rescue her. It sounds like their way into camp had been as eventful as ours!

Once inside the camp, the first thing that struck me was how different it looked in real life compared to what you see on the telly. It looked a lot bigger now I was actually standing in the middle of it. I looked at the beds and wondered if there were enough for everyone. I really didn't want to sleep on the floor where insects could run over me in the night. I assumed we would draw straws and I just hoped I would be lucky enough to be off the ground, even if it was in a hammock. If not, I would have made my own bed somehow from bits of the jungle. Luckily, there were enough beds for everyone.

At first, everyone was just saying 'Hi', and introducing themselves. No one had an ego where they assumed everyone knew who they were. I knew who everyone was, though. They were actual celebrities and had been for a while, unlike me.

Our bags were dropped into the bush telegraph hut and we sorted out who was sleeping where. Everyone was being so polite, like, 'I don't mind, I don't mind'. It actually took longer to sort the bed situation because everyone was so keen to make a good impression than if we'd all just run and claimed whatever one we wanted and then argued it out. Eventually I said to Scarlett, 'Do you want to come here with me?' I wanted to sleep away from the fire because I didn't want the smoke to further irritate my chest. I could see the wind was blowing the smoke over one particular bed. Lisa took that one at first but soon swapped with Adam Thomas, the actor from *Emmerdale*.

Scarlett did get the bed next to me and we used to sleep with both heads next to each other because we thought we could have a chat before we went to bed without disturbing anyone. But to be honest, after that first day – and every day after, actually – I was so physically drained that I've never slept so well in my life. We were always low on energy as food was restricted and life in camp was actually pretty physically demanding. We were constantly collecting firewood and water to boil and top up the drinkable water bag.

As well as hitting it off with Scarlett, I obviously knew Carol from Pride of Britain, so she was lovely. Lisa and Ola were lovely, too – completely the opposite of anything I might have thought beforehand. I remember very early feeling so lucky to have such a wonderful group of girls. Everyone just got on.

Pretty early on I struggled with the idea of constantly being on camera. I was acting naturally throughout but I was always aware we were being watched. It was quite a strange feeling. Everyone else seemed so comfortable with it, though. Soon it dawned on me that, with the possible exception of Wayne Bridge, everyone else was used to being on TV regularly. They managed to always act so full of energy. The mic packs didn't annoy them and they just seemed so much better than me when dealing with cameras. When I went into the bush telegraph, the confessional hut, it felt just like an interview. It made me feel uneasy at first, so I avoided it. For others like Scarlett, Adam and particularly Joel Dommett, a comic actor who had been in *Skins*, it was second nature. I think Joel spent almost as much time in the telegraph as he did the main camp.

Joel also wanted to set up an exercise regime from the second day. Adam and Wayne were into that, too. It was nice to have a group of lads with us that were so down to earth and had quite similar interests. They were always good to have a banter with. The Diversity dancer Jordan Banjo and I joined in the exercises for the first day but because our working days involve working out we wanted a different experience, so we stopped doing it. Instead I preferred to walk around, at least as far as the production team would allow us, and explore our surroundings. Once I had run out of places to go I then started doing a different type of circuit training, but it was hard because if you did even a little too much, you ended up really knackered.

It was strange living in the camp, but also really nice in some ways. It was such a simple existence and I enjoyed the peace and tranquillity of it all. No phones, no social media, no bills to pay or shopping to do. You also get to know people really well, very quickly. You sit around telling your whole life story basically. It's all, 'Have you got any kids? Are you married? How did you get proposed to? What was your best holiday?' etc.

Initially, I didn't open up as much as of some of the others. I kept my stories and my emotions to myself. I was quite guarded. I kept thinking, 'Ooh, can I say that?' 'Will the person I am talking about get offended?'

'Will the newspapers try to twist what I am saying?' I was aware of the scrutiny I was under by being on the show and I didn't want to let anyone back at home down. I think this led to me coming across much quieter than I naturally am.

One of our first group tasks wasn't actually broadcast. The producers had hidden boxes around the camp. In the boxes were questions relating to each celeb and the answer would be a number. For example, my question was, 'How many caps Sam has'. I think it was designed for us all to get to know each other better and learn things about each other that we may have been reluctant to share for fear of looking like we were blowing our own trumpets. We all shouted our answers to Carol and she had to work out a sum relating to the questions. Her board read something like 'What year Carol started on *Countdown*', minus the age of Adam's son, multiplied by how many England caps Wayne had etc. Carol did the maths and, as you would expect, she was insane. I had a real girl crush moment when she just came to an answer. Carol wasn't just the most intelligent 55-year-old I had ever met, she was also the most glamorous looking and funniest. She had the appearance, soul and outlook on life that felt like she was much younger than her years, whilst also having real-life worldly wisdom. She was my best friend in camp. When I eventually joined the real world again, someone said, 'Your relationship with Carol was lovely, like a mother and daughter relationship.' 'It wasn't like that,' I told them, 'we were like two naughty sisters.'

Once Carol had worked out the code to open a box, inside was a treat. I think they were brownies. No one grabbed them at first; we all just stood there in awe of Carol's maths skills.

We soon learned that producers had lulled us into a false sense of security with those brownies and the meal that night. On that first day we ate well. I think we had buffalo sausages, which were lovely, with rice and beans, and we also had vegetables and potatoes. We all thought, 'This is going to be okay; the years before us must have been right drama queens.'

Little did we know it wouldn't always be that good. The reality came when they showed us the size of the bags of the food that we'd be getting for each person. They were little more than a large tea bag in size. We were all shocked at first, but disappointing portion sizes soon became the norm. On the next task the reward was cheese, but it was like a cubed centimetre and a cracker each. Then one day we won crisps, but it was a tiny bowl between all of us. It honestly felt like they had emptied out a small packet and then decided to remove a couple of crisps before letting us have them. We got about two each.

As the days went on we soon adjusted and it wasn't long before I stopped getting hunger pains. Our stomachs seemed to just accept the inevitable.

Ola, Scarlett, Jordan and I faced the first bushtucker trial. It was called Tomb of Torment and involved the four of us being trapped in a pitch-black tomb for ten minutes while a host of creepy crawlies and all manner of horrible things were put in there with us. At the trials you could win up to a maximum of ten stars, each representing a meal for camp. If any of us left the trial at any point we would be heavily penalised by them taking stars away. Five would be taken if one person left, another two for the second, another two for the third person and if the fourth person left, we would win no stars. No stars meant no dinner for camp. All we would have were our tiny packets of rice if we all failed to complete the trail.

Before we had even started, Ant and Dec took great delight in telling us the tomb would contain the highest number of critters in the show's history. That meant over 120,000 insects, spiders and rats. Back at home I usually run out of the house if I see a single small spider. This was going to be something else.

Before we entered, Scarlett was in tears. I tried to reassure her by saying we were all in it together. In truth, I was crapping it, too! We decided to hold hands throughout and I tried to get her to take deep breaths. I really didn't want to do it. It was terrifying not knowing if you could handle it, or how you would react to being put into a situation like that.

But then a big part of me was thinking, 'This is on national TV, you are being marketed as the Olympian, you can't look like a wimp.' I also didn't want my campmates to go hungry.

I had to find a way. I am a believer that you can conquer anything if you put your mind to it. I remembered a famous quote by Franklin D. Roosevelt, the former American president, who said, 'The only thing we have to fear is fear itself.' If you start thinking, 'Oh my God, there's a rat on my ear' or 'Oh my God, there are spiders', then you are only going to freak yourself out.

I had a plan to hitch my socks up as high as I could and if anything crawled up my leg I would just shake it off. Worst case, they would bite my ankles. Then they revealed that we would actually be lying down throughout the entire challenge. We went in and strapped ourselves down, and I remember freaking out. President Roosevelt clearly hadn't been strapped to the floor in a pitch-black tomb while 120,000 bugs and rats crawled over and gnawed at him!

I think it was a blessing in disguise that it was pitch-black as it helped me zone out easier. I started to worry about my campmates, so I listened out for Jordan's voice. No doubt as the big strapping, chiselled man, he would be telling us 'Everything will be okay' and encouraging us throughout. It turned out that he was screaming the loudest out of all of us! It was going to be up to me to try to raise spirits.

'Right, we need to take our minds off it,' I shouted. 'Let's just count out loud in order.'

It worked for a few seconds, but then the critters came in and everyone started going nuts.

'Let's sing a song.' I shouted.

'What? ... WHAT?!' Scarlet screamed.

'Let's go with Spice Girls' *Stop*, I shouted back. We sang a few severely out of tune lines together until a rat crawled on my face and I screamed. I found out when I left the jungle that Emma Bunton (aka Baby Spice) had been watching and she tweeted saying she thought it was hilarious.

As cockroaches, rats, spiders, giant mealworms, everything you can imagine, clamoured over us and got into every nook and cranny I just kept on with the questions to try to keep people's minds off it.

'What do you fancy to eat if you were at home?' I shouted. 'A CHICKEN KEBAB ... A CHICKEN KEBAB!' Scarlet screamed.

Then some things fell on my face and I had to cover my nose and mouth. I was determined to keep calling things out, because if you stopped to imagine for one second what was crawling over you, it might make you panic even more.

I was on the end of the four of us as we lay down. I thought this was a blessing at first, because I was using my free hand to flick things off my face. But the problem was, because I was in the corner, all the rats congregated around my right shoulder and round my head. It was truly horrific, like a terrible nightmare coming true. I could hear squeaking and feel their whiskers; but what really freaked me out was a massive spider going down my right arm. I could feel its legs gliding across my skin. It was terrifying.

When the task had finished I crawled towards the door and then I really did freak out, because light flooded into the tomb and I could see what had been in there with us. I scrambled through and frantically brushed myself down. I think I just burst into tears from pure relief that it was over. Even though I couldn't see anything on me, my skin continued for hours to feel as though something was crawling all over it.

Ultimately, when we had calmed ourselves, the feeling was amazing. What a buzz – proper adrenaline. I couldn't believe we had done that. It felt a huge achievement.

As we made our way back to camp, we realised we absolutely stank. So that was the first opportunity for the three of us girls to have a shower. We made a pact that we'd shower together because we thought the cameras wouldn't be able to pick up as much. I didn't think anyone would feel comfortable being filmed showering and having it broadcast to the nation. There was a camera slightly to the right, one that was a lot further away and straight ahead of you. We felt if we stood at a particular angle they wouldn't be able to see much, but when you look at the clips now, you realise they can see everything.

The shower was just an artificial water pump and the water was freezing. Although the temperature in Australia was hot, under the tree canopy you didn't get a lot of sun, so it actually felt quite cold.

I never went in the shower on my own. In fact, I only went in when I absolutely had to after a task. I was so self-conscious and I even tried to cover my tattoo, just because I didn't get it to flaunt it on national TV.

It annoyed me a little that attitudes to women on the series were much different to those for the men. You had betting sites offering odds on which girl was going to be first in the shower but no market for the men because no one bats an eyelid. Knowing things like that were going on – and being aware that images of us showering would appear in newspapers, magazines and online – made me feel uneasy.

Women from all walks of life will be able to relate to the fact that it feels like there is enormous pressure to conform to a certain body type. I was a little bit aware of it before going in the jungle but obviously when you're exposed to it and you become the centre of attention it brings it into sharp focus. For some women they feel larger than what society deems normal, others may feel too skinny or dislike their cellulite or showing their stretch marks. For me I felt flat-chested, and that my muscles were overdeveloped. We had worked out particularly hard in the lead-up to the Olympics to ensure our bodies could deal with the demands of the schedule.

I knew in camp that plenty of column inches would be written about us and how we looked. I accepted it as a necessary evil and I signed up fully knowing what had gone on in previous seasons.

I was interested to see how the other women handled it. More often than not, Scarlett used to cover up with a T-shirt. I used to walk up with my towel to preserve a bit of modesty but then Ola, on the other hand, used to sunbathe in her bikini because she's not bothered. Ola was body confident and rightly so because she's got an amazing figure. All the girls had great bodies that they should be proud of, but some were definitely happier to show theirs than others. Lisa was also quite happy to sit there in a bikini top, because she felt comfortable to do so. More power to her, I say. I wish I had worried less. I might have just sat in a bikini on holiday, but not when I'm surrounded by cameras. Carol's attitude was hilarious. She was just like, 'I'm not giving them a free shot of the goods.'

Outside of the jungle spotlight and a little more covered up, I am generally quite comfortable in my own skin. I think being in a team helped me feel that way. I have to live with the fact that there are certain dresses and tops I wouldn't wear because I feel bulkier in them, and I've got quite muscular legs so often I can't fit into a certain style of jeans. There's no escaping some of those insecurities but hockey and sport taught me that if you can do the job and if you're happy in your body, then there's no issue. You're all in it together.

While in camp you had no idea how the public perceived you. That was until, of course, it came to the public vote. Our first experience of the public's opinion was in a vote to determine the camp president. We had to line ourselves up based on how we thought the public had voted. I knew that from everyone there I had the smallest following and by a distance, yet some of my campmates insisted I went nearer the top of the queue. Some genuinely thought that the pride of the team's Olympic achievement hadn't died down yet and that I would get some good votes. Others, I felt, didn't want to look too big-headed by putting themselves high up, preferring to play the underdog roll. Ultimately I came second to last in the vote. That was one place more than I had expected, in all honesty, and it reminded me to enjoy my time in camp as my days would likely be limited. I was determined to make the most of my time there.

There would be no public eviction for the first week. Instead, as is customary for the show, two more celebrities entered on day five – Martin Roberts, from daytime TV, and the radio presenter and comedy writer Danny Baker. I think they were added to spice things up. They were big personalities and we were all getting on so well there was no arguing or bitching. It was just a lovely environment. Their addition did disrupt the harmony but eventually everything settled down again. Rather than stir up rivalries in camp, Martin and Danny actually ended up starting a rivalry with each other.

In the second week there was an opportunity for us to gain immunity from the public vote by competing in a trial called Claim of Thrones. Every campmate would compete in a series of challenges over a number of days. At the end of the week, whoever was sitting in four thrones would have immunity in the first vote.

As the day of the first eviction came nearer, some people were saying, 'Oh I'm not bothered, I'd quite happily go home.' I never felt like that. I was desperate to stay. *I'm a Celebrity* was proving to be an amazing experience and I was thankful for every minute of it. I didn't believe anyone really was okay with going home. Maybe that's the competitor in me, but whilst I thought I would go out quite early, I just didn't want to be the first one to go.

I knew I was going to try my hardest to get immunity, and while others said they didn't really mind, I was honest. I put my hands up and said, 'I don't want to go, I'm going to be trying my hardest to get immunity. My following is tiny; I don't have the fan base voting for me that you guys do.'

Wayne was lovely and said that he thought I would be a lot more popular than I realised, but I knew from the camp president vote that I might be living on borrowed time. I found out afterwards that ITV aired me saying that to my campmates, which I didn't think they would. I thought they would want to make out that they had attracted some big celebrity names rather than self-doubters. I think that ultimately it helped me a little bit because some people thought, 'I like how honest she is' or 'She doesn't have an ego and is also being honest about not wanting to leave'. I think I showed that even becoming a gold medal winning Olympian and being asked on the country's biggest show, it still hadn't changed me. I was still just a normal, excited girl who was desperate to stick around and mess about with a group of celebrities.

The immunity task involved another confined space with more creepy crawlies. This time, though, I was in the zone. Whereas the other celebrities were used to the cameras and had the advantage in feeling more comfortable in camp, I was a competitor. This was going to be my time to show what I was about. It never entered my head that I wouldn't win, regardless of what the challenge would be. I wasn't just playing for food; I was playing for my very existence in camp. Even Ant and Dec, who always took the Mick out of me, said after the task, 'Whoa Sam, you really had your game face on today.'

We each lay in a see-through coffin that had three compartments – one from the chest up, a compartment from the chest down to our knees and then one from the knees to the feet. They put huge crabs in our feet, a load of cockroaches and crickets in the middle section and then snakes on our faces.

The task was to release a ball that was in a case secured by butterfly bolts in the middle section. Once you had the ball, you had to roll it down a drainpipe to a communal box. The first two celebrities' balls to roll into the box would win immunity. Usually the snakes would have been an issue, but I was just so thankful the cockroaches weren't on my face, plus, I was so focussed on getting the bolts off and then not dropping my ball. I smashed the challenge and won by a distance, even though on the TV, they made it look a close-run thing to add a bit of drama.

I was so chuffed that I got that immunity and weirdly, I hoped my family and friends back home were proud.

As camp life progressed it was clear that all the campmates wanted to be liked by the public. Why wouldn't you? It's always better to be liked than disliked but I didn't let my desire to be liked affect me. If I thought something was wrong and I had strong words for someone and the public didn't like me for that, I didn't mind so long as I was true to myself. Not everyone gets on and that's the reality, whether you're in a team, a business or in the jungle. People don't have to be best mates but they can still get on with one another. If someone's got an issue with me I'd much rather they said, 'I've got an issue with you, this is what it is.' More often than not we would then discuss the issue and it would be done with. I had a few arguments with Larry over the course of the experience. At times I didn't appreciate the way he undermined me when I was the camp chef and he interfered, claiming he always knew better. There were also times I thought he went a little too rude when talking about or to Martin, which I let him know, although it probably wasn't dramatic enough to warrant TV time. It might sound like I am hiding some juicy gossip, but there really were very few issues in camp as a whole. We all came from different walks of life and all grew up in different generations with different views on things. How someone deemed it appropriate to speak to or about someone else, others might not agree, but ultimately there was no malice behind it. I think I was really lucky to be in that group. Everyone bonded very quickly.

As evictions started I was doing a lot better than I ever could have imagined. Each vote-off was tinged with sadness because although I wasn't leaving, a new friend would be. After Danny went, Lisa followed, and within the next few votes, Ola. I was very sad when Ola went, because our girl group was really tight and it felt like it was disbanding. When Carol left I was gutted, because we were so on the same wavelength. Every morning I'd wake up and I'd hear, 'Good morning Samantha Quek.' I'd reply, 'Good morning Carol Vorderman.'

We always had each other's back. I think we're very similar in terms of our beliefs and how we behave in certain situations. She looked out for me. When I had a cockroach in my ear, after a trial called 'The Wicked Windmill' that I did with Joel, she would always insist on putting my eardrops in for me. She was really sweet.

While I enjoyed every minute in camp, when she left it was a different experience. During a vote-out, Ant and Dec would come into camp and read out our names in turn, leaving it hanging for a few tantalising seconds before they said either, 'It's not you', or 'It could be you'.

Every time I was expecting them to say, 'Sam, it's your time to leave', and I mean every time without fail. My heart was always pounding so hard that I worried you'd be able to see it going through my shirt. Over time you got to spot little clues to detect if you were safe. If yours was the first name mentioned by Ant and Dec, when they came into camp, you knew you were safe. Or if your name was mentioned right after they'd said to someone else, 'It could be you', you were safe. I always did a little gasp of surprise when I was saved.

Although I was desperate to stay in, I did miss home and Tom massively. When Martin and Danny came in, I saw a little opportunity to send Tom a message. After they entered camp we did a live team trial, so I knew the feed wouldn't be edited. I turned to the camera and signed '1, 4, 3' with my fingers, knowing he would be watching. When I played international hockey in the UK, Tom always came to watch me, but often he would turn up at the start of the game when I had been in a training camp for a week or so before. I couldn't exactly go up to him and give him a hug in the stands and say 'Hi!' One time he signed with his fingers '1, 4, 3' and I asked what it meant after a game. He said it stood for 'I love you'. After that, more often than not, when I was competing and hadn't seen him for a while, as we lined up and the anthems had finished, if I knew he was there and could see me, I would sign '1, 4, 3', and he would sign it back. It was just our thing and I felt it brought me good luck.

One morning, later on in the show, I wrote '1, 4, 3' on the front of my hat with a stone. When I came out there was a big hoo-ha, with the press suggesting, 'Sam Quek was breaking the rules and sending secret messages while in the jungle.' Hardly – I was just telling my boyfriend I was thinking of him.

Somehow, I made it to the final four along with Scarlett, Joel and Adam. Trust me, no one was more surprised than I was.

My final trial was the infamous Cyclone, where you have to battle through the craziest assault course, fighting water jets and objects being fired at you to collect stars. Cyclone is the trial used when there are only four celebrities left so I never imagined actually doing it. When I had seen it at home, I always imagined it would be the most fun thing to do in the whole experience. It didn't disappoint. In fact, it was even better than I could have imagined.

After the double eviction of Martin and Wayne, the camp had gone from six to four. It felt so empty and quiet. Sometimes during the programme, the producers would lower a laminated set of instructions to encourage a particular debate. As the final four, we had a laminate lowered into camp that asked us to talk about our favourite moments in the jungle, our worst moments in the jungle and things we'd learned about ourselves. It reminded me how close I had come to the end of the process because they were clearly getting ready to edit our leaving montages. There were only two days left in camp. I had made it to at least day twenty-one out of twenty-two. I had done a ton of trials, the worst of which was Head Museum, where my head was trapped for half an hour and my worst fears came true as creepy crawlies ran amok. It was the most frightened I had been during the whole show. After the trial had finished, I immediately burst into tears. I was just overcome with fear … but I completed it.

From being second to last in the first public vote of the series, I had outlasted eight other celebrities, all of whom had come in with much higher profiles than me. I wasn't so much proud, as completely flabbergasted and so thankful to the public for letting me live this journey for so long.

Winning honestly never crossed my mind because I knew Scarlett had such a massive following from her hit show *Gogglebox* and we saw Adam going up for every single trial, so clearly people were loving his character. Plus ITV's *Emmerdale* pulled in almost 8 million viewers on average for every episode, so I knew he was going to kill it. I was a little surprised how well Joel did, but his jovial character had clearly been well received by the public. But that was nothing compared to the surprise that I had made it to the final four.

When I left, it turned out to be the final Saturday night of the show. I didn't realise it at the time, but it meant I got my own primetime interview and highlight segment with Ant and Dec. Had I gone out the day before, I would have had to share with either Martin or Wayne as it was a double eviction. If I had made the final, I would have had my time split in three. It turned out quite well, as it gave me a chance to reflect on my time properly and also give hockey a plug to the nation when millions would be watching. It turned out that 9.94 million people tuned in live on the night I left – an incomprehensible number.

It was a joy to finally be able to see Tom again. He had flown out to be there for me when I left the jungle and had waited a lot longer than we both had thought. He came out to the rope bridge with a bunch of flowers for me and we had our pictures taken for the national press. When their cameras stopped snapping, we took a selfie of our own and he sent it to my mum saying, 'She's out!' We've had that selfie blown up and it hangs framed on the memory wall above our bed, alongside images from the European Championships, the Olympics and other important moments from our lives together.

Top of my list, though, after having a hug and speaking to my mum, was to get some food. We were whisked to the film crews' catering tent and I loaded everything on my plate. The first thing I ate was a sausage muffin with brown sauce. It tasted so good and I wanted so much more but I couldn't get it down because I felt a little sick from adrenalin. I had just had my own mini interview on Saturday night primetime on the nation's biggest show with the nation's favorite two presenters. Me … Sam Quek from the Wirral … Crazy!

I had lost about a stone in the jungle and soon after leaving you have to go for a check-up with the medic, Bob, who monitors your heart rate, blood pressure and weight and makes sure you're generally feeling alright. You then speak to a psychologist one-to-one about what to expect over the next few hours and days. They advise you stay away from highly sugary foods and alcohol because it can change your mood dramatically.

Finally, they asked if there was anything I was worried about now that I was emerging back into the big, wide world.

No, I said, there's nothing I'm worried about. After the incredible year I'd had, which saw me overcome the disappointment of missing two Olympics to win a gold medal that was beyond even my wildest dreams and after taking part in the toughest and biggest TV show there is, I was ready for anything.

I was just excited to see what the next chapter of my life would bring.

Epilogue

The BBC's *Sports Personality of the Year* is one of the broadcasting highlights of the sporting calendar. The great and the good of British sport gather to look back and celebrate some of the most remarkable achievements from the previous twelve months.

The event in 2016, held at the Genting Arena in Birmingham, would heavily feature athletes from the Rio Olympics, and the GB girls were going to be highlighted as one of the teams of the year.

Since coming out of the jungle we'd had one get-together – a Golden Ball held at the Tower of London by Great Britain Hockey to celebrate our success. On that occasion it had been great to see the girls. I remember having good catch-ups with Twiggy and Shona McCallin. I was very tired, though, as the ball was on the evening that I had flown back from Australia. Under normal circumstances I would have missed it, as I was severely jetlagged, but England Hockey were very keen for me to attend. I think they felt the event would get more coverage if I was there. That ultimately wasn't the reason I attended. I went because I didn't want to miss another team event after missing out on the palace visit and Olympic parade. I thought my teammates would appreciate the effort if I turned up, despite probably feeling and looking awful. Throughout the evening I felt singled out for attention because the press there were keen to speak to me so soon after my jungle exploits. *OK!* magazine were one of the sponsors and in their coverage I was the main feature, alongside photos of the Countess of Wessex, the patron of England Hockey, who was also in attendance.

Given that before *I'm a Celebrity* I was aware that there was tension with some of the girls because I was benefitting from, in their eyes, some undeserved exposure, or was somehow making it all about me, for the *Sports Personality of the Year* I just wanted to remain low-key.

It was a night to celebrate the team's efforts. Kate was one of the contenders for the main award – the first time a hockey player had ever achieved that – so I was happy to remain in the background. I didn't want to be treated differently. Before I left the house, I made a short video to explain why people should vote for Kate to win the top award, explaining why she was my sporting hero regardless of her being my teammate. I hoped the huge increase in followers I had gained after *I'm a Celebrity* could be harnessed into some much-deserved extra support for her.

The majority of the girls were meeting up in a hotel beforehand but I was working the following morning so couldn't have a boozy night. I was so busy around the time that I didn't even have time to get my hair done or find a dress. I managed to find one in the back of my wardrobes that I had worn at a previous event – a long, red number – and I drove down to Birmingham.

I met up with some of the girls and when we went along the red carpet, we got a lot of attention. Once again, I felt a little like I was under the microscope because I seemed to be the one singled out for interviews. I felt pressure to speak to everyone who requested a chat but by the time I was finished most of the girls had gone through and left me behind. I didn't blame them though. It would have annoyed me constantly stopping for someone to be interviewed.

To enter the main arena we had to go down two massive escalators. I had on my favourite shoes – a pair of Christian Louboutins that Tom had bought me in New York for my birthday. They were the first pair of shoes worth over £60 I had ever owned. I was so scared of ruining them, as I do most of my shoes, that I had only worn them once before, so they still looked brand new. They also had seriously high, thin heels. I was speaking to Unsy, who I had caught up to, and behind us were the bulk of the sportsmen and women, coaches and delegates. As I stepped to get off the escalator my heel got caught and sucked into the machine. It was completely jammed. Someone hit the emergency stop button. I couldn't get the heel out.

I was completely mortified.

Everyone had to walk past me.

I was dying of embarrassment.

Danny Kerry tried to pull it out but they had to clear the whole escalator. I felt like such a drama queen. One lovely lady said, 'What will you do when you go on stage? You'll need a pair of shoes. You can borrow mine.'

I hadn't thought of that. We were meant to be going on stage for a special presentation for Kate. If they couldn't free my shoe I might well have to borrow hers.

Eventually, security guards had to go to the top end and reverse it. My shoe popped out, incredibly with the heel still attached, but all the material was torn and chewed to pieces.

We had the best seats in the house, right at the front of the arena, and by the time I finally got through most people were seated. It was an incredible night, a truly memorable and moving occasion as the sporting world acknowledged some truly amazing achievements and mourned the passing of some real icons.

When it was our time to go up on stage, that was the first time I realised – I was the only one of the girls in a red dress. Everyone else was wearing black, which surely hadn't been chance. Had they perhaps forgotten to give me the memo? I felt a right dick, but knew it wasn't a deliberate thing to leave me out. I was more concerned that some of the team would think, 'Here we go again. Sam standing out from the team.' It really wasn't like that. There I was desperate to blend in, yet I was the only one with a red dress and I had also managed to render one of the escalators out of order thanks to getting stuck in my super skinny heeled shoes.

The way the night was shaping up, I wouldn't even blame them for thinking that it was all a ploy by me to be an individual, but it honestly wasn't.

Backstage they told us to line up with Kate at our head. When the call came we were all to walk out shoulder to shoulder. Some of the girls were a little worried, stepping out in our finery on live TV in front of a massive audience. The floor was slippery and a few were scared of falling.

Suddenly, I had a thought.

'Let's all hold hands,' I called along the line. 'When the screen goes up and we all walk out, let's lift our hands up. It'll look amazing and if anyone does slip we can save them.'

The screen went up. Out we walked. Everyone lifted their hands up and it did look amazing.

In that moment I was transported back to Rio. It didn't matter what had or hadn't been said about me. Watching them embrace what I'd suggested on board showed they still accepted me for being me. Ultimately I was still their teammate. Deep down we were all still on the same wavelength. We were still that group that brought home the gold together as the most successful women's hockey team in British history.

In January 2017 I had a decision to make. The squad for the next international cycle would be finalised and Danny Kerry, rightly, wanted to know where he stood. I had a conversation with Danny and told him I wouldn't be part of that cycle. I have not officially retired from England or Great Britain; I am just not part of the squad.

I did still want to play hockey and made the decision to go back to where it all started at club level. I left Holcombe, a club where I liked the supporters, team and the manager, Gaz, very much, and returned to Bowdon Hightown.

Ultimately Holcombe had become a bit of a job rather than a fun hockey environment. I never really felt at home there and I wasn't a fan of the way the head coach and the club management were running the team behind the scenes. It just stopped being fun, and I didn't want to play hockey and feel I was only doing it for the money, regardless of the wage on offer.

I rang my old friend Tina Cullen, who was the head coach at Bowdon, and told her I wanted to give back to the club that set me on my path to Olympic glory and that I was keen to help keep them in the Investec Premier Division. She was aware I was one of the top paid players in the country at this point and told me Bowdon didn't have the budget to match the salary I was on at Holcombe. I told her I wanted to play for free and, more than that, I didn't want any special treatment. I would pay my match and training subs just like everyone else did. In the last few seasons Bowdon had been in the relegation playoffs, having seen a lot of the international calibre players head down south to be close to Bisham. I wanted to be part of the squad that gave them a fighting chance in the league each season and perhaps be in with a shout of some medals. I also persuaded my very good friend Kirsty Mackay to join me there. I like to think we helped make an impact. The club has retained its top-flight status and in 2017–18 we also managed to win the indoor title.

Now when I see my old England and Britain teammates it is as opponents, but we always have a catch-up after the game, or at some point just look at each other as if to say, 'Hey you ... remember when we kicked the world's ass that summer not so long ago?'

It is so rewarding being back at Bowdon. There are some young players on the fringes of the first team who possibly look at me in the way I looked at Tina all those years ago. I've now become Tina Cullen, the one with the Olympic medal. I want to be that senior player shouting encouragement and being the one who can offer a consoling word if a player suffers a setback. One young girl very much reminds me of me. She narrowly missed out on selection for the Commonwealth Games and I had a long chat with her because I remember exactly how that felt.

I feel my hockey career has come full circle.

It's not just with hockey that I feel things have come full circle. Thanks to a great opportunity with LFC TV, the channel for all things Liverpool Football Club, I've been able to learn my trade as a sports presenter. An exciting new chapter in my life began in February 2017 when, after appearing as a guest on LFC TV, the editor Simon Ellis-Jones told me he was shaping the content and thought it would be great to have me as a co-presenter.

Since *I'm a Celebrity* I'd had further tastes of being on television with a second and third appearance on *A Question of Sport* and on Sky's *A League Of Their Own*, but this was a chance to try my hand at presenting. Simon was incredibly supportive and encouraging. He got me in to do a few run-throughs where I practised with the autocue and learned how much you have to accentuate everything so you don't sound monotone. He'd also sit in with me and pretend to be a guest so I learned how to interview. I also had to learn the art of talkback, when you have the producer, director, cameraman and timekeeper all speaking in your ear while you're conducting an interview and trying to pay attention to your guest. It was a great experience and a safe environment for me to learn the ropes.

My co-presenter was Rob Jones, who had worked with Sky Sports so was also very experienced. He, too, was excellent with me, putting me at ease and teaching me how to use the mic and the little tricks of the trade. I can't praise him enough.

It has been a dream to work for LFC TV. I couldn't believe it because I was getting to meet former players like Robbie Fowler and Steve McManaman, whom I used to pretend to be in my garden. He was my idol. Robbie Fowler we used to call 'God', because he was that good, and now I was interviewing them and getting to know them as individuals. I was in awe of them at first but now I feel we're on the same level. It's completely mad. Now, whenever I see him at a Liverpool match, he always makes the effort to come over, say 'Hi' and give me a hug. I even got the opportunity to play alongside him and Jamie Redknapp in the BMW PGA Pro-Am at Wentworth in May 2018. It was an awesome day and I can tell you that Robbie is a pretty decent golfer.

I have been extremely fortunate that a number of TV and radio opportunities have opened for me that I wouldn't have thought possible before Rio. One of the first opportunities I had after coming out of the jungle was to appear as a guest on *The NFL Show* for the BBC. I love American football. In fact, I think it's my favorite sport to watch on TV. It was a great opportunity to demonstrate my knowledge and eventually led to me presenting this show a year later, which was like a dream come true. Not only did it see me appearing on TV but also as the pitch-side host for NFL games at Wembley and Twickenham. That's a different challenge altogether – presenting to a camera and to a stadium packed with 80,000 fans. I'd be working live with Jason Bell, who was also on the BBC, or Darren Fletcher from BT Sport.

It's been amazing for me to work across a range of sports and I was thrilled to be asked to join the coverage for the women's football European

Championships in the Netherlands in the summer of 2017 for Channel 4, working with the likes of Clare Balding, Michael Owen, Ian Wright, Jermaine Jenas and Eni Aluko. Clare Balding is one of those presenters I really look up to. She is always so professional, so well researched, and whatever she turns her hand to it looks effortless. Working alongside her was a great opportunity and I tried to soak up any advice she gave me like a sponge.

With regards to Michael Owen, I had to pinch myself when I met him for the first time, remembering that day I was in the crowd to witness his two FA Cup winning goals in Cardiff. When I was a kid I had my photo taken alongside him in the players' lounge at Anfield. I look like a right geek, but I remember it being a great day. Now we regularly cross paths and take the Mick out of each other and have become friends.

Michael's love of football is equally matched by his love of horses and horse racing. He owns horses and has raced as a jockey as well. Our paths had first crossed at Aintree racecourse after I was approached by the Jockey Club to be one of its ambassadors. The club had found out I was an avid racing fan after *I'm A Celebrity*. Tom and I are annual badge members at our local course in Chester. They were looking for an ambassador for Ladies' Day. They already had Katie Walsh, the jockey, and Laura Wright, the soprano singer, and wanted me to be on board. I had never been to Aintree before then but I knew all about it. To go for the first time on Ladies' Day was amazing. The Jockey Club set me at a table with Liverpool legend Kenny Dalglish and his wife Marina, Michael Owen and his dad, and Dan Walker, the sports presenter. Like Clare Balding, Dan is another presenter I really respect. It was great to speak with him about his career and how he developed his craft. I am always fascinated to learn from those who have been in the business a while and become successful.

There have been times, certainly over the past two years, when I've had to step back and think, 'How on earth did you get into this position?' That day was one of those moments. It was insane to be in their company. King Kenny is revered by all Liverpool fans, not just for his heroics on the pitch and as a manager but for how he steered the club through the turbulent days after the Hillsborough tragedy.

After spending time in their company I just treat them as I would anyone else. My picture now hangs in the Champions Lounge at Aintree alongside theirs. What an honor. We are lucky because we've excelled in sport, which attracts a lot of attention, but I believe everyone has the opportunity to fulfil their potential, and I don't think I'm anything special just because I move in these circles or get to meet such people.

I've just had my second year this year as ambassador at Aintree and I love what the Jockey Club strives to do in terms of working in the community, promoting and supporting female jockeys and improving horse welfare. I enjoy working with them and am pleased to see they are so forward-thinking.

Some of the opportunities that have come my way have taken me by surprise. In 2017, Channel 5 contacted me to say they had the rights to broadcast the rugby Aviva Premiership and wanted to sound me out about being part of the team. I wasn't sure at first because apart from watching the odd international I didn't really know much about the Premiership and the technicalities of the sport. That's exactly what I said in the meeting with the producers but I also said I was perfectly willing to work hard, learn about the clubs, the players and the current issues to show I could deliver. They put a lot of faith in me and felt I suited the direction in which they wanted to take their coverage.

I covered my first match on 30 December 2017 and, while it was a steep learning curve, I thoroughly enjoyed it and was delighted it has carried on into 2018.

I'm now looking ahead to the hockey World Cup, which starts in London in July. It will be strange not to be playing but I will be part of the presenting team with BT Sport, which is the next best thing.

I didn't think anything would top winning an Olympic gold medal but going to Buckingham Palace to receive an MBE from Prince Charles is definitely up there.

Being awarded any kind of honour from your country is a huge privilege but the way I found out was quite amusing. I had just come out of the jungle and rang my mum. I had a camera filming me as I was speaking to her. They were making a show about coming out of *I'm a Celebrity* and back into the real world. She therefore couldn't tell me the news outright, so she just kept saying, 'Check your emails, check your emails.'

I thought, 'The last thing I am going to do is check my emails,' especially as I had quite literally just left the jungle. However, check my emails I did and I was thrilled to find out I would soon be a Member of the Most Excellent Order of the British Empire.

That night I went to dinner with the contestants who were already out, along with their friends and family. I sat next to Carol and wanted to tell her the news because she had also received an MBE some years ago. She had been to Buckingham Palace and I was keen to know what it was like. Instinctively I leaned in close and grabbed the collar of her blouse before I told her. For the previous three weeks, whenever I had wanted to whisper something to her or have a bit of a gossip in the camp, I'd held her microphone to muffle what we were saying and to maintain an element of privacy. Old habits die hard! We had a good giggle about that and she gave me a bit of insight into the day and what it would be like.

Even so, nothing prepared me for the day itself. I hadn't been able to make the first date sent to me but by happy coincidence the date I finally could make was my mother's birthday on 24 March. We made a day of it.

Most of the women's team had been through to collect their MBEs already. I felt it was an oversight that Danny Kerry hadn't been awarded one at the same time as we had. When I was being interviewed about the honours on BBC *Breakfast* I raised the issue and called for Danny to be recognised for the work he had put in and his genius in taking us to gold. I was delighted to see he did receive one in 2017.

For my mum and dad it was an incredibly proud day. They joined Tom and me at Buckingham Palace. We all entered through the same way we'd seen on royal weddings, up a grand staircase flanked by ceremonial guards. At the top of the stairs I turned right, while Tom and my parents went left. I went into a room where the other recipients were. I really enjoyed speaking to people, hearing their stories and how they came to be honoured. Each story was so varied. Among the medallists at Rio, from both the Olympic and Paralympic Games, there was a man who had painstakingly restored and preserved a steam train for a museum, and a woman who'd sadly lost her mum to cancer but had done so much to raise money for further research. It was inspiring listening to them all. In truth, I felt a bit of a fraud being there for services to hockey.

We were briefed beforehand what would happen. We were taken in alphabetical order and when it was your turn to be called, you walked in. Prince Charles would be on your left. You had to turn left, walk about three paces towards him and curtsey. You would then have a little chat before he hooked the MBE onto a strong pin we'd been given. Once he shook your hand you were to walk backwards three steps, curtsey again, turn to your right and walk out.

It sounds really simple but when you are so nervous and excited, you start to forget. When it was my turn to walk in I waved to my mum, dad and Tom like a little schoolgirl in reception class doing a Christmas play. What an idiot! Everyone else was so straight-laced but I couldn't help myself. I was so thrilled. I waited until I was sure they had seen me and then I walked over to Prince Charles. I noticed he had a little plaster on the tip of his forefinger and I was desperate to ask how he did it.

He spoke to me about hockey, how he had watched the final and what a great game it was. He said, 'Huge congratulations. You should be immensely proud of what you achieved at Rio.'

He then shook my hand, out I went and that was that.

I waited for the other recipients to collect their awards. Among them I spotted the actress Patricia Routledge, who has enjoyed a long and varied career but is probably best known for her role as Hyacinth Bucket in the BBC sitcom *Keeping Up Appearances*. She was made a dame. She had also gone to my school in Birkenhead.

It was such a lovely day and afterwards we went out for lunch. Mum and Dad had been majorly proud of the Olympic medal but to actually go to Buckingham Palace to be acknowledged on such a stage was very special for them. They were made up. My dad is not a man of many words but his face said it all. He was so proud – an immigrant walking the halls of Buckingham Palace while his daughter was honoured. Whenever we got into a taxi that day he would tell the cabbie, 'My daughter's just got an MBE.' I was so pleased to make him proud.

We headed back to our hotel, where we had a quick change before heading to Euston Station.

But after the pomp and ceremony of the palace, it was back to reality with a bump. There we were sprinting with our cases, me at the front, trying to hurry along my mum, while Tom went off with my dad. It was a Friday night and, as anyone who has made that journey from London to Liverpool knows, in the race for a table on a Virgin train, an MBE or a gold medal counts for nothing. If you're not fast, you're last!

I'm very lucky to have been able to forge a career away from playing hockey. However, I know that I wouldn't be in the position I am now if it wasn't for the support from the love of my life, Tom. He is the funniest, most intelligent, kindhearted man I could have wished to meet. Every day is an adventure with him, and I can count on him in a way that I could never have imagined. He loves me so very much and I am so thankful for that.

I cannot emphasise enough how much he has done for me. There are the small things like when there are times when I come back from a long day working in London very late at night and I have to leave in the early hours the following day for another engagement and Tom will make sure all the information I need for the next day is printed out ready for me on my side table. He also gets up with me at ridiculous hours and quizzes me as I get dressed so that I'm up to speed with all the essential knowledge I need for the following day. Then there are the bigger things like him putting his own career and aspirations on hold to allow me to achieve mine and following me to the four corners of the globe in the process. It's much harder than people realise being the partner of someone in the public eye, but I am very thankful to have someone like him in my corner.

Whilst 2018 will be a big year for sport, there is one date in my calendar that takes priority over everything else – our wedding day in August. I can't wait!

Unfortunately for Tom, he did have a bit of a wait until he popped the question. By the time we got engaged I knew he had a ring and I knew I wanted to marry him. It was on the way back from filming *I'm A Celebrity* in Australia that the cat literally was out of the bag. We were checking in at the airport and I went to get the passports out of Tom's bag, when out dropped a little box. I looked at him and then to the floor. Ant and Dec were at the next check-in desk and they both went, 'Ooooh'.

I said to Tom, 'Is that what I think it is?'

'Shut up, shut up, it's nothing,' he said and put the box back in the bag.

'Oh my god … is that a ring box?' I asked. 'It was, wasn't it? I didn't see anything I promise.'

'Sam, leave it!' he said, while hurrying to put it back in his bag.

His plan had been to propose in Australia because he feared I might come out early on, because I didn't really have a fan base to rely on for support. However, I surprised both of us by staying in right up until the day before the final, which was then just one day before we'd be leaving Australia to return home. When I did come out, he didn't think it was appropriate to propose when I was caught up with so many media obligations and receiving a lot of press attention. He thought it would just become another thing I'd have to deal with and he didn't want to take anything away from what I'd achieved.

For the next six months, almost from the moment we arrived back home, our lives were hectic. I was busy with my television work and Tom was also busy with his work. Besides, we felt under pressure because almost every interviewer I spoke to on coming home asked me the same question: 'Are you going to get married? And if so, when?'

From the jungle to June 2017, life flew by. We finally had a chance to take stock on holiday at a villa his parents have in Tenerife. It's one of our favourite places, where we can chill and just enjoy each other's company.

On 3 June, the day of the Champions League final, I said to Tom we should have a really late lunch and have dinner after the game. He went to the supermarket and got all my favourite foods and prepared lunch. Once we'd finished he cleared the table.

Then he got down on one knee and popped the question, presenting me with the ring. I had a fair idea what the ring would be like as every time I saw one similar in a magazine or on Instagram, I would always explicitly say, 'Wow … how lovely is that ring?' He'd clearly got the not so subtle messages. I had no hesitation in saying, 'Yes'.

It was a lovely moment; dead chilled – in a place we loved.

Within about an hour, we were in an Irish bar, watching the football, playing drinking games. He was Real Madrid and I was Juventus, and whenever either team scored we each had to do a forfeit. I came out worse because Juve were on the end of a 4–1 hammering!

We will be married at Chester Racecourse. Tom has done the majority of planning because I swear since coming out of the international hockey scene I cannot make a decision. He's also so good at organising things. We have really similar ideas of what we want. It's going to be a really personalised, unique, fun and relaxed day.

We will tie the knot almost two years to the day that Great Britain women's hockey team made history. It was fitting that Tom was with me in Rio that day, as he has been there for much of my remarkable journey. He is the first person I go to whenever something exciting happens and he is the first person who picks me up and motivates me whenever I suffer a setback. He has seen me at my worst, during the dark days when I didn't think I would ever fulfil my dream of competing for Great Britain at an Olympic Games and considered giving up hockey for good. I may no longer be part of Team GB, but with Tom we are a team that is looking forward to achieving more incredible dreams together.

Long before Tom came into my life, though, and also while he has been there, I have always had the love and support of my family, particularly my parents, to whom I owe almost everything I achieved. Their support for me over the decades should never go underestimated. I consider myself so lucky to have had parents whose hard work ethic allowed me to reach and then surpass my potential. It hasn't been easy for them. They have made a lot of sacrifices along the way and I'm sure my brothers and sister weren't always thrilled that me and my hockey would often monopolise their time. They made me the woman I am today and I hope they are proud of me.

Whilst I am so thankful for those who were alongside me throughout my journey, I am also very proud of what I managed to achieve at the times when I needed to step up and deliver on my own. My road to the Olympics was a very lonely one at times. It was bumpy, winding and long, and often I couldn't see the direction in which I was going or if there was an end in sight.

Others no doubt helped me along the way, but it was a road I ultimately had to be prepared to walk myself; no one was going to walk it for me and there were no shortcuts. I look back and at times I wonder where I got my strength from. Hopes and dreams are the most powerful motivation there is. I feel so lucky to have achieved mine; but the harder I worked, the luckier I got, and that doesn't feel like a coincidence.

There were so many times when I used to wonder whether it was all worth it – the agonies of rejection, the feelings of failure. However, those setbacks not only made success all the sweeter when it came, but they also made me a much stronger person. Now I am in the privileged position of being able to pass on what I've learned to younger players and I hope the next generation can take inspiration from my story and realise they too can live out their dreams if they keep fighting and never give up, no matter what goes on around them.

I hope I am living proof that dreams can come true and everyone has potential in them to achieve amazing things.

My life has been one heck of a journey up to now and my future looks equally as bright and exciting. But whatever my future may hold, I will be sure to remember a key lesson that my past has taught me …

Tough times don't last, but tough people do.